# THE TEXAS TONKAWAS

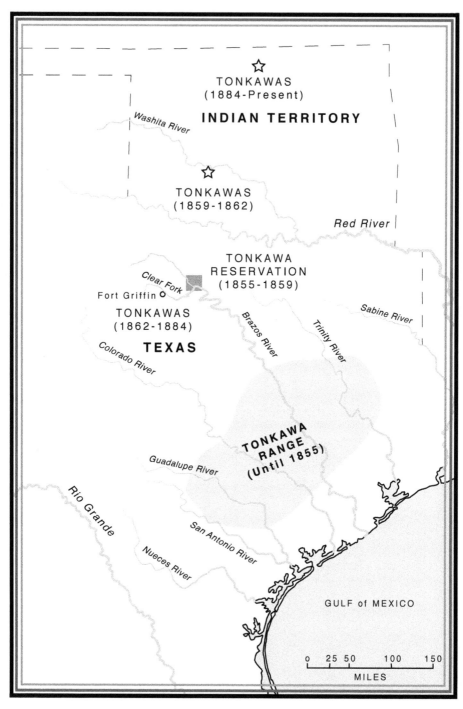

☆
TONKAWAS
(1884-Present)

Washita River

**INDIAN TERRITORY**

☆
TONKAWAS
(1859-1862)

Red River

TONKAWA
RESERVATION
(1855-1859)

Clear Fork

Fort Griffin ○

TONKAWAS
(1862-1884)

Sabine River

Brazos River

Trinity River

**TEXAS**

Colorado River

**TONKAWA
RANGE
(Until 1855)**

Guadalupe River

Rio Grande

San Antonio River

Nueces River

GULF of MEXICO

0    25 50      100        150
MILES

*Map by Donald S. Frazier.*

# THE TEXAS
# TONKAWAS

STANLEY S. McGOWEN

State House Press
The Texas Center
Schreiner University
Kerrville, TX
325-660-1752
www.mcwhiney.org

Cataloging-in-Publication Data

Names: McGowen, Stanley S., 1947-, author.
Title: The Texas Tonkawas / Stanley S. McGowen.
Description: First edition. | Kerrville, TX: State House Press, 2020. | Includes bibliographical references and index.

Identifiers: ISBN 9781933337920 (soft cover); ISBN 9781933337937 (e-book)
Subjects: LCSH: Tonkawa Indians – History. | Texas – History – 19th century. | Indians of North America – Texas.
Classification: LCC E99.K23 (print) | DCC 976.4

First edition 2020

Cover and page design and production by Allen Griffith of Eye 4 Design.

Distributed by Texas A&M University Press Consortium
800-826-8911
www.tamupress.com

For the people called Tonkawa

# CONTENTS

# LIST OF IMAGES

# PREFACE

When writing a history of American Indians, the author must remember that he oftentimes writes with the view, concerns, and information left by the conqueror. Many times, histories are written by the victors, not the vanquished. Compounding the problems of historical events, time, fading memory, or personal agendas alter oral histories. Historians must remember that many past reporters of American Indians based their accounts on myth, lore, and hearsay, never personally visiting any Indians. Unfortunately, many historians solely rely on white perceptions of America's native peoples, with all the inherent cultural misconceptions and ethnic biases. When analyzing primary documents, "professional" historians must realize that all mortals are rather ethno-centric, no matter how open-minded we consider ourselves, and must guard against interjecting that bias into our writing.

European chroniclers of America's past invariably asserted that the Indians were "uncivilized" or "savages" that lacked a civilization without understanding the complexity of native social structures. This lack of understanding thus created a great disparity of cultural perceptions. What distinguished a "savage" from a "civilized person?"

Spanish explorers read the *Requiremiento* to Indians who had no concept of the Spanish language and then, according to Spanish friars, attacked the Indians as savagely as wolves for failing to follow decrees issued by the King of Spain. The majority of Mexican and Texian officials also considered Indians, including the Tonkawa tribe, uncivilized savages. Despite United States government policies that, generally, required Native Americans be treated with humanity and dignity, the mass of American pioneers considered all indigenous people savages. Most settlers believed the only way to end the violence along the frontier was to relocate the Indians, or failing that, exterminate them entirely. According to most nineteenth-century American frontiersmen one could not trust the Indians to keep their promises and remain on reservations set aside for them.

In mid-nineteenth century Texas, as well as the rest of the United States, a precursor of social Darwinism prevailed along the frontier. Most Americans deemed settler encroachment onto millions of acres previously inhabited by native peoples ample "evidence of the innate superiority of the American Anglo-Saxon branch of the Caucasian race." Racial ideology rode as a saddle partner with every white settler of the Texas plains and imbued them with the certainty of their actions, expelling Indians from their lands or relegating "uncivilized savages" to reservations where they could be rehabilitated. Ignoring the tribal diversities of language and culture, the vast majority of Americans referred to all indigenous peoples as "Indians," accepting what an Austin editor wrote, "the whole race are thieves and murderers. Lying, stealing, and murdering are in their nature and it cannot be eradicated." Referring to the "friendly Indians" who occupied the Brazos River Reservation in the late 1850s, Texas Ranger John S. "Rip" Ford commented, "They are trying to imitate the whites in manners, interest in agriculture, and in all essential particulars." Without a doubt, the reservation system, like the Spanish missions, was a trade school in how to become a white man.[1]

An essential understanding of those who study American Indians is the realization that conflicts between "redskins and palefaces" occurred because of vast cultural schisms. Indians and white frontiersmen desperately battled for control of the land, and to settle which culture would prevail. As Elmer Kelton often said, "It was root hog or die on the Texas frontier."[2]

I first encountered the Tonkawa tribe in my teens during a Boy Scout encampment at "Camp Tonkawa," located near Buffalo Gap south of Abilene, Texas. Over the years, as a result of my interest in Texas history, I frequently stumbled across mentions of the tribe and wondered why more was not written about this native group. During my collegiate studies, and researching my last book, I realized that most of what people knew about the tribe was innuendo and myth. The Tonkawas were different than other Texas Indians, vainly attempting to retain their culture as they aligned with settlers who wrestled control of Texas lands away from other Indian tribes.

To the best of my ability I wrote this book with an open mind, attempting, with my limited expertise in Tonkawa society and custom, to narrate an unbiased chronicle of the tribe. I endeavored to glean every insight possible from primary and secondary sources, as well as personal and telephonic interviews with tribal members. Understandably, because of previous experience with Anglo-American authors, some members of the tribe were reticent during interviews. On the other hand, others openly discussed their knowledge of Tonkawa tribal history and customs. For these insights I am extremely grateful. Any inaccuracies or misconceptions are completely the fault of the author.

# ACKNOWLEDGEMENTS

As a blind historian and author I must offer my thanks to several people who cheerfully assisted me in completing this book. To my research assistants/readers, Nancy Grace and Jennifer Tucker, who also became chauffeurs now and again, I must say that without your valuable assistance my research would have been very shallow indeed. I also owe much thanks to the staff of several archives and museums. The National Archives and Records Administration; Texas State Archives; Center for American History at the University of Texas at Austin; the Institute of Texan Cultures at San Antonio; the Southwest Collection at Texas Tech University; the Texas Collection at Baylor University; the Panhandle Plains Museum at Canyon; and The Old Jail Art Center in Albany. The staffs at all these facilities afforded me their very best efforts in assisting me with my research. Dr. David R. Hunt and Bill Billeck from the Department of Anthropology, National Museum of Natural History, deserve my thanks for quickly responding to a request and confirming the existence of Texas-the-Tonk, a female Tonkawa scout who was killed in 1872. For the exceptional photographs I must thank three repositories. Two photo archivists, Lou Stancari of the National Museum of the American Indian and John Anderson of the Texas State Archives, did yeoman service searching their holdings for their best Tonkawa images. Margaret Blagg, former Executive Director of The Old Jail Art Center, courteously opened the doors for me when the building, displays, and archival holdings were undergoing major renovations.

Several other individuals provided valuable time and their unique expertise in preparing my manuscript. Dr. Caroline Castillo Crimm, Sam Houston State University, translated several documents from archaic Spanish to West Texas English. I'm sorry to admit that my abilities in Spanish do not include ciphering documents written by Spanish and Mexican clerks more than 185 years ago. In San Antonio, Sharon R. Crutchfield waded through more journals than most libraries possess, and Wayne Cox sifted through the entire Béxar Archives at The University of Texas at San Antonio, both proving that they are true historians. Helen J. King added her proficiency in searching the internet for documents that I overlooked in my archival perusals. Shirley Caldwell and Joan Farmer, both of Albany, in addition to offering suggestions of other sources, freely opened their private collections of Texana for my perusal.

When I visited the Tonkawa Tribe in Oklahoma the tribal council welcomed me, provided me open access to their museum, and several tribal members graciously shared their food with my wife and me during our visits to the Tonkawa powwows.

As for the others to whom I must extend my thanks, Gary Zaboly magnificently depicted the inter-racial character of the Texas frontier with his superb cover art, *The Tonkawa Scout: Spotting the Enemy.* And to those whom I have forgotten to mention, a grateful thank you.

My patient wife Jolene, as she did with my other books, provided more support and understanding than I deserved throughout the trying process of research, writing, and editing this book.

Stanley S. McGowen, 2018

# INTRODUCTION

One of the least known and probably most misunderstood Indian tribes of the Southwest was the Tonkawa tribe of Texas. Previously considered indigenous to the state, more recent research pointed to the fact that a few bands who comprised the tribe may have migrated from as far north as the Southern Plains of Kansas. The remainder of the tribe coalesced from a scattering of small family groups that roamed Texas from near the mouth of the Brazos River, to the forks of the Trinity River, across the Edwards Plateau, and near the Texas Coastal Plain from the Rio Grande back to the Brazos. Tonkawa clans initially formed loose, shifting alliances with various Comanche bands that invaded their territory from the northwest. By the end of the eighteenth century, however, the Tonkawas had allied themselves with the Lipan Apaches and became mortal enemies of the entire Comanche Nation. Fearing annihilation by raiding Comanche warriors the family groups in Central Texas merged with the few bands migrating from the north to form the Tonkawa tribe.[1]

The name Tonkawa derived from a Waco Indian word meaning "they all stay together." Although little is known of the true Tonkawan tongue, scholars collected and translated what remained of the language, allowing some insight into the tribe's culture and society. The Tonkawas called themselves Tickanwatic, which roughly translated meant "the most human of people." Despite the fact that several disjointed bands of Tonkawas roamed the edge of the Texas Coastal Plain, anthropologists do not believe that the Tonkawas actually lived on the Texas coastline because words like canoe, island, and fish were not simple, but compound words. The Tonkawas did, nonetheless, provide a trading conduit between the coastal tribes and the people of the Southern Plains.[2]

Rumor and innuendo distorted surviving descriptions of Tonkawa culture, society, and language. Early accounts of the tribe described both men and women wearing skins of deer and antelope, buckskin moccasins and, in cold weather, buffalo robes. Men adorned themselves with facial tattoos, body painting, and numerous earrings and necklaces. Women also tattooed their faces, as well as their breasts.[3]

Initially the Tonkawa people inhabiting the river valleys of Texas lived in dome-shaped dwellings constructed of long willow poles, measuring about four and a half feet in height and ten feet in diameter. To weatherproof their homes, women covered the willow framework with fresh branches and animal skins. A fire burned in the center of the lodge to repel insects in the summer and to warm the dwelling in winter.[4]

After the clans composing the Tonkawa tribe merged and moved to the fringes of the rolling plains, they adopted the buffalo hide tipis and lifestyle of the Plains Indians. By the mid-1800s, Tonkawa villages resembled those of other Plains Indians. Women skinned game and tanned the hides, while the men lounged around the village or prepared for war. Herds of horses grazed near the camps and packs of dogs scavenged the villages.[5]

Without the Tonkawa Indians, white explorers would have found frontier life in Texas much more difficult. The Tonkawas openly offered not only their friendship, but buffalo jerky, robes, deer hides, tallow, pecans, honey, and furs. The Tonkawas, however, vacillated between befriending the Europeans or opposing exploration of their traditional hunting grounds. With the exception of a few minor transgressions the Tonkawa tribe gave most early Texas pioneers little cause for concern. White retaliation, however, was always out of proportion to the Tonkawa's petty crimes.[6]

The main reason the Tonkawas found themselves chastised by the white frontiersmen and settlers, and vehemently despised by other Indian groups, was their practice of ritual cannibalism. The Tonkawas were not unique in this practice as several other Texas tribes participated in some form of cannibalism. According to Tonkawa cultural beliefs, consuming small portions of a vanquished enemy's body demonstrated superiority in warfare, and deprived that enemy of an opportunity to take revenge on the Tonkawas. Therefore, ritualistic cannibalism became part of the tribe's victory celebrations.[7]

Trapped between the advancement of white settlers and several Plains Indian groups, Tonkawa chiefs made a pivotal decision to ally themselves with the settlers. The Tonkawas opened a flourishing trade with Stephen F. Austin's colonists, while the settlers attempted to convert the Tonkawas into farmers. The Tonkawa's major chief, however, informed Austin that the "Great Spirit" told him that the Tonkawas should continue hunting as was their custom.[8]

To prove their friendship Tonkawa warriors guided the Texians on reprisal raids against other native peoples. In 1822, a Karankawa party raided Austin's colony near Skull Creek, and Tonkawa warriors accompanied the settlers on a reprisal raid that killed nine or ten Karankawas. When Tonkawas were caught with stolen horses Austin prescribed corporal punishment and banishment from the white settlements. To confirm their friendship with the pioneers the Tonkawas returned several head of livestock stolen by other tribes.[9]

Although remaining friendly with the Texians, the Tonkawas apparently did not actively assist them during the revolution against Mexico. After Texas gained its independence, however, Tonkawa chiefs soon signed a treaty with the new Republic and maintained the tribe's unceasing conflict with the Comanches. Despite President Mirabeau B. Lamar's reversal of Sam Houston's "peace policy" toward Indians, the Tonkawas remained friendly with the Republic of Texas and participated in several punitive expeditions against other tribes. Due to the Tonkawas' continued allegiance, Lamar did not target the tribe for extermination.[10]

In 1840, Chief Plácido and twelve Tonkawa warriors participated in the Plum Creek Fight near Lockhart. The Tonkawas joined the Texans in a running fight against a large force of Comanches, who had recently raided through Central Texas to the Gulf Coast. Commanded by Felix Huston, Matthew "Old Paint" Caldwell, Edward Burleson, and Ben McCulloch, the combined forces killed an estimated 138 Comanche warriors. Throughout the existence of the Republic of Texas, the Tonkawas continued their faithful alliance, even though many Texans considered them "shiftless and lazy." At one point the Texas government actually promised to protect the Comanches from the Tonkawas.[11]

On February 12, 1845, Robert S. Neighbors assumed the duties of agent to the Tonkawas and established himself as one of the most important Indian Agents in the history of the tribe. Acting under government instructions, Neighbors instituted a policy of moving the Tonkawas away from the advancing line of settlements. This policy of removal became the theme of white/Tonkawa relations for almost fifty years. A major portion of Neighbor's duties included preventing war between the Tonkawas, other Indians, and white traders: "the white man's path should not be soiled with blood."[12]

Under Neighbors' direction the Tonkawas relocated north of Austin and west of Waco. He provided the tribe with seed corn, hoes, and knives hoping the Indians would learn the "arts of civilization" and become agriculturalists. In September 1845 Tonkawa chiefs met with state commissioners and several chiefs from other tribes, and unaccountably agreed to move even farther north into the domain of the Southern Comanches—long-time bitter enemies of the Tonkawas.[13]

Warriors from other tribes continued to ambush isolated settlers and steal livestock, which resulted in demands for extermination or removal of all Indians away from any settlement. Neighbors agreed that to protect the diminishing number of Tonkawas from both the Comanches and frontiersmen the tribe should be relocated to reservations established along the Brazos River. In July 1855, Plácido led the majority of the Tonkawa tribe to the Brazos River Reservation, near Fort Belknap in Young County.[14]

Exhibiting their loyalty, the Tonkawas continued to guide both Texas Rangers and U.S. troops in campaigns against other tribes who persistently raided along the Texas frontier. In May 1858, 113 Tonkawa and Shawnee scouts, accompanied by their new agent Shapley Ross, guided 102 Rangers under John S. "Rip" Ford to a large Comanche village near Antelope Hills, north of the Red River. Led by Ross, the Tonkawas "gave a good account of themselves in battle, fighting like demons." During the fight a Tonkawa named Jim Pockmark downed the legendary Comanche Chief Iron Jacket.[15]

In 1859, ignoring the Tonkawa's valuable service and attempts to acculturate into white ways, John R. Baylor, and several of his Indian-hating associates, attacked the Brazos River Reservation, finally forcing the Tonkawas to relocate to Indian Territory. Most settlers accused all Indians of any depredations and clamored for all tribes to be moved north of the Red River. In August, Neighbors and the U.S. Cavalry escorted about 1,400 Tonkawas and other Indians from the Brazos Agency to a reservation south of present-day Anadarko, Oklahoma.[16]

Not all Tonkawas remained north of the Red River. A few young warriors returned to Belknap and, enlisting with Lawrence "Sul" Ross, participated in one of the most famous campaigns against the Comanches. Ross, with forty Rangers, twenty-one soldiers, and twenty-five Tonkawa scouts, located a Comanche camp on the Pease River. On December 18, 1860, Ross' force attacked the camp, scattered the Comanches, and recovered two captives, a Mexican boy and a white woman, who proved to be Cynthia Ann Parker, the wife of Peta Nocona.[16]

In the first months of the Civil War, the Tonkawas signed peace treaties with Confederate Indian Agent Albert Pike, and continued their tradition of friendship with Texans by guiding both state and Confederate troops against Comanche bands that raided into Texas. Their collaboration with Texans against the Comanches and their reputation for cannibalism caused the reservation Tonkawas to suffer an attack by a coalition of other Indians that killed more than half of the Tonkawas. Of the 300 Tonkawas who lived in Indian Territory, only 137 survived and fled back to Texas, settling near Fort Belknap. Reversing their previous attitudes many Texans welcomed the Tonkawas back into the state and provided subsistence for the destitute tribe.[17]

In July 1867 the United States Army resettled 143 Tonkawas near Fort Griffin in Shackelford County. Under Chief Castile and medicine man Campos, the Tonkawas heightened their reputation as dependable frontier scouts. To deter Comanche raids on their dwindling tribal population the Tonkawas lived near Fort Griffin for more than ten years. The United States Army supplied the tribe with rations, clothing, and some weapons in return for the services of twenty-five scouts and guides. Officers who supervised the Tonkawa scouts described them as "superior trailers" that could follow "a dim trail at a gallop." Several army officers employed Tonkawa scouts in numerous successful campaigns against Comanche and Kiowa bands that steadfastly refused to surrender their North Texas domain. Tonkawa scouts guided Col. Ranald S. Mackenzie across the Llano Estacado and were, in great measure, responsible for his victories in both the Tule and Palo Duro Canyon battles.[18]

With the end of major Comanche threats to the Texas frontier the Tonkawas became wards of the United States government—a people without a home. The Bureau of Indian Affairs refused to accept responsibility for the tribe until it moved to a federal reservation. The Tonkawas, however, resisted relocation to Indian Territory, fearing another attack like the 1862 massacre. The tribe remained near Fort Griffin, eking out a pitiful existence from limited hunting, small garden plots, and infrequent largess from the fort's commander. Residents near the fort described the tribe as "drunken, dirty, and debauched."[19]

In 1884, after a series of failed negotiations with several other tribes to locate the Tonkawas on their reservations, the United States government finally granted the remaining ninety-two Tonkawas a separate reservation in Indian Territory. The United States Army loaded the Tonkawas on a few rail cars and permanently moved the tribe out of Texas. The Tonkawa tribe had barely settled onto their reservation in present-day Kay County, Oklahoma, before they experienced another injustice. Under the 1887 Dawes Severalty Act they lost their reservation land, and almost disappeared as a tribal entity. The Tonkawa's faithful commitment to first the Republic of Texas, then the Confederacy, and lastly to the United States Army, was ignored, even though native groups considered "hostile" received more attention and government assistance than the friendly Tonkawas. Today, a little more than 600 Tonkawas remain on tribal rolls.[20]

# THE TEXAS TONKAWAS

One of the least known and probably most misunderstood Native American tribes of the Southwest was the Tonkawa tribe of Texas. Previously considered indigenous to the state, more recent research pointed to the fact that a few bands who comprised the tribe may have migrated from as far north as the Southern Plains of Kansas. The remainder of the tribe coalesced from a scattering of small family groups that roamed Texas from near the mouth of the Brazos River, to the forks of the Trinity River, across the Edwards Plateau, and near the Texas Coastal Plain from the Rio Grande back to the Brazos. Tonkawa bands initially formed loose, shifting alliances with various Comanche bands that invaded their territory from the northwest. By the end of the eighteenth century, however, the Tonkawas allied themselves with the Lipan Apaches and became mortal enemies of the entire Comanche Nation. Fearing annihilation by raiding Comanche warriors the family groups in Central Texas merged with the few bands migrating from the north to form the Tonkawa tribe.

Although most of the scattered bands of hunter-gatherers which eventually made up the Tonkawa tribe ranged over Texas, Oklahoma, and Kansas as early as 800 BC, these family groups had not coalesced into a single unit by the time European explorers first encountered the Tonkawas. As many as two hundred small indigenous groups of loosely associated and linguistically related clans roamed Texas, forming the nucleus of the Tonkawa tribe. A few of the clans absorbed by the Tonkawa tribe probably came from as far south as Northern Mexico. Other immigrant groups, forced from the South Plains by expanding Indian nations and the spread of Europeans west of the Mississippi River, constituted the remainder of the tribe. Trapped between the warriors of the onrushing Plains Indian horse culture and the encroaching white frontiers, these migratory units joined together for mutual protection and survival.[1]

Contradicting previous historical theories, more current research indicated that not all family groups eventually absorbed by the Tonkawa tribe spoke the Tonkawan tongue. A small number that ranged into Central Texas from Northern Mexico spoke a language called Sana. The Sana speakers, forced northward by Spanish expansion, merged with the Tonkawas in the late eighteenth century, becoming the Sana clan of the Tonkawa tribe.[2]

Around 1670, Spanish documents reported the Ervipiame clan located in Northeastern Coahuila. Because of their location, the Ervipiame probably spoke Coahuiltecan. In 1701, conflicts with both the Spanish and Apache tribes forced the Ervipiame north of the Rio Grande where they joined about twenty smaller displaced groups in a settlement called "Rancheriá Grande," located near the confluence of the Little and Brazos Rivers near present-day Cameron, Texas. Between 1714–1755 a few of these "pernicious pagans," as a Spanish priest called them, relocated into missions near San Antonio de Béxar, but the majority traveled even farther north to join the Tonkawas, eventually becoming another clan of the tribe. As late as 1759, Spanish missionaries and traders reported members of the Tonkawa tribe communicating daily with sign language, indicating that other non-Tonkawan-speaking family groups lived with the Tonkawas. The sundry Indians fleeing Spanish mission life always found a ready welcome among the Tonkawas.[3]

Between the years of 1528–1691 several Spanish and French explorers encountered Tonkawas, but extant records fail to reveal which Europeans first stumbled into the tribe's antecedents. Recounting his exploits, Álvar Núñez Cabeza de Vaca did not specifically mention the Tonkawa, but from the route of his travels, he undoubtedly met, and probably lived with, the Tohoor Tohaha, clans that became part of the Tonkawa tribe. More than likely he also contacted the Mayeye and Yojuane, who spoke a Tonkawan tongue. Some evidence suggested that Luis de Moscoso Alvarado's men may have skirmished with Tonkawa clans in 1542 at the fringes of the Caddo Confederacy, east of the Trinity River.[4]

In 1687, Henri Joutel, one of René Robert Cavlier, Sieur de La Salle's lieutenants, pinpointed the Mayeye, another of the Tonkawa clans, just inland from Matagorda Bay. Exploring the coastal plain the next year, La Salle's men came into contact with mounted Indians described by the Frenchmen as "Tonkawas" using saddles, bridles, and other equipment of "Spanish design." Searching for the French intruders in 1689, Spanish Capt. Alonso De León reported Emet and Cava Indians living in present-day Victoria and La Vaca counties, clans that would eventually amalgamate with the Tonkawa tribe. De León's journals also list the Toho, which meant his expeditions came across southern branches of the future Tonkawa tribe scattered between the Nueces and Brazos Rivers.[5]

Members of two Spanish explorations of the Great Plains probably contacted the northern Tonkawa clans first. In 1540–1542, Francisco Vázquez de Coronado led an expedition across the plains of modern New Mexico, Texas, Oklahoma, and Kansas. In the canyons of the Llano Estacado Coronado met a band of Indians that tattooed themselves like "the Berber women of North Africa," a trait unknown to most Plains Indians. Perhaps these Indians were the Toho clan of the Tonkawas. In 1601, Juan de Oñate undoubtedly encountered members of the Tonkawa tribe. Oñate's expedition traipsed eastward from Santa Fe across what is now the Texas panhandle and onto the southern plains. In a skirmish with Indians the Spanish called Aguacanes, Oñate's men captured a young man named Miguel. Under interrogation, Miguel revealed to the Spanish that the Aguacanes captured him during a raid on his home "pueblo" called Tancoa. Spirited away at twelve years of age, Miguel remained with the Aguacanes for several years and spoke the local dialect fluently. Miguel disclosed that his people tattooed themselves and painted their faces before going into battle. Other Indians of the region related that Miguel's people were cannibals, a trait later ascribed to the Tonkawa tribe.[6]

The Aguacanes belonged to a branch of the Wichita tribe, thus part of the Caddoan linguistic family, which greatly influenced European use of southwestern native tongues. Logically, Miguel used his captors name, Tonkawa, for the Titskanwatits. More than any other linguistic group, Spanish and French explorers came into contact with the Caddo, or Hasinai, and several Wichita bands of East Texas. Therefore, these explorers and missionaries apparently adopted the Caddo and Wichita word for Tonkawa, making Tonkawa the accepted name for the tribe. French explorers, such as Jean Baptiste Bérnard de La Harpe, used the word Tancaoye, meaning "wanderer," in their reports concerning the Tonkawas.[7]

Tonkawa came from the Waco word Tonkaweya meaning "they all stay together." Although little is known of the true Tonkawan tongue, scholars collected and translated what remained of the language, allowing some insight into the tribe's culture and society. The Tonkawas called themselves Tickanwatic or Titskanwatits, which roughly translated meant "the most human of people" or "Real People." Despite the fact that several disjointed clans of Tonkawas roamed the fringes of the Texas coastal plain, most anthropologists agreed that the core of the Tonkawas did not inhabit the Texas coastline. They postulated that because Tonkawa words for objects such as canoe, island, and fish were not simple but compound explanatory words, the Tonkawas resided inland. Island, or Tacamai ay-kapai, meant "dry ground piece of land in the water." Some studies in the late 1950s linked the Tonkawan language to the Algonkian linguistic family, based in the eastern United States. Several Plains tribes, however, speak a tongue that share common descent with Algonquin, including the Blackfeet, Cheyenne, and Arapaho. If the northern Tonkawa clans had any roots in Algonquian tribes, the Tonkawas had been separated from them for centuries.[8]

Whatever language they spoke, the Tonkawa progenitors provided a trading conduit between the coastal Indians and the Plains-dwelling nations.

Tonkawa traders, for example, exchanged sea shells from the coast and arrow points fashioned from flint picked up in Central Texas to the East Texas and Plains Indian tribes for buffalo and wolf skins. When Europeans arrived in Texas the Tonkawas continued to serve as middlemen between other Indian groups and the Spanish and French traders.[9]

Records of Oñate's expedition place the Titskanwatits on the plains of modern Oklahoma and Kansas. During his time with his Spanish captors, Miguel drew a rough map of all the Indian villages with which he was familiar. Miguel's map, along with Oñate's journals, place the Titskanwatits' range along the Salt Fork of the Arkansas River in present-day Oklahoma, and at the confluence of the Little Arkansas River and the main Arkansas River in Kansas.[10]

Further evidence pointed to the Tonkawa inhabiting both the banks of the Arkansas River and eastern Texas. In April 1716, Spanish missionary Father Francisco Hidalgo, on his way to establish Catholic missions in East Texas, came across a large Tonkawa village on the Trinity River containing an estimated two thousand people. In June 1719, French explorer and trader de La Harpe described six men and two women of a tribe arriving at his trading post in French Louisiana. The visitors came from a village located on the Arkansas River, and this was the first documented time this particular group sojourned into the region. From the Frenchman's account, the visiting Indians appeared to be Tonkawas. De La Harpe presented several presents to the leader of the little group, but lacking a competent translator, he failed to learn much about his guests.[11]

Later on, a scouting party returned from Spanish Texas and reported to de La Harpe that, "seventy leagues to the westward," they had encountered a group of "nomadic tribes," including Tonkawas. De La Harpe's scouts related that the nomads had defeated a band of Lipan Apaches camped on the Red River about "sixty leagues" from where the meeting occurred. De La Harpe recorded that the nomadic tribes were warlike and great fighters, with the Tonkawas "renowned above the others." The Frenchman wrote that their chief was one-eyed from an arrow wound received in battle. De La Harpe continued, "these nations . . . are so hostile towards one another that the victors eat the vanquished." The nomadic tribes, according to de La Harpe, carried bow and lance as their primary weapons, but possessed no firearms because the Spanish refused to furnish "any to the savages."[12]

At least the Spanish government officially refused to provide guns and powder to Indians in Spanish Texas; not so with several Spanish soldiers and traders. In 1760, Gov. Ángel de Martos y Nazarrete conducted an investigation that verified that since 1751, the Tonkawas, and several other tribes, received weapons through illegal trades with Spanish soldiers and settlers. According to several sworn testimonies, Jacinto De León, Jacinto de Barrios y Jáuregui, Pedro de Sierra (a warrant officer assigned to the San Antonio garrison), Domingo del Rio (a sergeant in the Spanish garrison), and his brother Cristobal, along with several others, carried on an "illicit traffic" with the Tancagues (Tonkawas). Most testified that they did not remember what items were traded, but later learned that the "barbarians" received clothing, knives, guns, and powder in return for animal skins. Lazaro Ybañes testified that some Indians traded bison hides at the French Presidio of Nachitos, and that the Catholic priests at the East Texas missions of Nacogdoches and Los Adaes bought "bear grease for their annual sustenance," but he could not remember what the clergymen used as trade items.[13]

Wandering bands such as the Emet, Mayeye, Yojuane, Ervipiame, Caua, Sana, Toho, and Tohaha formed shifting alliances between themselves and the Tonkawan-speaking clans in Texas, forming the basis for the Tonkawa tribe. Because of the convoluted alliances between these groups and their nomadic nature, early European explorers identified the Tonkawas, sometimes mistakenly, in several widespread locations. Between 1746 and 1749, the Spanish founded three missions on what was then called the San Xavier River (now known as the San Gabriel River) northwest of modern Rockdale, to subdue and Christianize the Tonkawas and several other small tribes. Established on the edge of the blackland prairie, the missions drew in several clans of Indians that the Spanish identified as Tonkawas. Ervipiame, for example, inhabited the region of present-day Milam County, and fought numerous skirmishes with the Spanish before moving to the missions. Despite the avowed purpose of enticing the petitioning Tonkawas into the missions, registers of the San Francisco Xavier de Horcasitas Mission listed only "a few" Tonkawas as residents.[14]

As with many Spanish garrisons, soldiers assigned to protect the missions treated the Indian neophytes "with excessive insolence." This brutal treatment by the soldiers and frequent raids by Apaches caused most of the apostate native people to flee the missions by 1752. Fearing French expansion from Louisiana toward Santa Fe, and desirous of the gold and silver reported in the hilly region northwest of San Antonio, the Spanish transferred the priests and soldiers from the San Xavier missions to a new mission and presidio on the San Saba River in 1756. With this move, the Spanish shifted their priority from converting the Tonkawas to cementing an alliance with the Apaches against the Comanche and their French allies.[15]

At least one other band from the Southern Plains migrated south and assimilated into the Tonkawa tribe. Spanish records identified the Yojuane living in southern Kansas in 1601, but described them as a Wichita tribe and enemies of the Titskanwatits. Forced south by other tribes, the Yojuane allied themselves with the Tonkawas. Several Yojuane and Tonkawa warriors participated in the March 1758 destruction of the Mission Santa Cruz de San Sabá northwest of San Antonio in present-day Menard County, linking the Tonkawas to a large body of Indians the Spanish dubbed Norteños. The Spaniards categorized any Indian tribe north of San Antonio hostile to Spanish expansion as Norteños. Further proof of the amalgamation of the Yojuane with the Tonkawas stemmed from the fact that the Yojuane became a large Tonkawa clan and a Yojuane warrior, known as El Gordo, ascended to chief of the Tonkawa tribe in the late eighteenth century.[16]

Most Tonkawa clans lived too far away to be attracted by the San Xavier missions. As early as 1741, Fray Mariano Francisco de Los Dolores y Viana journeyed from San Antonio to the upper Trinity River to deliver presents to the Tonkawas and entice them to enter the Spanish missions, but the Tonkawas declined to move into the missions. In 1759, Spanish soldiers and traders recorded branches of the Tonkawa tribe in widely scattered locations: north of San Antonio on the San Marcos River; at the point where the Clear Fork of the Brazos joins the main river; near Spanish Fort on the Red River; as well as along the Brazos River in the vicinity of present-day College Station. On July 4, 1772, French explorer and trader Athanase de Mézières y Clugny, then Spanish lieutenant governor of Natchitoches post, stated that the Tonkawas ranged between the Trinity and Brazos Rivers in Northeast Texas. In 1774, Gaspar Fiolas, another French trader, journeyed into East Texas to a Tonkawa encampment where he traded various merchandise for tanned deerskins. Some of the Tonkawas returned to Natchitoches with Fiolas, who had several horses and mules loaded with the tanned hides.[17]

On a trading expedition in 1778, de Mézières visited the Tonkawas at a place he called La Tortuga, probably located in the northwestern corner of present-day Limestone County. Most of the archeological discoveries in this area, however, have since been attributed to the Tawakoni, a branch of the Wichita tribe. The nomadic lifestyle and miscellany of Indian tribes inhabiting Spanish Texas prevented archeologists from definitively identifying a Tonkawa encampment dating before the mid-1850s.[18]

Although the varied clans that constituted the Tonkawa tribe remained semi-independent for decades, events in the mid- to late-1700s forced these groups to unite into one tribal unit. Until this time, as they traveled from one area to another, Tonkawas by and large maintained friendly relations and trade with various Wichita, Waco, Caddo, Apache, and Comanche tribes with which they came into contact. External pressures from France and Spain, however, destroyed these fragile alliances, and by the late-1700s open hostilities erupted between the Tonkawa subunits and most other Indian tribes, especially the Comanche, who carried on a lucrative trade for guns with French coureurs de bois from Louisiana. The powerful Comanche forced the Tonkawas to seek an alliance with the Spanish for self-protection. In the summer of 1773, thirty-five Tonkawas, including two chiefs and a French interpreter, rode into the presidio near Mission Concepción in a quest to "ratify a peace pact with the Spanish soldiers." To assure "the fruits of a sincere peace," both the governor and viceroy in Mexico accepted the agreement.[19]

Factors other than warfare with the Comanche Nation forced the scattered clans to mass into a single Tonkawa tribe. For example, in September 1796 a hunting party of eight Choctaws from Louisiana ventured west of

Nacogdoches and was attacked and defeated by "warlike Tonkawas." The defeated Choctaws retreated first to the Red River Valley and then to the Ouachita River. Continued intertribal warfare and an epidemic, probably smallpox which swept through Eastern Texas and Louisiana, devastated Indian populations. As a result of declining numbers, as well as for self-protection, the scattered Tonkawa clans joined together into a single tribe.[20]

Even after consolidation the Tonkawa tribe tallied far fewer members than their enemies. In 1778, de Mézières reported that the Tonkawa warriors numbered three hundred, indicating an estimated total tribal population of one thousand. A smallpox epidemic the next year reduced the tribe by as much as half. Disease and relentless warfare continually reduced the population of the Tonkawa tribe. By 1847, the tribe could field only fifty fighting men. Anthropologists estimated that by 1890, the Tonkawan tribal population dropped by at least seventy-five percent from pre-Columbian numbers.[21]

Despite promises to establish a permanent settlement and discontinue associating with French traders from Louisiana, the tribe remained only semi-loyal to Spain and continued their nomadic lifestyle. In 1779, Capt. Antonio Gil Ibarvo, lieutenant governor of Spanish East Texas, reported to Domingo Cabello y Robles, Spanish governor of Texas, that although the Tancahues (Tonkawas) traded with the Spanish, the tribe refused to remain in one area and sow grain for their livelihood. Ibarvo added that a few apostates, who had fled from several missions, lived among the Tonkawas along the Trinity River and refused to return and "establish themselves in a suitable place" and take up an agrarian life. Disregarding the Tonkawa's recalcitrance, Cabello issued a proclamation offering a reward for some articles, including three muskets, stolen from a Tonkawa delegation visiting the San Antonio de Béxar Presidio in September 1779. The Tonkawas had journeyed to San Antonio to discuss a permanent settlement, but seemed disinclined to abandon their roving existence.[22]

The seventy-five man Tonkawa delegation, which arrived with de Mézières and Andres Courbiere as interpreters, also sought Spanish affirmation of their new chief. De Mézières recorded that an Apache named Tosche, called El Mocho by the Spanish, had been captured at a young age and rose to lead the tribe. During a fight with the Osage he lost his right ear, earning him the sobriquet El Mocho "The Cropped." On October 8, 1779, hoping to gain favor with the Tancagues (Tonkawas), Cabello appointed El Mocho "Capitan Grande" of the tribe, to replace the deceased Chief Neques. In return, El Mocho promised loyalty to "His Catholic Majesty," "to make war against [the enemies] of the Spanish Nation," and to settle the Tonkawas in a permanent town called La Tortuga, "in the area inhabited by the Taguacanes [Tawakoni] and Quiches [Keechi] Indians, building houses and sowing crops for the well being of the Indians of his nation." El Mocho also promised to return any Indians that fled Spanish missions and sought "asylum in his town," and to cooperate with all "Spanish subjects" in Texas. As a symbol of authority the governor presented El Mocho with a silver-headed baton and several gifts of brightly colored cloth and clothing, including a scarlet frock coat and a cockaded hat.[23]

While they were in San Antonio, Cabello lavished numerous gifts on the Tonkawas, including horses, swords, tobacco, salt, bolts of cloth, ribbon, glass beads, combs, awls, and scissors. He also provided the delegation firewood, and treated them to twenty boxes of cigars, a cooked beef daily, and "ears of tender corn." The Tonkawas declared that "they had never been more well attended and cared for," and that Cabello obviously loved the Tonkawa tribe.[24]

While Cabello dealt with the Tonkawa delegation, a larger number of Lipan Apaches arrived near San Antonio to discuss gifts with the governor. When the Lipans discovered the Tonkawas were already in the city, they encamped in the hills of Puerto Viejo about twenty miles northwest of the presidio. First alcade Joseph Antonio Curbelo reported that at least three unarmed Lipan men, including the Chiefs El Joyoso and Joseph Chiquito, slipped into the city to ascertain why an enemy might be entertained by the Spanish governor. The arrival of both Tonkawas and Lipan aroused some consternation with both Cabello and de Mézières. The animosity between the two tribes might flare into open combat, or arouse the suspicion of both tribes as to the true intent of the Spanish.[25]

Cabello assured the Lipan that he was friendly to both tribes and urged the Lipan not to destroy that friendship by "taking revenge" upon the Tonkawas when they left the confines of San Antonio. The governor provided boxes of cigars as a symbol of his fealty. The gifts satisfied the Lipan chiefs and "they went away very contentedly," despite being "extremely resentful" of the Tonkawas. To insure the "care and custody" of the Tonkawas, Cabello provided them an armed escort of a lieutenant and twenty-one soldiers as they rode away from the Lipan and east of the Colorado River. Cabello wrote Teodoro de Croix, commandant general, that "it is no concern of mine whatever incidents might befall [the Tonkawas]," after they crossed the Colorado.[26]

Sometime after the incident in San Antonio, notwithstanding previous animosities, the Tonkawa and Lipan Apache tribes commenced a longstanding interrelationship, which became the only unbroken alliance in either tribe's history. The surviving Lipan creation legend even states that the Lipan and Tonkawa people were created at the same time. In November and December 1782 the Tonkawa, Lipan Apache, Mescalero Apache, Natage Apache, Akokisa, Bidai, Coco, and some Caddo met on the Guadalupe River for a trade fair. The Tonkawas traded French firearms to the Lipan for stolen Spanish horses. For the next three years the Tonkawas carried on an illicit trade in guns and whiskey with the Lipan tribe, strengthening, for a time at least, the bond between the Tonkawa and Lipan Apaches.[27]

In July 1784, the Spanish murdered El Mocho at Nuestra Señora de Loreto de La Bahía, near present-day Goliad. Concerned over the developing Tonkawa/Lipan alliance, Cabello contrived "the final extermination of that [El Mocho] malefactor" more than a year previously, planning to blame the killing on the Lipan. The Spaniards hated El Mocho for years because of suspected Tonkawa thefts of Spanish horses, as well as the chief's resistance to Spanish authority and open assistance to French traders in Texas. Cabello even instructed his soldiers who discovered Tonkawas with stolen horses to "treat the [Tonkawas] the same as if they were Cumanches [sic]." With the elimination of the "accursed" and "traitorous villain" El Mocho, the Spanish authorities hoped for a more malleable Tonkawa chief. Cabello expressed some concern that the Tonkawas might retaliate for the murder but, because El Mocho was born a Lipan, the Tonkawas might choose one of their own for a new leader.[28]

Fortunately for the Spanish, the Tonkawas "had no complaints or regret whatsoever on the death [of El Mocho]." Although the Tonkawas maintained "trade and communication" with the Lipan, bartering French firearms for stolen Spanish horses, the new chief, Yaculchen, moved his tribe to a semi-permanent village on the banks of the Navasota River, where the majority of the Tonkawa tribe remained for about ten years, and opened a lucrative trade in deer skins with the Spanish.[29]

In 1785, the Spanish concluded a fragile peace with the Comanche, who promised to annihilate the Lipan Apaches for the Spanish. In 1786, the Spanish convinced the Tonkawa to join the Comanche and Wichita in warring upon the Lipan Apaches. One hundred and fifty Tonkawa warriors joined a coalition from other tribes which attacked the Lipan and forced them to retreat southwest to small rancherías between the Nueces River and Rio Grande. The frangible alliance between the Comanche and Spanish rapidly crumbled, however, and the Tonkawas rejoined the Lipan as mortal enemies of the Comanche and Wichita tribes.[30]

Incessant warfare with the more populous tribes pushed the dwindling Tonkawas farther south and east into the fringes of the blackland prairie, a post oak savannah where the tribe found partial shelter from the mounted Comanche warriors. To maintain the friendship and economic dependency of the Tonkawas, as well as several other tribes, and to use the Indians as a shield against Comanche raids, the Spanish altered their policy concerning trade with the Indians. Beginning in 1785 the Spanish, following the French example in Louisiana, began including firearms and powder in their trade goods. In September 1785, the Tonkawas gathered with a few other small tribes to receive their share of gifts and trade items from the Spanish. These included:

| | |
|---|---|
| 12 | rifles [probably fusils] |
| 46 | pounds of powder [another 40 pounds ruined en route when it became wet] |
| 92 | pounds of bullets |
| 23 | worms [for firearms] |
| 276 | flint stones |

| | |
|---|---|
| 9 | pounds of wire |
| 10 | axes and hatchets |
| 10 | hoes |
| 95 | knives |
| 89 | shaving blades [razors] |
| 84 | awls |
| 100 | needles |
| 64 | "steel pieces" |
| 36 | pairs of scissors |

The Spanish governor included beads, combs, bells and jingles, tobacco, shirts, bolts of wool and cotton cloth, blankets, mirrors, and iron pots to the list of gifts and trade items. When Tonkawa dignitaries visited San Antonio the Spanish not only provided food and lodging, but offered gifts of valuable horses and "saddle trappings." When the Tonkawas departed the presidio they received the "customary gifts" of corn, beans, salt, cigars, and other provisions. These arrangements left the Tonkawas "full of contentment, for the good hospitality for which they were attended [when visiting San Antonio]."[31]

Despite the amenable visits with the governor in San Antonio all did not remain peaceful between the Tonkawas and the Spanish. On November 12, 1787, Ibarvo recorded a Tonkawa mistreatment of Christóbal Equis, a resident of Nacogdoches, and an employee of a licensed Indian trader. Equis reported that he had to abandon the bulk of his trade goods and "retreat in haste" from a Tonkawa encampment. Because Equis angered the chief by a paucity of gifts, the Tonkawas beat Equis and "cursed him atrociously," at the direction of the chief. Ibarvo commented that "this kind of bold outrage can produce nothing but evil consequences in the depraved spirits" of the Indians, and he prohibited any contact with the offending Tonkawa village.[32]

Ibarvo also proposed to cutoff trading with the Tonkawas until "we receive from them the satisfaction we must demand in order to keep these barbarians from increasing the bold excesses toward which they constantly lean." Concerned by increased hostility with the Tonkawas, and typical of a Spanish colonial bureaucrat, Interim Gov. Rafael Martínez Pacheco cautioned

Ibarvo to "handle these matters with the proper tact and skill" and instruct the traders to "behave with wisdom and prudence." Pacheco then forward Ibarvo's letter to Commandant General Jacobo de Ugarte y Loyola for instructions, which were as ambiguous as those issued to Ibarvo. Pacheco continued to blame the Tonkawas for horses stolen from ranchos in Texas, further compounding the settler's distrust of the Tonkawa tribe.[33]

Continued pressure from marauding Comanche, and pursuits by Spanish soldiers, persuaded the migrant Tonkawas to seek more congenial relations with the Spanish governor. On June 1, 1788, a "Christian" Tonkawa named "Francisco" entered San Antonio and, in fluent Spanish, reported to Pacheco that four Tonkawa chiefs, accompanied by ten other leaders, sixty-seven warriors, thirteen women, and ten children, awaited just outside the presidio to meet with the governor. The Tonkawas stated that they wanted to meet Ugarte, who had just visited Texas, but were delayed because of swollen rivers and Indian enemies. The chiefs sought gifts of food and affirmation of the "peace agreement" between the Spanish and Tonkawa nation.[34]

News of Spanish prosecution of a war with the Mescalero Apaches had reached the Tonkawas and convinced them of the military prowess of the Spanish. Knowledgeable of his advantage, Pacheco informed the Tonkawa leaders of "the proper manner in which they should comport themselves." After a "parlay," the governor presented the Tonkawas with the usual gifts and "they [Tonkawas] left greatly pleased." An escort of soldiers accompanied the Indians for several miles outside San Antonio, both to protect the Tonkawas from their enemies and insure that none of the Indians "furtively returned" to steal horses from the Spanish. For the remainder of the eighteenth century, and the first few years of the nineteenth century, the Tonkawa tribe maintained a rather capricious peaceful coexistence with the Spaniards, while attempting to survive unremitting raids by the Comanche and Wichita warriors.[35]

## 2  TONKAWA CUSTOMS AND SOCIETY

Surviving descriptions of Tonkawa culture, society, and language vary, with factual information distorted by rumor and innuendo. Sometimes considered part of the Plains Indian culture, the Tonkawa exhibited a conglomerate of disparate native cultures, from the small family groups of the Coahuiltican forgers of South Texas to the even more nomadic buffalo hunters of the South Plains. Early accounts described the Tonkawas as tall, resembling most Indians, but shorter than their coastal-dwelling Karankawa neighbors. In the 1700s, Father Isidro Félix de Espinosa recorded that most Tonkawa men wore nothing, but the women "were decorously covered" in tanned deerskins. By the nineteenth century, both men and women dressed in skins of deer and antelope, held up by a leather thong that served as a belt. In warmer weather men adopted long breech clouts and leather leggings, while the women wore only a simple short leather skirt. Both sexes wore buckskin moccasins, called teguas, year round and, in cold weather donned long buckskin overshirts and buffalo robes for warmth.[1]

In June 1807, American explorer Zebulon Montgomery Pike, while being escorted out of Texas by Spanish soldiers, visited a Tonkawa village on the Colorado River, near present-day Bastrop. He wrote that the "Tancards [Tonkawas]" were "tall handsome men, but the most naked savages I ever saw." In the "encampment of Tancards, [there were] more than 40 lodges. Their [Tonkawas] poverty was as remarkable as their independence."[2]

According to early European explorers both men and women adorned themselves with facial and body tattoos, along with considerable body painting. Both sexes tattooed a single line through the middle of their forehead, down the bridge of the nose, and over the center of the chin. The male tattoos usually consisted of two or three additional horizontal lines across the forehead and chin, with vertical lines on the cheeks and nose. Men also sported numerous earrings, amulets, and necklaces made from bone, shells, animal claws, and later brass, iron, and copper. Tonkawa warriors gathered their hair at the back of their neck and festooned their hair at the gather with brightly painted feathers and beads. Women tattooed their faces with horizontal and vertical lines down their cheeks and nose, but not as many as their male companions. Women of the Tonkawa clans also decorated their breasts with blue tattoos of concentric circles beginning at the nipples. Both men and women rubbed vermillion, ground charcoal, and lime into tattoos to add color and permanence to their personal embellishments.[3]

Apparently most antecedents of the Tonkawa tribe lived in close-knit, self-governing matrilineal clans. Led by a single chief, up to forty families composed these village organizations. Mature men, in a council, selected both peace and war chiefs. Depending on his skill in battle and reputation for wisdom in providing for the tribe, one chief might lead the clan, and later tribe, during both peace and war. These clans were the Tonkawa social structure as well, with the children belonging to their mother's clan. Tonkawa men married women outside their clan because the tribe considered marriages within the clan incestuous. After marriage, men remained members of their mother's clan, thus forming ties between the two families and uniting the clans into a larger familial group. When a warrior died his remaining property went to his sister's children, not his own who belonged to another clan.[4]

After the Tonkawa clans became a single tribal band, each clan leader, or sub-chief, maintained an important role in both clan and tribal management.

Each of the twelve clan leaders held an equal voice in tribal councils. Additionally, a clan leader assumed the responsibility of maintaining a mental record of blood relationships between members of his wife's clan and individuals of other clans. Tonkawas considered each clan as an extended family descended from a common mythical, or totemic, ancestor. Within a clan, Tonkawa culture grouped persons of the same generation under a single kinship term. Known as the Crow system, several Plains Indian tribes adopted this method of family organization whereby a person's father, uncles, and the male children of his father's sister were addressed, in Tonkawa, as ha-ago-n gwa-lou, meaning father, or "a male of my father's lineage." Similarly, an individual addressed his mother and her sisters as kwan k-w'alo gwa-n gwa-lou, meaning mother, or "female of my mother's lineage."[5]

With one or two notable exceptions, Tonkawa culture and societal practices reflected those of neighboring tribes. Women remained with the clan except during childbirth, when they confined themselves to an isolated birthing hut. Tonkawa taboos also prohibited a prospective father from touching birds or breaking the marrow bones of animals in order to prevent his child from being born with weak legs. Not all Tonkawa women, however, allowed their pregnancies to reach full term. Spanish archives recorded that priests asked Tonkawa women "did you take something to kill the child in your belly?" Excavating mission sites where Tonkawas resided for short periods, archaeologists recovered several fetuses from cemeteries. According to Cabeza de Vaca, the Mayeyes and Yojuanes practiced female infanticide to prevent their daughters from falling into enemy hands and possibly producing warriors for another tribe. In the 1800s, Texas cattleman Charles Goodnight wrote that Tonkawa women did not want to bear children for their enemies to kill so they induced abortions with native herbs.[6]

Overall, the Tonkawas handled their children comparably to other American Indian tribes. They treated their youngsters with tolerance, never physically punishing "youthful infractions." Tonkawas used a type of cradleboard and considered their children babies until they were about three years old. Like other tribes, the Tonkawas named their offspring after the children reached a few years of age. Adult Tonkawa men and women might also change their name later in life. Tonkawa clans sometimes practiced polyandry, and less often polygyny, because marriage and reproduction insured survival: "Unmarried men and women could not survive in the rugged environment of the nomadic hunter-gathers."[7]

All the Tonkawa clans subsisted as hunter-gatherers. Living a transient life, these groups seldom attempted agrarian practices, and when they did, the experiment usually failed. Bison or buffalo, deer, and antelope provided meat and clothing for most of the tribe, but the Tonkawa also ate almost anything they could catch or kill. Javelina, rabbits, squirrels, raccoons, opossums, skunks, rats, turkeys, prairie chickens, snakes, turtles, fish, and freshwater clams added variety to the Tonkawa diet. The Tonkawa women and children combed the riverbanks for the abundant pecans and berries that grew along the water courses of Central Texas.[8]

The women pounded dried meat, ground pecans, and dried berries together to make pemmican, to which they added hot grease and stored the mixture in rawhide bags. Preserved in this manner, pemmican lasted for months. During lean times the Tonkawas ate the storage bags as well, and tribal dogs probably added to the hungry tribe's larder. Wolves and coyotes held an esteemed role in the Tonkawa creation legend, and the tribe refused to eat, or even injure, these animals. In 1830, naturalist Jean Louis Berlandier noted that the Tonkawas endured hunger "better than any human beings I have ever known." According to Berlandier the Tonkawas, during times of hunger, just drew their belts tighter and tighter around them until they found something to eat.[9]

Except for their legend of creation, and resulting wolf dance, little of early Tonkawa culture and religion survived to the present. According to Tonkawa ideology, the wolf dug into the earth and released the first Tonkawa people from a dark cave. After liberating the Tonkawa from the earth, the wolf accepted responsibility for the tribe and provided the humans with the necessities of survival. The wolf presented them with fire, the bow and arrow, and taught the Tonkawa how to use the weapon in both hunting and warfare. The wolf also taught the people how to survive in a hostile land, instructing them which plants were sources of food and medicine, and showing the Tonkawa how to build shelters from the weather. The wolf explained to the Tonkawa that they, now safeguarded by the most powerful predator on the plains, were hunters not farmers. According to their traditions, the wolf forbad the first Tonkawa from cultivating the earth, instead tutoring the humans in survival by hunting, raiding, and stealing from their enemies.[10]

Tonkawa clans gathered once a year to celebrate their creation with a ceremony and dance dedicated to the sacred wolf. In the opening of their crescent-shaped village, the Tonkawas constructed a large brush arbor especially for the dance, which they performed at night. Dancers dressed completely in wolf skins, representing their benefactor, cavorted around the ceremonial fire growling, snapping, and snarling at one another. The wolf dancers rhythmically capered around the fire, sniffing the earth as if searching out a particular scent. A preselected dancer howled and began to dig in the earth. All the other wolf dancers then circled around him and scratched at the ground, digging up a Tonkawa man buried especially for the purpose, thus symbolically releasing the Tonkawa people from their earthly confinement. Other dancers, representing the newly released humans, entered the circle, where the wolf dancers solemnly presented the Tonkawas with the bow and arrow, along with the knowledge to use the weapon. The humans danced with delight and the "wolves" threw off their skins and became Tonkawa as well. Because the Tonkawa considered the wolf sacred and refused to harm the animals, they had to trade for the ceremonial wolf skins from other Indian tribes.[11]

Another Tonkawa legend, which explained how the people entered the High Plains, also involved the wolf. According to the legend, long in the past the Tonkawa were a numerous people, and their neighboring tribes feared the powerful Tonkawas. The other tribes joined together to attack the Tonkawas. In a vision a chief foresaw the future and tried to warn the tribe of the coming attack. Most ridiculed the chief's dream, but several followed his advice and the gray wolf led the people westward away from the doomed village. All who remained in the village died.[12]

The handful of survivors followed the wolf spirit guide until a rock cliff blocked their way. The wolf led the Tonkawa into a cave, where Tonkawa warriors defended the opening against their pursuers. Out of food and starving, the Tonkawa survived by eating those who had starved to death until a man discovered a green plant, which he gave all to eat. The plant, peyote, caused all to go to sleep for seven years. The Tonkawa enemies believed the Tonkawas starved in the cave and went home. After the Tonkawas awoke from their long nap the wolf led them out of the cave onto the plains. This legend contains the three major themes affecting the Tonkawa tribe. First, the tribe was small and the enemy of most other Indians. Secondly, the reference to cannibalism, which became part of their culture and caused other Indians to castigate them. Thirdly, the peyote, which later became a central part of their religion that they passed on to numerous other Plains Indians.[13]

According to several sources, the Tonkawa clans conducted a death watch on dying family members. When the death of a male or female appeared imminent, friends and relatives gathered around the sick or wounded. Forming a tight circle around the dying person, those nearest placed their hands on the dying and those behind placed their hands on the shoulders of the inner circle. Until death came, all swayed and sang a death chant. The Tonkawas believed that the soul went to an afterlife, where it lived a better life than on earth. By being near a dying tribal member the Tonkawas believed they might catch a glimpse of that afterlife. Chiefs, medicine men, and respected leaders lay in state for a short time, but most of the dead were interred immediately in concealed graves.[14]

Accounts varied as to whether the Tonkawas buried their dead lying prone or in a sitting position. Prior to burial the family members painted the deceased's face yellow. Relatives wrapped the corpse in the person's best robe with their favorite accouterments: men with weapons, tools, and prized scalps; women with tools, jewelry, and pottery; and children with their toys. Friends also placed provisions and gifts in the grave to guarantee a pleasant journey to the afterlife. At the conclusion of the ceremony, to serve as a companion in the afterlife, the burial party killed a warrior's favorite dog or mount atop the burial mound. Often, to hide the grave, the animals were buried with the remains.[15]

Some sources contradicted one another as to the actions taken after a death in the clan. Noah Smithwick, author of *Evolution of a State, or Recollections of Old Texas*

*Days*, noted that by daylight on the morning following a Tonkawa death the entire village had decamped with no trace of the village or grave. Those who later reported Tonkawa ceremonies, John C. Jacobs for example, related that official mourning lasted three days, with at least three paid women mourners who wailed and cried all night. The professional mourners also slashed their breasts with sharp stones. Jacobs wrote, "they are almost dead from lost blood, and they are a sight to behold." Spanish observers recorded that women sometimes cut off their nipples when a son died in battle. According to Jacobs, during the official mourning, seven warriors sat in a circle smoking a pipe. Each man in turn would draw in a lung full of smoke and exhale it toward the ground. If the smoke rose the departed spirit had gone to the supernatural world.[16]

Like the Comanches, the Tonkawas never spoke a deceased person's name, nor used one to name a child. The Tonkawas did not fear the dead nor believe the spirits of the dead were evil, just lonely and sought to return to their relatives. Tonkawa warriors, however, seldom traveled or fought at night, but this reluctance did not appear to reflect any fear of evil specters haunting the darkness.[17]

Generally, the clans of the Tonkawa tribe inhabited two distinct geographical regions, which determined the societal and cultural heritage they brought into the coalescing tribe. The northern division roamed over the plains on both banks of the Red River and the southern clans made their homes along the lower reaches of the Trinity, Brazos, Colorado, and Nueces Rivers. The people who composed the southern subunits of the Tonkawa tribe lived in temporary, dome-shaped dwellings called yetsoxan, roughly translated as "interwoven," or "brush lodge." Between 1687–1690, the journals of both René Robert Cavalier, Sieur de La Salle, and Alonso De León describe the Emet, Cava, and several other tribes of the region living in small brush shelters.[18]

Much later, in 1828, Berlandier described these lodges, which Tonkawa women constructed of long willow, or cane, poles. The women implanted the poles in a circle, bent them over, and tied the ends of the poles together in the middle. These structures measured about four to five feet in height and ten feet in diameter. Sometimes in summer one or two sides were left completely open. To weatherproof their homes, women covered the framework with fresh green branches and animal skins. Spanish moss and furs provided beds for the family, sometimes numbering as many as fifteen. A fire burned in the center of the lodge to repel insects in the summer and to warm the house in winter. A low door served as both entrance and chimney. De León observed no horses with these native peoples, noting that they used dogs for beasts of burden.[19]

The Tonkawas who inhabited the fringe of the blackland prairie and Southern Plains adopted the buffalo hide tipi and lifestyle of the Plains Indians. Tonkawa villages resembled those of other Plains Indian tribes, although some observers opined that the Tonkawa tipis were not quite as tall as those constructed by other Plains Indians. A bed of animal skins or sometimes Spanish moss, covered the tipi floor. All twelve clans of the Tonkawas constructed temporary brush arbors and isolation huts in their villages.[20]

In addition to "a healthy and savory" meat, the buffalo furnished the Tonkawas with horns for spoons and drinking cups, bones for tools, sinew for thread and bowstrings, hair for ropes, and the hides for shelter, saddles, clothing, and moccasins. Tonkawa women skinned game and tanned the hides with buffalo brains, while the men repaired or made weapons and equipment when not out hunting or on the war trail.[21]

Like other Plains Indians, the Tonkawas faced the opening of their lodges toward the rising sun, celebrating the beginning of each day and preventing their souls from inadvertently entering the next world. The Tonkawas believed that the spirit of the dead departed to the west and, during sleep, their souls sometimes left their bodies through their heads. If a person slept with his head to the west, he might unwittingly send his spirit to the afterlife. When the clans gathered together in a large village, for the annual wolf dance for example, tribal leaders directed that the village be constructed in a crescent shape, with the open end also toward the east. Tradition directed that each of the twelve clans occupy a certain section of the crescent, with specific clans at the horns of the crescent guarding the "doors" of the encampment. Nineteenth century Tonkawa clans included the Bear, Wolf, Long Genitals,

Snake, Meyei, and Sanux, the last two undoubtedly remnants of the Mayeyes and Sanas. Unfortunately, the tribe lost the knowledge of where each clan should be placed in the crescent. Returning hunters and warriors always approached the village from the east, entering the open end of the crescent. During tribal rituals the people arrayed themselves in such a fashion that the dancers could formally parade into the ceremonial circle from the east.[22]

In June 1807, Pike recorded his expanded perceptions of the Tonkawas as:

> a nation of Indians who rove on the banks of Red [R]iver, and are 600 men strong. They follow the buffalo and wild horses, and carry on a trade with the Spaniards. They are armed with the bow, arrow, and lance. They are erratic and confined to no particular district. [They] are a tall, handsome people, in conversation have a peculiar clucking, and express more by signs than any savages I ever visited . . . They complain much of their situation and the treatment of the Spaniards; are extremely poor, and except the Apaches, were the most independent Indians we encountered in Spanish territories. They possess large droves of horses.[23]

After the Spanish introduced the horse into the Southwest the Tonkawas switched from dogs to horses as their major means of transportation. As with the other Plains Indians, the Tonkawas became expert mounted warriors and hunters. Horses with the same bloodlines as those grazing the plains of Andalusia carried Tonkawa riders on the warpath and on the trail of the buffalo. By the mid-nineteenth century large herds of mustangs grazed near Tonkawa camps while numerous dogs scavenged the village for scraps of anything edible left over from meals and hunts. John Sibley, United States Indian Agent in Natchitoches from 1805 to 1814, described the Tonkawas thusly: "They plant nothing, but live upon wild fruits and flesh: are strong, athletic people, and excellent horsemen."[24]

Tonkawa weapons differed little from those of other American Indian tribes. Sometime in prehistory, the Tonkawa discovered the bow and arrow which became the principal tools of hunting and warfare. Few descriptions of early

Tonkawa weapons survived, but stories of the Tonkawas' skill and accuracy with the weapon abound. Several nineteenth-century accounts, supported by oral history, indicated that the Tonkawa used a short bow, fashioned from a single length of wood, usually hickory or Bois d' Arc (Osage Orange), with a strand of animal sinew for a string. The few remaining examples of Tonkawa bows suggested that the tribe used the short bow of equestrian warriors, but the Southern clans may have utilized a longer bow, such as the five-and-a-half- or six-foot red cedar Karankawa bow described by Stephen F. Austin in 1822. When fully drawn, a Tonkawa bow provided enough energy to drive an arrow completely through a deer or deep into the lungs and heart of a buffalo bull. Arrow makers used slim branches of willow, dogwood, and other pliable trees to make arrows tipped with stone, and later metal, points. The makers fletched the arrows with three "wing feathers" to stabilize the arrow in flight. Warriors sometimes poisoned their war arrows by dipping the points into mistletoe juice.[25]

Mounted Tonkawa warriors carried the stabbing lance of the plains, tipped with either stone or metal points and decorated with strips of animal fur and brightly colored feathers. Warriors also employed buffalo-hide shields, which they decorated with animal skins and eagle feathers. Eagle claws, porcupine quills, elk teeth, bear claws, and after European contact, beadwork adorned Tonkawa weapons. Using the brightest pigments possible each warrior emblazoned his war pony and shield with his personal talisman. Tonkawa men and women carried a variety of stone and metal knives, war clubs, and tomahawks. Firearms, both rifle and pistol, revolutionized Tonkawa life and became essential weapons in the nineteenth century. Tonkawa warriors quickly recognized the advantage of firearms in hunting and war, especially repeating rifles such as the Spencer, Henry, and Winchester.[26]

The primary reason the Tonkawas found themselves chastised by the whites and vehemently despised by the Comanches was their practice of ritualistic cannibalism as part of their supernatural beliefs. The Tonkawas, however, were not unique in this practice. The term itself came from a corruption of the Carib Indians of the Antilles Islands. The Northeastern tribes of the Iroquois, Hurons, Miamis, and especially the Ottawas consumed parts of their dead enemies bodies. On the Great Plains, Cheyenne warriors of certain societies cleansed themselves by eating the cooked heart of an enemy. Lipan Apaches, allies of the Tonkawas from the early 1800s, also indulged in ritualistic cannibalism by flaying off and consuming parts of their slain enemies. Several white mountain men followed this Indian custom of eating part of an enemy. "Liver Eating" John Johnson, for example, earned his sobriquet by devouring part of the liver of the Crow warriors he dispatched in retaliation for Crow warriors slaying his Flathead wife.[27]

In Texas, several tribes practiced some form of cannibalism. According to at least one source the Kiowa Nation, a close ally of the Comanche, included a secret warrior society whose members pledged to devour the heart of the first enemy they slew in battle. Coastal dwelling Aranama, called either Cheraname or Jaraname by the Spanish, Atakapas, and Karankawa tribes often demonstrated a predilection to consume parts of their fellow man. Several families of Aranama, either fleeing Comanche raids or tiring of a life of servitude as Spanish mission apostates, joined Tonkawa bands; Aranama culture may have influenced the Tonkawa's reputation for cannibalism. Seventeenth-century accounts often mentioned various Texas native tribes eating their prisoners and torturing captives to death. According to Tonkawa cultural beliefs, consuming small portions of a vanquished enemy's body demonstrated superiority in warfare and transferred a slain enemy's courage and "spirit power" to the victor.[28]

The Tonkawa also believed that by eating part of a slain foe they deprived that enemy of a second life and an opportunity to take revenge upon the Tonkawa. Therefore, ritualistic cannibalism, and mutilation of enemy dead, became part of the tribe's victory celebrations. The Tonkawa believed that if an enemy's body was destroyed, the soul died too. If an enemy arrived in the afterlife with no eyes, he could not see to harm the Tonkawa, and if he had no legs he could not fight. Berlandier mentioned that Tonkawa warriors left the scene of a battle "carrying the bleeding severed limbs" of Tawakonis. According to Noah Smithwick, John Henry Brown, John Salmon "Rip" Ford, and several other early Texans, Tonkawa celebrations, or "scalp dances," included roasting and consuming portions of their enemy's arms or legs. Texas settlers recorded that the Tonkawas said human flesh tasted "like bear meat." Mountain men and frontiersmen claimed that bear meat tastes like pork. Possibly, this is where the Tonkawas acquired their craving for the settlers' free-ranging hogs.[29]

Most accounts of Tonkawa cannibalism mention consuming smaller pieces of flesh, but Smithwick's tale recounts a ghastlier scene. According to Smithwick several Tonkawa warriors accompanied a group of white Texas frontiersmen pursuing a band of Comanches who had stolen several horses near Bastrop. Three of "the most expert" Tonkawa scouts quickly overtook and slew the single Comanche rear guard, who was mounted on a stolen plowhorse. After dispatching the Comanche, the Tonkawas quickly scalped him and started home to celebrate their victory with "a feast and scalp dance." Smithwick related how the Tonkawas "fleeced off the flesh of the dead Comanche," and borrowed a big wash kettle. Into the kettle they put the "Comanche meat together with a lot of corn and potatoes." Smithwick described the contents of the kettle as "the most revolting mess my eyes ever rested on." Continuing his yarn, Smithwick recounted that the "whole tribe gathered round . . . and eating it [the stew] as freely as hogs," explaining that the Comanche tasted "better than bear meat."[30]

Smithwick wrote that after the "feast" the Tonkawas gathered for a scalp dance. He described the men "in all the hideousness of war paint and their best breechclouts, the warriors gathered round in a ring. Each one armed with some ear torturing instrument, which they operated in unison." Chanting and keeping time to a deerskin drum, the men moved with a grace "that would have pleased a French dancing master." While they danced an old woman presented "an arm or leg" to the warriors, who would "bite it viciously . . . and shaking it like savage dogs." While the warriors danced, a "patriotic squaw" held aloft a lance with the "dressed and painted" scalp attached to the tip. Smithwick wrote that the scalp dance continued until all dropped from exhaustion.[31]

John H. Jenkins, another Texian frontiersman, described an incident he witnessed involving Tonkawa ritualistic cannibalism. Jenkins recalled that about thirty Tonkawas came to him and asked him to point out the body of a Waco warrior he recently killed. According to Jenkins, when the Tonkawas saw the body "they seemed wild with delight, or frenzy." The Tonkawas scalped the body, "cut off both legs at the knees, both hands at the wrists," and strung the Waco's finger and toenails around their necks. The Tonkawas proceeded to shoot the corpse in the head "for good luck." The Tonkawas then begged some beef from Jenkins and went back to their camp where they boiled the beef and Waco's body parts together. The Tonkawa men informed Jenkins that the women would eat part of the enemy's hands and feet, "believing this would make them [the women] bring forth brave men, who would hate their enemies and be able to endure hardness and face danger." The Tonkawas erected a pole, which they topped with the scalp and added the hands and feet. Jenkins continued, "with horrible yells and gestures, all danced around it." The women danced up to the pole and took bites of the hands and feet and then danced away again. Jenkins recalled that the Tonkawa scalp dances sometimes lasted, "three, five, and sometimes ten days."[32]

The vast differences in culture causes one to question the veracity of many Anglo-American and European reports on the Tonkawas. Spanish soldiers and missionaries mentioned the war-like nature of the Tonkawa, and their treachery and cannibalism, generally degrading the tribe. Spanish accounts, however, invariably reflected their pejorative attitude toward any native group which did not possess volumes of accumulated gold and silver, or who failed to unquestioningly follow Spanish directives. A number of explorers and traders, along with some Indian tribes, contradicted the general deprecatory claims of many whites by praising the Tonkawas for their affability and indulgence of others. Some accounts maintained that Tonkawa hospitality included offering young women to visiting males.[33]

Smithwick's assertions should be questioned for several reasons. First, the inherent bias of many white settlers toward natives may have prejudiced his version of the incident. The shock of seeing the Tonkawas eating human flesh may have also hidden the ritualistic meaning of the ceremony. Smithwick's choice of words and phrases, such as "hideous," "vicious," "savage," and "as freely as hogs," exemplified the nineteenth-century white attitude toward American Indians. Secondly, Smithwick's story of cooking an entire human being may have been sensationalized in order to make it more interesting. Additionally, the similarity of Smithwick's tale to stereotypical cannibal stories cast doubt upon the truthfulness of his statements. The oft-told anecdote of missionaries cooked in a cannibal's pot all too closely resembled Smithwick's portrayal of the Tonkawa "feast." Jenkins, conversely, seemed to understand the ceremonial significance behind the Tonkawa ritual.

Actions by other native tribes equally appalled whites raised in Judeo-Christian cultures. Comanche victory celebrations invariably resulted in what whites considered atrocities. Herman Lehmann, captured as a child near Fredericksburg by Lipan Apaches, spent several years among different Indian tribes, eventually becoming a Comanche warrior. Lehmann described a life and death battle between his Comanche band and a group of "Tonkeways." Trailing their enemies, the Comanches discovered a Tonkawa camp and rushed in, driving the Tonkawas from their campsite. When the Comanches discovered a leg of a Comanche roasting over the fire, they cried out for vengeance and gave chase to the fleeing Tonkawas. Lehmann avowed that "we meant utterly to annihilate our enemies." When the Comanches cornered the Tonkawas in a ravine, a Tonkawa warrior killed two Comanches in single combat. Enraged, every Comanche "loaded his gun" and charged into hand-to-hand combat.[34]

The cornered Tonkawas "fought bravely," slaying at least eight of the Comanche warriors and wounding "forty or fifty" more. The Comanches, however, emerged victorious and Lehmann described his war party's actions: "We scalped . . . the [dying enemy], amputated their arms, cut off their legs, cut out their tongues, and threw their mangled bodies and limbs on their own campfire." The Comanche warriors then piled more wood on the fire and, according to Lehmann, "Piled the living, dying, and dead" Tonkawas on the fire. Some of the Tonkawas begged for mercy as the Comanches "danced around with great glee as we saw the grease and blood run from their bodies and were delighted to see them swell up and hear their hides pop as it would burst in the fire." After the slaughter, the Comanches rode away with twenty-eight scalps, thirty-five horses, thirty rifles, saddles and tack, and "a great quantity of ammunition . . . which barially [sic] satisfied our bloodthirsty band."[35]

## 3 SHIFTING ALLIANCES, 1800–1836

As the nineteenth century dawned, intrusions of people and cultures caused a radical shift in the geo-political structure of Texas. An incipient independence movement against Spanish rule brought numerous Anglo-American adventurers into Spanish Texas, who were followed by an even greater number of settlers from the United States and Europe. Among the native peoples, Comanche warriors thundered off the High Plains, riding their painted ponies deep into Chihuahua, Coahuila, Nuevo Santander, and onto the Texas Coastal Plain.

The Comanches fearsome onslaught almost wrecked a teetering economy as it drove other Indians from their traditional lands, and toward the ever-advancing white frontier. The Wichitas dispersed into small villages along the Red River, while the Wacos and Tawakonis settled near present-day Waco. The Tonkawas, with only two hundred warriors in 1805 by John Sibley's reckoning, retreated to the post oak savannah and the woodlands fringing the San Antonio River. The tribes east of the Brazos River continued to occupy their traditional homeland, bartering with Louisiana traders, but facing increasing competition from Indians forced into East Texas by the inescapably approaching United States frontier. The Lipan Apaches, fleeing from the constant pursuit of both the Spanish and Comanche, eked out an existence in the arid regions of southern Texas and northern Coahuila and Chihuahua.[1]

During the last decade of the 1700s and first two of the 1800s, Tonkawa relationships with other tribes altered dramatically. In 1714, the Tonkawas destroyed a Caddoan village and burned the main temple of the Hasinai Confederacy on the Angelina River and, over the years, captured hundreds of Caddo women and children and sold them to Spanish slave traders in Mexico. By the early nineteenth century, however, the Tonkawas had joined the Caddos in an alliance against encroaching eastern Indians and the Comanche raiders from the west. The short-lived 1780s Tonkawa alliance with the Comanches and Wichitas disintegrated rapidly and the Tonkawas refused to join the Comanche and Wichitas in attacking the new Spanish settlement of San Marcos de Neve in 1812. Nevertheless, Spanish authorities sent a punitive expedition against the Tonkawas for harassing the Spanish settlements. Responding to the Spanish offense, in 1812–1813 a few Tonkawas joined with Hasinais and Wichitas in the Gutiérrez-Magee Expedition to liberate Texas and Mexico from Spanish control. Some four years later, several Tonkawa warriors living in East-Central Texas apparently joined the Cherokees in a bloodthirsty war against a traditional Tonkawa enemy, the Osages.[2]

Beset by Comanche raids the Tonkawas established an everlasting alliance with the Lipan Apache and a series of transitory alliances with the Spanish, Mexicans, and Texians, serving as scouts and guides for the whites against the Comanches and their allies. Unfortunately, the Tonkawas remained in some type of conflict with most Indian tribes throughout the nineteenth century. Tonkawas went to war for various reasons, most prevalently over thefts of horses and women, or to avenge the killing of a tribal member. Fights usually consisted of a large number of participants, with a garish display of color and horsemanship. Most battles between warring factions, although bloody, usually resulted in few fatalities. Indian tribes could little afford to lose scarce warriors. For example, in 1819 explorer Juan Antonio Padilla estimated the entire Tonkawa tribe contained no more than five hundred warriors. Wars and raids cannot be minimized; however, the very survival of the Tonkawa tribe rested on victories over their enemies. Each Tonkawa clan depended on the skill of a warrior's bravery, both in battle and in hunting. Warriors held "an honored niche" in Tonkawa society.[3]

Pressure from their native enemies and the desire for manufactured goods, especially firearms, caused the recently consolidated Tonkawa tribe to move into the post oak savannah of Central Texas. Here they remained for several years, establishing friendly relations with the newly arrived immigrants to the region. From the post oak territory, mounted Tonkawas sallied out on buffalo hunts, then returned to the relative sanctuary of the woodlands, where they continued in a lucrative trade of hides and furs for horses, metal tools, and guns. Sibley reported that one trader claimed that he acquired five thousand deer skins from the tribe in one year, "exclusive of tallow, rugs, and tongues." The Tonkawa's central location also provided a haven for any Indians who relished a nomadic life over that of a sedentary farmer.[4]

Amidst the turmoil the Tonkawas attempted to maintain a congenial atmosphere between themselves and the shifting political and economic powers in Texas. In February 1818, the Tonkawas concluded a peace treaty with Antonio María Martínez, the last Spanish governor of Texas, who hoped because of the tribe's strategic location the Tonkawas would "constitute a safeguard" by "observing any traveler from the United States." In June 1820, Martínez reported a band of amicable Tonkawas camped northeast of San Antonio on the Brazos River near Garrapatas Creek. The Spanish, however, did not fully trust the Tonkawas. Martínez wrote in a letter that, "I doubt that their peace treaty was made in good faith because they all are untrustworthy and are influenced only by gifts, and they receive none from us . . . they have no ambition at all."[5]

Padilla reported in 1820 that the Tonkawas "although not entirely lacking in valor and disposition to carry on offensive warfare . . . were not to be exceeded as the laziest and greatest of knaves." Padilla suspected the Tonkawas remained at peace with the Spanish only "because of the war they are engaged in with the other nations." Contradicting Padilla, an unsigned

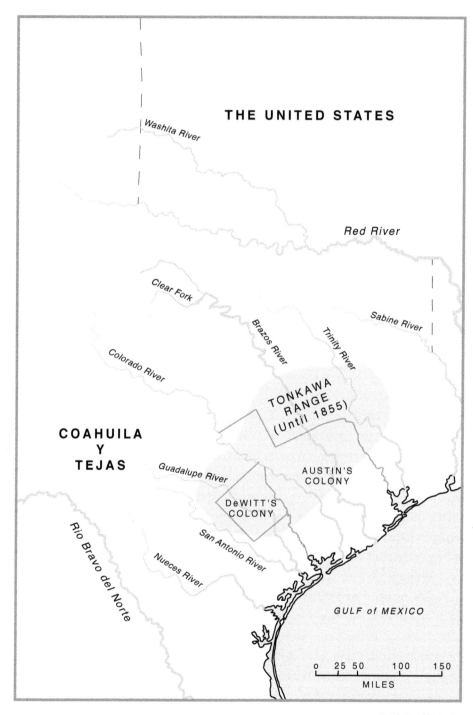

THE UNITED STATES

*Washita River*

*Red River*

*Clear Fork*

*Brazos River*

*Trinity River*

*Sabine River*

*Colorado River*

TONKAWA
RANGE
(Until 1855)

**COAHUILA
Y
TEJAS**

*Guadalupe River*

AUSTIN'S
COLONY

DeWITT'S
COLONY

*San Antonio River*

*Rio Bravo del Norte*

*Nueces River*

GULF of MEXICO

0   25  50      100      150
MILES

*Map by Donald S. Frazier.*

report in the Arkansas Territorial Archives reported the Tonkawas as "the most expert with firearms and warlike Indians of any in the province in Texas." In 1822, a Tonkawa chieftain visited the Mexican governor in San Antonio seeking to sustain an alliance between the new Mexican government and the Tonkawas. The chief offered to guide Mexican soldiers against the Comanches and Wichitas, as well as lead the Mexicans to the lost silver mines on the San Saba River.[6]

On August 22, 1821, Stephen F. Austin first encountered the Tonkawa tribe. On an exploratory trip the empresario met the Tonkawa Chief Gocoso, presented him with some tobacco, and noted in his journal that the chief was "pleased" that Americans would soon settle in Tonkawa territory. Typical of white misunderstandings of Indian culture, Austin refused to take the time to "smoke" with Gocoso, which somewhat angered the chief. The next year, Austin's colonists met the tribe along the Brazos River in present-day Washington County. The Tonkawas opened a profitable trade with their new neighbors, exchanging tanned hides and horses for food and other goods.[7]

Meanwhile the settlers initiated their first attempts to convert the Tonkawas to an agrarian lifestyle. Austin supplied the Tonkawas with hoes and other farming implements and "an ample supply" of seed corn, hoping the Tonkawas would become sedentary farmers. The Tonkawas made bread from the corn; however, Carita, the Tonkawa's major chief, informed Austin that the "Great Spirit" told him that the Tonkawas should continue hunting as was their custom, because the "whites could grow food enough for all."[8]

In addition to trading with Austin's settlers Tonkawa warriors guided the Texians on several reprisal raids against other Indian tribes. In 1822, a Karankawa party raided a settlement near Skull Creek, severely wounding Robert Brotherton. A few Tonkawas, led by Chief Carita, as both scout and hostage, accompanied the frontiersmen on a reprisal raid that killed "9 or 10" Karankawas. In 1824, several Wichita raiders slipped into the Kuykendall settlement near Washington-on-the-Brazos and rode away with some good horses. Tonkawa scouts tracked the thieves to a spot near San Felipe where settlers captured the Wichitas and recovered their horses. Unfortunately, most of Austin's settlers failed to recognize the friendly Tonkawas and adopted a policy of "shooting down red men wherever they were found."[9]

Further cementing their commitment to the Texians the Tonkawas even submitted to corporal punishment instituted by Austin for stock thefts. In October 1823, five Tonkawas stole several horses from the colonists. The colonists trailed the Tonkawas to within six miles of Fort Bend on the Brazos River and then rode to San Felipe where Austin gathered a party of about thirty men to recover the horses. Carita received word of the pursuit and endeared himself to the colonists by meeting Austin and admitting that the thieves were Tonkawas, and promising that the valuable animals would be returned to San Felipe. Carita led the Texians to a camp where Austin's men captured the thieves and recovered their horses. Austin sentenced the culprits to fifty lashes and banishment from the settlements, promising the scoundrels they would be shot if they were again caught stealing livestock from Austin's colonists. Carita himself administered half the lashes, but "laid them on very lightly."[10]

In Spring 1826, settler's complaints disrupted the peace between Austin's colony and the Tonkawas. One colonist complained about the theft of several hogs, another a theft of several bushels of corn and other provisions, and still another settler, a Mr. Dyer, complained that a group of Indians rode up and so frightened his wife that she fled from her home. The settlers blamed all these events on the Tonkawas and gathered a group of at least fifteen men to chastise the Tonkawas. When the Texians rode into the first Tonkawa camp they stumbled upon, they opened fire and, in the ensuing battle, at least two Tonkawas and one settler died. J. H. Kuykendall claimed that six Texians fired into the Tonkawa camp, killing four and wounding three other Indians—awfully good shooting for single-shot, muzzle loading rifles.[11]

Austin investigated the incident and, "from my investigations, I felt satisfied that the presumed depredations of the Indians were not sufficiently established to justify the attack, although there were good reasons to suspect them [the Tonkawas]." Austin considered the whites the aggressors, and more at fault than the Tonkawas. On April 29, a group of Tonkawa leaders summoned by Austin participated in a four-day conference, whereupon they agreed that the Tonkawas might have been involved in some of the thefts and promised that any Tonkawas involved in further stealing would be surrendered for punishment. According to Austin, the Tonkawas also understood that any Indians caught stealing would be shot.[12]

Stealing horses from other Indians also brought the ire of Austin's colonists down on the Tonkawa. As part of their raiding economy the Tonkawas stole horses from other Indians, especially the Comanches and Wichitas. In retribution, the Comanches followed the Tonkawas back to their villages on the fringes of Austin's colony. Soon horses and cattle from the settlement fell prey to Comanche raiders as well. A few settlers, such as James J. Ross, exacerbated the problem by buying stolen Comanche horses from the Tonkawas. William Rabb complained to Austin that several colonists, "for the sake of dishonest self interest," brought the wrath of the Comanches down upon the colony. Rabb believed that if the Tonkawas and Lipan Apaches stopped stealing Comanche horses, which were in turn brought among the settlers, then the colonists "should not be troubled with the Comanches"—wishful thinking at best.[13]

During the next decade, the Tonkawas living near the settlements helped to recover numerous horses stolen from white settlers by other native tribes, and some eighty Tonkawa warriors served as scouts and guides for the Texians. Reciprocating the favor, Austin's colonists also returned horses stolen from the Tonkawas, while overlooking the alleged theft of several hogs by the Tonkawas. In 1830, a group of whites stole a cavvy of horses belonging to some Tonkawas living near San Felipe. Some of Austin's colonists caught the thieves and returned the horses to the Tonkawas. These reciprocal actions solidified the friendship between the Tonkawas and Austin's pioneers.[14]

Ever the adroit politician, Austin maintained a friendly relationship with the Tonkawas and used them as a barrier to more hostile tribes to the north and west of his colony. William Pettus described the Tonkawas as "a small impertent [sic] and contemptible tribe," who claimed no territory and roamed the countryside at will. Pettus observed that the tribe remained close to the colonist because "they were involved in difficulties with other tribes," not venturing very far north "less they should meet with the Comanches." The Tonkawa camped along Yegua Creek, making the location the northern boundary of Tonkawa protection from the Wichita in Washington County.

In 1837, the Tonkawa fought the Waco and Wichita south of Yegua Creek near Evergreen Mountain. Both sides claimed victory, but the Wacos were never again reported south of the creek.[15]

In 1826, Jean Louis Berlandier, in his *Journey through Texas*, described the Tancahueses [Tonkawas], as "one of the most wretched [tribes] in Texas." Led by principle Chief Joaquin, who spoke perfect Spanish, this particular band of Tonkawas camped on the banks of the Guadalupe River. Driven off the buffalo plains and "diminished daily" because of continual warfare with Comanches and their allies, many of the Tonkawas were hungry, and their elderly were in a "state of decrepitude." Berlandier met one old man "of at least 70" who bore a scar from a spent conical ball, which "made a cavity of half the size of its caliber in one of the frontal bones [of his head]." Berlandier verbally depicted an old woman so starved that she appeared "to have emerged from the empire of the shades." He wrote that "the muscles had dried on her boney frame . . . her skin was blackish," and he viewed the old woman as "a type of spectre." Berlandier portrayed the tribe as so hungry that when a horse drowned the "savages threw themselves into the water (the temperature standing at 0) to fish it out and eat it."[16]

Several Tonkawa clans also roamed over Green De Witt's colony, established south and west of Austin's "Old Three Hundred." These Tonkawas experienced numerous devastating Comanche raids and, according to available records, caused more turmoil than in Austin's colony. In February 1827, James Kerr reported a battle on the San Marcos River near Gonzales in which a combined group of Tonkawas and Lipan Apaches suffered a bitter defeat at the hands of a large raiding party of Comanche and Wichita warriors. Throughout 1829–1830, De Witt's colonists complained that both Tonkawas and Karankawas slipped into the settlements and stole numerous horses. One settler who maintained a trading post provided guns to both tribes, hoping they would eliminate each other, but the Indian's poor marksmanship foiled the perverse merchant's scheme. During these incursions, the Tonkawas also killed several hogs, which caused considerable consternation among De Witt's colonists.[17]

In one instance, De Witt and about seventeen men trailed a much larger group of Tonkawas that had stolen a few farm implements and several horses from the colony. When another band of forty Tonkawas joined the party that De Witt was trailing, the combined group turned and "commenced a fire on me with guns and arrows." De Witt's men repulsed the first attack, killing two Tonkawas. De Witt and his men then took cover in a creek bed and fought the Tonkawas until dark, killing two more Indians during the second clash. After suffering these losses, the Tonkawas allowed the whites to withdraw and then rode away with the stolen horses.[18]

The outnumbered Texians thought themselves fortunate that their attackers were not Comanches, as they believed such an encounter would have been fatal. To preclude future thefts by Indians, De Witt offered to provide inexpensive provisions for a detachment of Mexican soldiers if the commandant at La Bahiá would station the men in his colony. Noteworthy in all the livestock and property thefts perpetrated by the Tonkawas in De Witt's colony, recollections failed to include a single settler injured. Not so with Mexican rancheros farther south. According to Vicente Filisola, commanding troops at Matamoras, a party of Tancahues [Tonkawas] and Lipans "killed Don Clemente Guzman and wounded a worker of his" during a stock raid in 1838.[19]

Capitalizing on the Tonkawas need to protect themselves from escalating Comanche raids, De Witt proposed what he considered an amicable solution to the local Tonkawa chiefs. He attempted to convince them to accept a grant of land from the Mexican government and become farmers. De Witt promised to raise money to buy axes and other necessary tools, organize people to teach the Tonkawas to farm, and assist them in securing proper titles to lands as bona fide citizens of Mexico. De Witt added that the Mexican government "had a great regard for them and wished them to become a great and good people." The Tonkawa chiefs nonetheless declined De Witt's offer, clinging to their wolf culture of hunting, raiding, and stealing from their enemies. Local Tonkawas, however, ceased their larceny in De Witt's colony, probably hoping to engage the Texians as military allies against the Comanches.[20]

Cognizant that any enduring amity with the whites depended on their continued assistance, the Tonkawas offered their skills to the Texians at every opportunity. In 1836, a small party of Comanches stole Bartholomew

Manlove's favorite "huge powerful horse." Manlove offered his best slave and his daughter Dolly's "hand in marriage" to her suitor for the return of his horse. The young man engaged several Tonkawas as scouts and rode off in pursuit of the Comanches. As they followed the trail a Comanche warrior appeared on Manlove's prized horse, shook his spear in "contemptuous gestures" toward his pursuers, calling the Tonkawas "cowards and squaws" then rode away.[21]

Unfortunately for the Comanche, a large horse did not translate into a fleet horse, and the Tonkawas soon overtook the brazen warrior. He agilely dismounted and rapidly loosed a flight of arrows at the onrushing Tonkawas. Fighting "like a tiger" the Comanche fell before the Tonkawas, who scalped him and cut off his hands and feet. The Tonkawas then flayed his hips and thighs, saying they would leave the rest to "the wolves and buzzards." The Tonkawas supposedly took the flesh of the Comanche for the "washpot feast" mentioned in the previous chapter. From all accounts, Manlove lived up to his bargain and Dolly married her beau shortly thereafter.[22]

Despite that for more than a decade the Tonkawas exhibited little hostility toward the Texians, several colonists openly derided the tribe as mere opportunistic thieves. Pettus disagreed with several estimations of the Tonkawas, writing that they were "never warlike or brave," but like many other colonists thought the Tonkawas "the damnedest of all thieves." Pettus remembered that the Tonkawas bartered skins for green corn and other foodstuffs, but resorted to stealing when they lacked trade items. He related a story in which a settler agreed to give several Tonkawas half of his corn crop in return for two horses to be provided at a later date. When the Tonkawas failed to live up to their part of the bargain, the settler had one of the guilty Tonkawas brought before Austin for adjudication of the contract. According to Pettus, the Tonkawa assented that he had incurred the debt but had eaten the corn and had no horse to provide the farmer. Pettus wrote that the Indian defended himself, saying "Did de white tink I ever pay? He know better. He fool to tink so . . . Indian no pay and de white should not trust him. He fool too much and ought to lose horse." Surprisingly his plea worked and Austin voided the Tonkawas' debt.[23]

George W. Bonnell commented that the Tonkawas had a "natural proness [sic] to steal [which] will manipulate itself whenever they [Tonkawas] have a good opportunity." In 1833, an incident occurred that apparently substantiated his comments. A trader from the United States named Reed journeyed into Texas and spent several days at "Falls of the Brazos," in present-day Falls County. Seven friendly Toncahuas [Tonkawas] coincidently camped there with Reed and swapped horses and goods with him. The Tonkawas, believing that Reed cheated them in a horse trade, lay in ambush as the trader returned to the United States. After killing Reed, the Tonkawas kept his horse and baggage, which identified them as the perpetrators of the murder. Canoma, a Caddo, enlisted several of his followers and took up the trail of the Tonkawas. Eight days later, the Caddos returned with Reed's horse and belongings, along with seven fresh scalps. For their actions the Caddos earned "substantial commendation" from the colonists. A group of Texas settlers later killed Canoma and his son as the two were returning several horses stolen from the whites by Comanches.[24]

The smoldering insurrection to separate Texas from Mexico erupted into a gory revolution in the mid-1830s, but the Tonkawas did not actively participate in the conflict against Mexico. Tribal leaders seemed more concerned with maintaining advantageous commercial relationships with their white neighbors than fighting Mexicans. The tribe did, however, continue raids against other native groups. In 1834 or 1835, J. H. Kuykendall recalled that Mexicans around Victoria instigated a Tonkawa attack against a nearby Karankawa village. According to Kuykendall, the Tonkawas "treacherously assassinated" fifteen or twenty Karankawa after a small Tonkawa boy slipped into their camp and cut all the Karankawas' bow strings. When the Tonkawas attacked they killed all but two or three occupants of the village.[25]

## 4 TONKAWAS AND TEXIANS, 1836–1845

While the Tonkawas remained friendly with the Texians, they did not actively assist their white friends during the revolution against Mexico, and the new Republic did not recognize the Tonkawa tribe as an ally. On October 12, 1837, the Standing Committee on Indian Affairs listed the Tonkawas, Lipans, and Karankawa as part of the Mexican nation and "no longer to be considered as a different people from that nation." The Texas government, however, shortly reversed its decision concerning the Tonkawa tribe. On November 22, 1837, encouraged by President Sam Houston's peace policy toward Indians, Tonkawa Chiefs Ouchcala, Gosata, and Harshokena signed a treaty with the new Republic with the "promise to bury the Tomahawk and live upon terms of Peace and Amity with the government of Texas." This, and several other subsequent treaties favoring the Texians, provided trading posts for the tribe, and appointed Nathaniel Lewis as the tribe's first agent, "who shall regulate and have a controlling influence over the trade which may be carried on between the Tonkawa and the citizens of Texas." In reciprocation the Tonkawas promised to end any "depredations" against white Texans. The Tonkawas also continued their informal alliance with Texas against the Comanches.[1]

A short five months later, the Republic of Texas and the Tonkawas further affirmed their commitments to one another. On April 10, 1838, Secretary of War Barnard E. Bee and Col. George W. Hockley, along with Tonkawa Chiefs Campos, O'Quinn, Plácido, and Benevido signed a "Treaty of Peace and Amity" in Houston. By affixing their "X" to the document, the Tonkawas consented to "bring to just punishment" any Tonkawas who "commit any depredations upon the property or injure the persons" of the Republic of Texas. To prevent the Tonkawas from "being cheated by bad men," the Republic promised to appoint an agent to superintend Tonkawa business and "protect their rights."[2]

The treaty also delineated certain reciprocal actions required by the signatories. The Tonkawa chiefs assented to trade only with authorized agents and allowed those traders "free and safe" conduct through Tonkawa territory. The treaty stated that the Texas government "will punish any Citizen" of the Republic, according to law, who "may infringe on the rights" of the Tonkawas, "or injure them in any way." Concerning any property stolen or that "may otherwise fall into the hands" of the Tonkawas, the Tonkawa leaders promised that the property would be "forthwith restored to the owner or the agent of Government." The Tonkawas agreed not to steal horses or any other livestock from settlers along the Texas frontier. After the treaty was signed, Houston authorized an expenditure of $20 for a beef as a gift to the Indian delegation and the Tonkawas returned home. Over the next few years the Indian agent's main duty became preventing the Tonkawas from wandering into white settlements near the frontier.[3]

According to many Texas frontier folk, the Tonkawas, through both instruction and trade, provided needed food and clothing to frontier communities. The Tonkawas tutored the newcomers in the arts of hunting, gathering pecans, and basic woodsmanship. German immigrants arriving around New Braunfels and Fredericksburg in the mid-1840s commented that they became much more proficient hunters, and thus better providers for their families, after receiving guidance from friendly Indians. After tutoring from nearby Indians, German settlers killed several deer on one hunt, instead of one deer during several days of hunting. The Tonkawas also brought in wild game of all types for sale, most commonly venison. When asked by a female customer why he did not bring in wild turkeys the Tonkawa hunter answered, "Turkey too hard to kill." A Tonkawa considered deer easily stalked and killed, but a turkey demonstrated a completely dissimilar demeanor. "Turkey look [and think] Injun by God, and he duck his head and run." Texas frontiersmen, as well as modern hunters, confirmed the extreme difficulty in bagging a wild turkey.[4]

Noah Smithwick recounted that there was little conflict between the settlers and the Tonkawas, except for the annual pecan harvest from which the Tonkawas derived "a rather large revenue." The Tonkawas chopped off the limbs of several large pecan trees to expedite gathering the nuts. When the Tonkawas ignored the citizens' complaints, they bolstered their protests "with a shotgun in one or two instances." According to Smithwick, the "old chief" Plácido "stood in the breach" and kept peace between his tribe and the Texians. Plácido's proudest boast was that he had "never shed a white man's blood," and would not do so over such a trivial matter.[5]

The Tonkawas not only knew how to hunt and gather pecans, but how white immigrants acquired their land in Texas. John J. Linn, a Victoria merchant during the Republic, related a story about a Tonkawa named Joe. The Indian came into Linn's store and inquired from where Linn came. Linn told Joe that he had arrived in Texas from Louisiana. The Tonkawa then asked from whom the white man had purchased his land. After Linn informed Joe that he had bought his land from a white man, Joe commented that the whites bought and sold Indian land without any regard whatsoever to the Indian's claims. Joe continued, that although God had given the land to the Indians who occupied it, the Tonkawas would soon be dispossessed of their homes. The Indian astutely observed that if he wished to buy an article from Linn's store, he must pay the price asked, but "when the white man want a piece of the Indians land, he goes to another white man and the trade is made." When asked if he thought this system was honest, Linn was unable to provide "some ethical defense," stating only that he had paid for all that he owned "to a white man."[6]

Smithwick also related that Tonkawas exhibited a guileless curiosity toward their new white neighbors, appearing at any and all social gatherings without invitation, and provided some levity on several occasions. When the settlers gathered to hear an itinerant preacher, several Tonkawas assembled at the door, "watching and listening as intently as if fully understanding all that was being said." A Tonkawa mother, tiring of holding her "chubby baby boy," stood him in the doorway, where "his highly original costume . . . a tiny bow of pink ribbon in lieu of the traditional fig leaf attracted much attention." Another time several Tonkawas gathered near a trading post. Smithwick recalled that a woman, "presumably over the propensity of her lord for gambeling [sic] off everything he could get his hands on," became very angry and proceeded to give her husband "a genuine tongue lashing." The Tonkawa man only laughed at first, but as the harangue intensified, went out the door "on a dead run." The Tonkawa woman grabbed his braids as he fled and the pair disappeared to the laughter and "applause of the spectators."[7]

Not all encounters with Tonkawas seemed so amusing to white settlers, and many were filled with erroneous innuendo and hearsay. Recalling an event occurring on June 12, 1838, Mary Maverick, who had never seen a Tonkawa before this time, described them as "treacherous and cruel and noted thieves and murderers." According to Maverick, seventeen Tonkawa warriors rode up to a Texian camp proclaiming mucho amigo, "dear friend," and "were loud and filthy and manifested their intention to be very intimate." She remembered that it was "No exaggeration to say, they annoyed us very much." Fresh from a victory on the Nueces River over several Comanches, the Tonkawas wore war paint and were well armed. The Indians openly displayed two scalps, a hand, and "several pieces of putrid flesh from various parts of the human body." Maverick recounted that the Tonkawas intended to take the flesh to their camp "to be eaten and danced over by their tribe."[8]

Maverick continued her narration, "I was frightened, almost to death and tried not to show my alarm." The Tonkawa warriors rode up to the carriage where Maverick sat in order to see "papoose." The frightened woman held up "my little Sammy" and smiled, but "took care to have my pistol and Bowie knife visible." She also refused to hand her baby out so the Tonkawas could "see how pretty and white he was." Maverick suspected that the Indians intended to kill all in her party, eat the baby, and ride off with their horses. Constantly vigilant, the Anglo settlers remained armed, broke camp, and loaded up their wagons to depart. The Tonkawas followed them eighteen miles through a "bright moonlit night" but "fell away" when the Texians "kept up their guard." By morning all the Indians had disappeared and Maverick believed that she had barely averted "a narrow escape from a cruel death."[9]

Despite the reversal of Houston's Indian policies by President Mirabeau B. Lamar, who assumed office in December 1838, the Tonkawas remained friendly with the Republic of Texas. Lamar's Indian policy focused on either absolute eradication or complete eviction of all Indians from Texas, and many Texians agreed with their new president. In November 1838, V. R. Palmer sent a letter to Lamar which suggested that the Tonkawas created problems and several citizens intended to remove them elsewhere. Palmer pointed out that "our frontier is again agitated with the alarm of Indian depredations and threatened with all horrors of an Indian War." According to Palmer, he and others intended to force the Tonkawas to "their old range," because the settlers were not happy with the Tonkawas living in close proximity. Palmer charged that the "mischief which had been done" along the frontier was committed by "northern Indians . . . Tankewas [Tonkawas]."[10]

Regardless of such disparaging attitudes the Tonkawas participated in several punitive expeditions against other tribes. In the 1839 Cherokee War, the Tonkawas turned against a one-time ally. Plácido and forty warriors joined Col. Edward Burleson as scouts and guides, assisting in expelling the Cherokees from Texas. Of one skirmish between Burleson's force and the Cherokees John Henry Brown wrote that "stately and never faltering" Plácido would have faced "devils and demons dire" rather than abandoning his friends and "bold warriors."[11]

During the same year Tonkawa warriors scouted for both Burleson and Col. John H. Moore on expeditions against raiding Comanches. In February, twelve Tonkawas and forty-two Lipans joined Moore's force of fifty-five whites in an attempt to rescue Matilda Lockhart, recently captured by a Comanche war party. Moore's scouts located a Comanche camp on the banks of the San Saba River, but failed to realize the size of the camp. At dawn on February 12, the "wily old" Castro and thirty Lipans stampeded the Comanche horse herd, while the remaining Indians joined Moore's men in attacking "the buffalo tents." The unexpected large number of Comanches quickly recoiled against the surprise attack, and in a "fierce and bloody" battle, Moore suffered an ignoble defeat at the hands of the "enraged savages." Moore lost all his horses, but managed to fight a defensive action, withdrawing with his six wounded men. Moore's second attempt proved more successful when his men, guided by Tonkawas, destroyed a large Comanche camp on the crescent bend of the Colorado River near present-day Colorado City.[12]

On December 23, a group of Tonkawas, again scouting for Burleson, discovered the trail of a herd of stolen stock east of the Pecan Bayou. For two days the Tonkawas followed the trail to a point near where the San Saba River flowed into the Colorado. "By great caution and the cunning" of his Tonkawa guides, Burleson led his command to within a few hundred yards of a Cherokee camp, when a running fight ensued. Bending low over their horses, Burleson's men rode through the thick brush, killing seven Cherokees during the fight, including Chiefs John Bowles and The Egg. They also captured another man, five women, nineteen children, and all the Cherokees' stock and camp equipment. Burleson lost one officer killed and a Tonkawa slightly wounded.[13]

In late February 1839, Ben McCulloch convinced War Chief Captain Jim Kerr and thirty-four Tonkawa scouts to guide McCulloch and four other whites in pursuing Comanche marauders. Camped in Gonzales County, at the juncture of Peach and Sandy Creeks, the Tonkawas and their white compatriots reluctantly left their warm abodes to sally forth against the Comanches. According to Brown, Chico accompanied the Tonkawas as their medicine man. On the second day of the expedition the Tonkawas struck a fresh Indian trail leading back toward Gonzales. Two of the swiftest Tonkawas left out on foot, leading McCulloch's party on a spirited chase for about four hours.[14]

When overtaken, the Comanches and Wacos disappeared into an "almost impenetrable thicket," where they remained unseen while covering every ingress to their position. During sporadic firing over several hours, the Comanches killed one Tonkawa hiding behind a tree. Finally, McCulloch split his forces and encircled the thicket. The Tonkawas formed a blocking force on one side, while four of McCulloch's men entered the brush on the other side. In the melee, McCulloch's party killed five Comanches, but the remainder slipped out of the cordon. McCulloch later blamed Captain Jim for allowing the "hostels" to escape. According to McCulloch, the victorious Tonkawas scalped the Comanche dead and cut off their hands and feet, as well as slicing strips of flesh from their thighs, to be used in the scalp dance. On the return to Gonzales, McCulloch said the Tonkawas stopped and "went through most of the mystic ceremonies attending the war dance . . . thoroughly commingling weird wails over their fallen comrade with their wild, and equally weird, exultation over their fallen foes."[15]

On August 12, 1840, Plácido, one of the Tonkawa's most famous chiefs, and twelve Tonkawa warriors participated in the Plum Creek Fight near Lockhart. After the infamous Council House Fight in San Antonio the previous March, several hundred Comanche warriors swept across Texas to Victoria and the coastal town of Linnville, killing and wounding numerous Texans along the way. After razing Linnville on August 8, the Comanches headed back toward their haunts on the South Plains, encumbered by loads of booty and a caballada of three thousand horses and mules. Several groups of Texans, commanded by Felix Huston, Matthew "Old Paint" Caldwell, Burleson, and McCulloch, headed off the retreating Comanches at Plum Creek, a tributary of the San Marcos River. "Bedecked with red streamers and ribbons," and several wearing "top hats," the unsuspecting Comanche raiding party rode into the open near the creek where a force of about two hundred white Texans and Tonkawas, identified by white armbands, sprang their trap. In a running fight, covering some fifteen miles, the combined command killed between fifty and eighty Comanches, with the Tonkawas dealing "death with every hand." After the fight the Tonkawas scalped the Comanches, cut off the hands and feet of their perennial enemies, and carried the trophies home for a scalp dance celebration.[16]

According to several retellings of the Plum Creek engagement, Plácido saved Maj. Monroe Hardeman's life during the melee. Startled by the cacophony of sudden gunfire Hardeman's horse took the bit into its teeth and bolted toward the Comanches. Seeing Hardeman's plight, Plácido dashed through the "flying arrows and bullets" toward Hardeman and his unruly mount. Reaching the horse Plácido grabbed the headstall and bridle of the terrified animal and led the horse and rider back into the Texan lines. For saving his life Hardeman reportedly gave the Tonkawa chief a "fine horse" and Burleson presented Plácido a medal which the Indian wore around his neck for years.[17]

Describing the Tonkawa actions at Plum Creek, Brown wrote that "the heroic actions of Placido . . . attracted universal praise. He seemed reckless of life and his twelve followers, as rapidly as mounted, emulated his example. All being on foot [upon entering the battle] they could only be mounted by each vaulting into the saddle of a slain Comanche. But they [Tonkawas] were all mounted in a marvelously short time after the action commenced."[18]

Throughout the existence of the Republic of Texas, the Tonkawas continued their faithful alliance even though many settlers considered them "shiftless and lazy," and blamed them for missing livestock stolen by other Indians. On January 22, 1841, just outside the new capital of Austin, a band of five Comanches attacked and killed James W. Smith, and took his nine-year-old son Fayette prisoner. Fayette's uncle William and a group of "Tonkaway" men took to the trail and followed the raiders for a short time, and then made an abortive trip to Santa Fe to ransom the boy from traders there.[19]

After Houston again assumed the presidency in 1841, his peaceful policy toward Texas' Indians paid some dividends for the Tonkawas. Frontier settlers slowly became aware that the Tonkawas were not responsible for the atrocities committed by other tribes. A letter to Houston from J. C. Eldredge, one of Houston's Indian Commissioners, exemplified such attitudes. Eldredge discovered that complaints against the Tonkawas were unjustified and, placing the blame on another tribe, vindicated the Tonkawa's reputation. Eldredge wrote in part, "A long time ago peace was made with all tribes including the Tonkawa," and when the "Wichita stole Tonkawa horses they [Tonkawas] retaliated on other tribes" and "war broke out." Eldredge pointed out that when peace was restored "the Wichita interfered and after involving all the tribes in war retreated into the United States leaving the Texas tribes who were innocent to bear the brunt of the war."[20]

Contrary to myth and legend, the German settlements founded in Central Texas during the mid-1840s did not escape Comanche raids, but the German immigrants did establish enduring, amiable relations with the Tonkawas. In 1845, the German verein established its first settlement of New Braunfels on Comal Creek north of San Antonio. Prince Carl of Sommes-Braunfels, director of the new settlement, initiated friendly relations with the Tonkawas by an agreement allowing the Indians to maintain a village near New Braunfels. In October, an Indian raiding party, probably Comanches, killed and scalped two settlers returning to New Braunfels from Austin. The next Spring, verein settlers led by Johann O. Meusebach moved northwest to the Pedernales River and established the second colony of Fredericksburg.[21]

In Spring 1847, Meusebach sought out the leaders of the Penateka band of Comanches and, with the assistance of Indian Agent Robert S. Neighbors and Jim Shaw, a Delaware Indian, as interpreter, concluded a peace agreement with six Penateka chiefs. The agreement held for years between the groups, but not with other Comanche chiefs not present at the peace conference. In October, raiders killed four surveyors west of Fredericksburg, but contemporary accounts did not identify the Indians as Comanches. During Spring 1849, Comanche chiefs, including the influential Buffalo Hump, voiced serious dissatisfaction with the number of survey parties traipsing over Comanche lands. While tensions heated between the Comanche and the settlers, around New Braunfels and Fredericksburg whites maintained cordial relations with the Tonkawa and Delaware Indians living near the settlements by an exchange "of small gifts" and trade for the manufactured items, including firearms, and "cheap beads and trinkets" that the Indians admired.[22]

Relationships between the German settlers and Comanches changed radically when smallpox and cholera exploded among several Indian tribes in 1848–1849. The epidemics killed several peaceable Comanche chiefs, leading to an increase of hostilities between German settlers and the Penateka Comanches. In 1850, raiders killed at least five settlers near Fredericksburg, and some of the perpetrators were recognized as Comanches. After 1850, immigrants reported a growing number of murders, kidnaping, and live-stock thefts by raiding Comanches, which increased during the Civil War and continued through the mid-1870s. German relations with the Tonkawas, however, remained noncombative, even after the tribe's removal to the Brazos River Reservation in 1855.[23]

William Bollaert, an English traveler in Texas during the 1840s, left his recollections of the Tonkawas and their interdependence with Texas settlers along the Colorado River. On August 22, 1843, Bollaert met a young Tonkawa man who was clothed with only a "girdle around his loins, and a long, narrow strip of cloth hanging before and behind. His body painted with vermillion." The Tonkawa twisted hair stripped from the main and tail of a mustang into a cabresto, or rope, for a local resident. Later the same day Bollaert visited the Tonkawa band headed by Chief Campos. Bollaert estimated that the camp contained about one hundred warriors. The Tonkawas were drying and jerking venison and buffalo meat. Campos informed Bollaert that the Tonkawas had just returned from a buffalo hunt in the "mountains." The "mountains" may have been the Edwards Plateau. The chief said he would soon move his people nearer the coast where he could see the ocean and hunt wild horses and deer.[24]

The next day, Bollaert journeyed to Bastrop and noted that Tonkawas filled the only dry goods store in town, bartering buffalo robes, tanned hides, and moccasins for powder, cloth, beads, "finery for their squaws," and "an occasional bottle of whiskey from the tippling shop," which was against "executive orders." To the Tonkawas' detriment, alcohol was culturally foreign to them and the most destructive manufactured product introduced to the tribe.[25]

Between 1843 and 1845 the Republic of Texas appointed three different agents to the Tonkawa tribe, all of whose principal responsibilities evolved into preventing the beleaguered Tonkawas from roaming through white settlements and protecting them from Comanche marauders. On February 12, 1844, Cambridge Green succeeded Benjamin Bryant, who followed Lewis as agent to the Tonkawas and Lipan Apaches. Green pledged to "well and truly and to the best of his ability discharge his duties according to law and instructions of the Government." The same month Green visited the Tonkawas main camp on Cedar Creek in Bastrop County. According to his reports, the Tonkawas possessed no, or very few horses, and visited local communities to find work just to survive. On May 27, citizens reported several Tonkawas in the vicinity of Gonzales, where they were "drinking liquor, stealing cattle, and committing depredations." By September 1, Chief Campos moved the Tonkawas from around Gonzales and established another camp near Bastrop. Some of the women picked cotton, while the men "spent some of their time in town drinking." O'Quinn, however, informed Green that most Tonkawa warriors left to steal horses in Mexico, forcing the tribe to remain close to white settlements for protection and to "obtain sustenance."[26]

Waco Chief Ah-ho-dot, translated as either Shot Arm or Lame Arm, ostensibly confirmed some of Green's reports by relating that he and several other Indians participated with Tonkawas in several horse thefts. According to Lame Arm's tale he started south with ten warriors to make war on the Mexicans. When near Gonzales, Tonkawa Chief David Warwick, taken from white settlers when a young boy and raised as a Tonkawa, convinced the Wacos to change plans and steal horses from the white settlements. The band filched about twenty-eight horses and turned to ride leisurely back to the Waco village. A party of Texians soon overtook the Indians, and Warwick led several of them into a fight with the settlers. During the ensuing battle the Texians killed Warwick and one Waco warrior. The rest of the Indians scattered and took refuge in an Anadarko village on the Trinity River. Lame Arm claimed he regretted stealing the horses, and blamed the Tonkawas for persuading the Wacos to steal from the Texians and not Mexicans.[27]

On March 21, 1844, noted Comanche Chief Mopechucope (Old Owl), from a camp near the headwaters of the Colorado River, dictated a letter to President Houston that included his demands for a peaceful settlement with the Tonkawas and Lipan Apaches. The chief stated that although the Comanche bands were scattered from the Salt Plain of the Arkansas River to the Pecos River and south to the Rio Grande, they were maintaining peaceful intentions and "no mischief done" by Comanches "neither to Texians, Tonkawa, or the Lipan." Old Owl claimed that depredations blamed on his band were not committed by his people and he would tell Houston who "created any mischief if he [Old Owl] knew who it was." Old Owl's letter related that the major Comanche bands claimed all of Central and West

Texas, disregarding the obvious fact that the Comanches had only recently forcibly displaced the Tonkawas, Lipan Apaches, and several other Indian tribes.[28]

During Summer 1844, intermittent conflicts erupted between the Tonkawas and a few other tribes, with the other Indians blaming the Tonkawas and Lipans for the discord. A duplicitous Waco chief sent a message to Houston indicating that he "wanted path with the white man wide and clean." The Wacos reported that the Tonkawas and Lipans would not have anything to do with the other tribes, but the Wacos "Would not molest them but would not associate with them" either. In May, a group of Delawares, Shawnees, Caddos, Anadarkos, Keechis, Tawakonis, Wacos, and Cherokees met on Tehuacana Creek with a delegation from the Republic of Texas. During the meeting a Tawakoni chief made the following statement:

> Tonkawas and Lipans are friends and live near us and will be kept at home and not permitted to steal from our red brothers or to do harm. We want all red brothers to treat them [Tonkawas and Lipans] as friends and not to steal their horses or make war against them. They will be kept as far from our other red brothers as they can. Should any of their [Tonkawa or Lipan] bad and foolish young men steal horses, do not make war on them but send [word of the theft] to our agent and we will try to return stolen horses to owners.

The chief continued, "Young men sometimes steal and get killed. Do not want white path to get bloody, yet by stealing and killing it will be so." He would not promise lasting peace with the Tonkawas and Lipan Apaches until he consulted with his Comanche allies, but promised if the Comanches made peace with the Tonkawas, he would also.[29]

At the end of June, Neighbors visited a Tonkawa camp on Cibolo Creek near the "old Gonzales crossing," and confirmed that other tribes continued to raid the forlorn Tonkawa people. Neighbors reported that the Wacos raided the Tonkawas near the "Dutch Settlement" on the Comal River, killing an old woman and stealing a few horses. Neighbors payed for repairing some Tonkawa weapons because the Tonkawas "subsist entirely by hunting," and they "had not the means of paying for it themselves." Although the Tonkawas appeared "much exasperated" against the Wacos, both they and the Lipans planned to attend an upcoming council with several other tribes. The Lipans urged the Tonkawas to accompany them "on a long buffalo hunt" on the upper Colorado and Brazos Rivers. Neighbors informed Thomas G. Western, Texas Superintendent of Indian Affairs, that he hoped to join the Tonkawas and Lipans together at one place to better "keep both under his eye at the same time and have better control."[30]

On February 12, 1845, Neighbors officially assumed the position as agent to the Tonkawas and Lipan Apaches. Receiving an annual salary of $500, Neighbors moved to live among his charges to gain their trust. Neighbors' instructions from Western included locating all the Tonkawas and Lipans, assembling them, and "remov[ing] them out of the settlements as fast as practicable." Western empowered Neighbors to select suitable camps on the San Marcos River above or below the old San Antonio Road. Western cautioned Neighbors that "old feuds probably still exist," and with this in mind "do not place them [the Tonkawas] so high up as to expose them to Collision with those Tribes [Comanches, Wichita, and Wacos] with whom they are not at Peace." Western emphatically reminded Neighbors that "No blood must be shed by them [Indians] . . . the 'White Path' must be kept 'unsullied.'" Along with his missive, Western sent along a "pipe of peace" to smoke at councils and "tobacco for that Purpose."[31]

Western also notified other departments of the government, especially those dealing with Indians, that the Tonkawas "will hunt and make peltries for trade at Torrey's Trading House on the Brazos." His letter continued, treat the Tonkawas "kindly . . . and be particularly careful that their trade is upon just and equitable terms." A "show of liberality on the part of the camp traders at the onset will operate as an incentive to their [Tonkawas] energies to hunt and become industrious." The tribe requires "something to Stimulate them to activity and bring their minds to Industry." Western reminded everyone that the Tonkawas were "old friends and allies of ours," now "poor and needy, deal with them accordingly." Additionally, Western warned his agents that several unscrupulous men were illegally trading with the Indians and that all measures should be taken to arrest these culprits.[32]

In his instructions to Neighbors, Western included impressing upon the Tonkawas the importance of self-sufficiency, hunting, and inducing the tribe to select a single chief as head of the tribe. Neighbors followed these directions to the best of his ability and on April 11, 1845, he reported to Western that the Tonkawas had reorganized under Chief Campos, and relocated to a reservation near San Marcos. Western authorized Neighbors to provide the Tonkawa women with one hundred bushels of seed corn and two dozen hoes to plant a crop and to give the men knives, powder, and lead, "solely for hunting." The men could also expect their guns to be repaired free of charge by the armorer at Torrey's Trading House. In May 1845, Neighbors reported the hunting excellent near the Tonkawa's new camp and they were generally contented, but because of persistent Waco horse thefts, war between the two tribes seemed imminent.[33]

Between September 12–25, 1845, at Torrey's Trading House, representatives of the Republic of Texas and various tribes met in a general council. Neighbors and his associates attempted to keep the peace among the tribes, and between the Indians and the Texans. Campos, Plácido, Benividez, and "war chief" Jose represented the Tonkawa at the meeting. Another five warriors and one female accompanied the chiefs to the meeting. Comanche, Cherokee, Lipan Apache, Caddo, Anadarko, Ioni, and Delaware chiefs also attended. Each chief addressed the others. In his turn Campos stated:

> I have heard nothing today but what I am pleased with, for it is all good talk. It is not worthwhile for me to promise anything more than I have already promised. I have always been friendly with the whites, and have fought for them and I shall continue to do so . . . and I want now to be friendly with all my red brothers and walk with them on the white path of peace. I want all of our women and children to be no more afraid in traveling about, either of their lives or property . . . all are welcome to come to my camp and among my people. I will treat them well and I want all to treat me and my people in the same way. If there are any of my red

brothers who have not made peace with my people I want them to do so now. If young men of other tribes come among my people I want them to dance with my young girls and marry them, for I see none here that I am not willing to meet as brothers. We are now without horses for the Waco came down and stole all we had, but we will soon have more and then we intend traveling about and see our red brothers and all live in peace. If the great white chief tells his people to make war with the Wacos I want them, and all others who make war against them to try and get the horses which they stole from my people.

The council cost $2,617.93 for gifts to the Indians, more than the treasury could afford, but peace prevailed for a time.[34]

During the council proceedings, Tonkawas agreed to relocate even farther north into the lands claimed by their mortal enemies, the Southern Comanche tribes. Extraordinarily, the Comanches did not object to the move. Perhaps both tribes realized the benefits of peace with one another in the face of increasing white demands for native lands.[35]

For their part, the Texas commissioner's motives remained unclear. Conceivably, the whites thought of only moving the Tonkawas northward away from "civilization" or, perhaps, they hoped that the tribes would resolve the state's dilemma by killing off one another away from the settlements. Whatever the case, Neighbors opined that the Tonkawas deserved their own lands, separated from the Comanches. Of his charges Neighbors wrote, the Tonkawa's "devotion . . . to the government and their [Tonkawas] willingness at all times to serve them [Texians] to the best of their [Tonkawas] ability in every respect . . . it would be . . . justice and very beneficial to the country for the Gov[ernmen]t to locate [the] Tonkawa and assist them in acquiring the arts of civilization."[36]

Neighbors and the Tonkawa leaders Plácido and Campos fervently hoped for a treaty with the Republic of Texas that would protect the dwindling numbers of the tribe from Comanche incursions, but their hopes never came to fruition. In December 1845, the United States annexed Texas as the twenty-eighth state, transferring all negotiations for Indian treaties to the United States federal government. Peace remained the fundamental goal between the Tonkawas and Texans and, despite several trivial disturbances, the Tonkawas continued to be a reliable ally for the Texans. Most settlers endeavored to remain at peace with the tribe, oft times disregarding the Tonkawa's missteps to sustain a stable relationship between the two cultures. Be that as it may, no matter whether under state or federal administration, the remaining seven hundred or so Tonkawas were treated differently from other Indian tribes, sometimes favorably, but often just simply ignored. One untoward topic, however, constantly beset the Tonkawas for the remainder of the nineteenth century: removal from Texas.[37]

## 5 WARDS OF THE U.S. GOVERNMENT, FRONTIER SCOUTS, AND FIRST REMOVAL, 1846–1859

On May 15, 1846, at Council Springs in Robertson County, Col. Pierce M. Butler and Maj. M. G. Lewis, United States Indian commissioners, formally signed a "treaty of peace and commercial alliance" with eleven Tonkawa chiefs, including Campos and Plácido, effectively making the tribe economic wards of the United States government. The previous September, four months before Texas became a state, the two officers received orders to negotiate a treaty with several Texas Indian tribes, and may have attended the council at Torrey's Trading House that month. The U.S. government followed the long-standing practice of giving gifts to the Indians, but made it plain in the treaty that the signatories should trade or negotiate with authorized U.S. agents only. In February, Robert S. Neighbors reported that the Tonkawas lived along the San Marcos and San Antonio Rivers, "remaining clear of white settlements," and planned to attend the treaty council called by Butler and Lewis. Unfortunately for the Tonkawa tribe, U.S. officials concentrated on placating "hostile" tribes and shunted most Tonkawa interests aside.[1]

In a report to the U.S. House of Representatives concerning their mission in Texas, Butler and Lewis wrote that, "the Ton-que-was and Lipans, the first numbered about 700 souls, the latter about 125." They "have been uniformly the friend and ally of Texans." Both tribes relied on "game alone for subsistence. They do not cultivate the soil, or have any stationary place of abode." The report stated that both tribes seemed "extremely depraved in their habits, great drunkards, and fond of gambling." According to the two officers, the "vice of drinking ardent spirits" appeared common among the Tonkawas and Lipans. The mention of "depravity" may have alluded to cannibalism. The report recorded that the majority of both tribes spoke "the Spanish language with great fluency."[2]

Through Neighbors' influence, David G. Burnet, former Interim President of Texas, sent Henry Rowe Schoolcraft, a noted ethnologist, several letters. On August 20, 1847, Burnet sent Schoolcraft a paper entitled "The Comanche and Other Tribes of Texas, and the Policy to be Pursued Respecting Them," in which he briefly described the Tonkawa tribe. Burnet wrote that "the Tonkawa are a separate tribe, having no traceable affinity to any other band of Indians in the country. They are erratic, living on game and are quite indolent, and often in extremity of suffering." Burnet acknowledged that the Tonkawas had "generally been friendly to the whites though often suspected of stealing horses from the frontier." Burnet also recognized that the Tonkawa's "rendered good service" to the Texas Army during the 1839 Cherokee War in Texas. Burnet estimated that the Tonkawas could field about 150 warriors at the time of his report.[3]

Although the Tonkawas usually professed mutual congeniality with most settlers, especially the Germans, at least one event marred that relationship in 1849. A few Tonkawas evidently killed a German settler while he was plowing his fields along the Guadalupe River. After dispatching the farmer, the Tonkawa men took two scalps, one from his head and the other from the settler's long flowing beard. The Tonkawas reportedly dined on portions of the portly immigrant. Cooperating with Neighbors, Maj. Ripley A. Arnold led a small detachment of soldiers to round up the suspected perpetrators. Neighbors charged the Tonkawas with the murder, but they contended that they had killed and eaten "a bearded one," not a white man. Several years later John S. Ford asked O'Quinn, a Tonkawa scout and Ranger, "O'Quinn, you have eaten all sorts of people. What nationality do you think makes the best eating?" According to Ford, O'Quinn promptly replied, "A big, fat Dutchman." This story seems to indicate that some Tonkawas adopted the prejudices against German-speaking immigrants, or at the least, the Tonkawas were familiar with the racial tensions within Anglo settlements between various groups of white settlers.[4]

As early as 1847, tension between Texas frontiersmen and the Tonkawa tribe escalated dramatically because of horse thefts and several killings. In previous incidents, settlers blamed "the wild Indians" but, because of the Tonkawas' proximity to the settlements, many accused the Tonkawas of the spate of "depredations." The Tonkawas, along with many other settlers, believed the accusations arose from immigrants who coveted the Tonkawa land north and west of Austin. In December 1847, Neighbors wrote to Gov. Pinckney Henderson that he believed the Tonkawas and most other Texas Indians honored their 1846 agreement to a boundary line. Some "citizens however show a determination to violate that agreement by locating themselves above that line, thereby threatening to disturb our peaceful relations with these tribes."[5]

Meager federal annuities and continued Comanche incursions forced the Tonkawas to remain near the Anglo settlements, and some Texans assisted the impoverished tribe in various ways. Several members of the tribe resided on Edward Burleson's farm, where they helped recover Burleson's and his neighbor's livestock stolen by other Indians. In 1848, Plácido and his sons sat visiting with Burleson when the chief heard the "hoot of an owl," immediately recognizing it as "a Comanche fake." Before anyone could react the Comanches stole Scurry, a "fine horse of Burleson's," and Plácido and his two sons mounted their ponies and tracked down the thieves. In the resulting fight the Comanches wounded Plácido with an arrow, but failed to prevent the Tonkawa chief from killing the rider of Burleson's stolen horse with a thrust of his lance. The Tonkawas slew two more Comanche warriors and triumphantly returned with Scurry and three fresh scalps.[6]

Other settlers helped Tonkawa warriors defend against attack and provide food for their families. Peter Mercer, a gunsmith who lived on the San Gabriel River, repaired several Tonkawa guns and made "iron spikes" for their arrows. Many settlers blamed the federal government for the Tonkawa's plight. By 1852 an informal, and erroneous, census of the Tonkawas tabulated the tribal population at only 240 members. In August 1853, Neighbors wrote that "the Tonkawa [actually just more than 600 souls] reside on the Colorado, driven from point to point, and have no assurance that they would be permitted to occupy a tract of land long enough to gather their corn if they were to plant." A prominent newspaper, *The Telegraph and Texas Register*, blamed the federal government for any problems with the Tonkawas because the United States did not provide "promised annuities nor horses" in ensure that Tonkawa men could properly provide food and protection for their families.[7]

Although Neighbors and his sub-agents verified that the Tonkawas, for the most part, remained innocent of most accusations and should not be held responsible for the offenses of other native peoples, many Texans wished to exterminate all Indians, friendly or not. Just prior to leaving office, however, Gov. George T. Wood offered an alternate, "peaceable" solution. The governor suggested that the only realistic plan to assure peace along the frontier, and prevent the Indians' extermination from white settlers, was to remove the Tonkawas "by their own consent to lands where they could have their own government and develop their true national character." Cooperating with Neighbors, Plácido gathered the remnants of the Tonkawa tribe and moved them farther north toward the upper reaches of the Brazos River, exposing the tribe once again to Comanche and Kiowa war parties.[8]

For the next several years Comanches, Western Apaches, Kiowas, and Wacos continued to ambush isolated settlers and steal livestock along the Texas frontier, increasing white demands for the extermination of all Indians, or at the very minimum, removal of all tribes far from any settlement. When Neighbors investigated areas of reported Indian outrages he "found that the depredations committed is conferred to two or three parties of Comanche and Apache Indians." Ignoring evidence to the contrary, Gov. E. M. Pease promised the citizens of several Central Texas counties that the Tonkawas would be forced away from white settled areas. Pease also authorized the citizens "to turn out and punish them [Tonkawas]" without waiting for government action.[9]

Neighbors, who on May 9, 1853, became United States Supervising Agent for all Texas Indians, agreed that to protect the diminishing number of

Tonkawas from the rifles of both the Comanches and Texans they should be relocated to reservations away from frontier settlements. In Spring 1854, after the U.S. Congress agreed to fund removal, Neighbors and Capt. R. B. Marcy, U.S. Army, rode through the upper Brazos River valley searching for suitable sites for reservations. In July 1855 Plácido, although convinced that only empty government promises filled his tribe's future, led the Tonkawas to the 35,424-acre Brazos River Reservation located at the juncture of the Clear Fork and main branch of the Brazos River, near Fort Belknap in present-day Young County. The reservation, administered by resident agent Shapley P. Ross, was shared between several small tribes including the Tonkawas, Caddos, Anadarkos, Ionis, Delawares, and Shawnees. In 1856, the reservation population swelled to 1,112 natives. The Tonkawas began cultivating corn, beans, and pumpkins and, by 1858, attended school to learn English under schoolmaster Z. E. Coombs.[10]

Although most Tonkawas and members of other tribes agreed to move onto lands set aside for them, not all Indians readily accepted restricted boundaries. A small number of Tonkawa traditionalists abrogated Plácido's leadership and fled to Mexico. In 1927, Peyton Meyer established a ranch near Sabinas, Coahuila, Mexico, 150 miles south of Eagle Pass, where he reported a flourishing community of Tonkawas living near his ranch that had fled to Mexico instead of going to the Brazos River Reservation.[11]

Only a few miles up the Clear Fork from the Brazos River Reservation about five hundred Penateka Comanches moved onto the Comanche Reservation in present-day Throckmorton County. While this relatively small number of Comanches agreed to live on the reservation, most of the Comanche Nation categorically refused reservation life, continuing to roam at will over the Texas Plains. Lt. Col. Robert E. Lee deemed the reservation natives capable of "horrifying depredations," and about one thousand free-ranging Comanche warriors even "more able and hostile" toward white settlers. In 1856, Col. J. K. F. Mansfield toured the Texas frontier and reported that approximately five hundred to eight hundred natives living off the reservation were "so wild, inhuman, and thievish that they were not yet disposed to accept the protection of the government."[12]

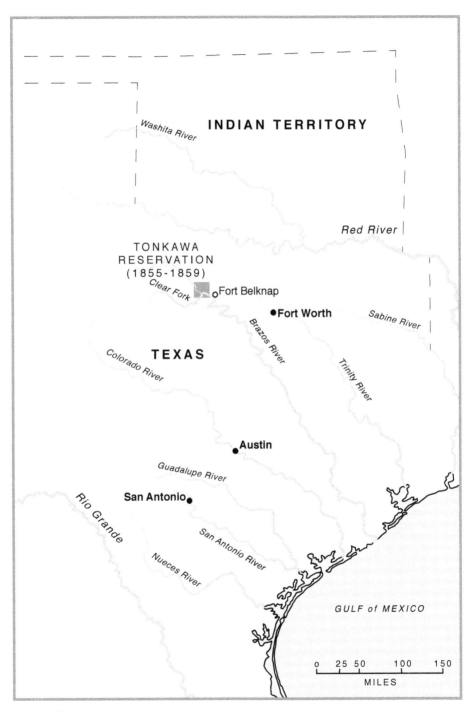

GULF of MEXICO

```
o   25 50      100      150
   |___|__|_____|_____|
          MILES
```

Map by Donald S. Frazier.

Relocating several smaller tribes to the Brazos River Reservation failed to halt the discord between native people and white Texans. During the decade of the 1850s, Texas' population almost tripled and white settlers moved onto much of the land surrounding the various native reservations. Along with the population, livestock in the vicinity of the Brazos River Reservation increased as well. The horse represented a major part of the plains culture of both frontiersmen and Indian, epitomizing prosperity in both races. In a six-month period between October 1857 and April 1858 several hundred head of horses and cattle disappeared and twenty-five settlers were killed near the reservations.[13]

Natives who refused reservation life and white outlaws disguised as Indians committed most of these outrages, but since much of the stolen livestock were driven onto the reservations, ranchers and farmers blamed the reservation Indians. Ranchers trailed the livestock raiders through the reservation, north across the Red River, and into Indian Territory. James B. "Buck" Barry tracked a party of horse thieves through the reservation and eventually identified a Comanche riding "Blue Dog," one of Barry's swiftest horses. John R. Baylor, who became an inveterate Indian hater, even said that "Northern Indians were responsible" for the thefts. Barry agreed, believing that Comanches and Kiowas raided the Brazos River Reservation and stole horses from the Tonkawas and other tribes, as well as from white settlers. Francis R. Lubbock remembered that the Tonkawas committed "petty crimes," but were not "otherwise troublesome." A number of citizens near the reservation claimed that "friendly Indians" stole their horses and then returned the animals for the $10 reward offered for stolen stock.[14]

Many Texas citizens understood the "northern Comanche's" propensity to steal livestock, and believed the Tonkawas adhered to the peace agreement between their tribe and the federal government. On October 6, 1855, the *Texas State Gazette* reported:

> Mr. Skidmore . . . was killed . . . The Indians . . . belong to a band of Northern Comanche . . . Major Neighbors dispatched an express to the lower reserve for a pursuing party-including Placido and eleven [Tonkawas]. The readiness with which the Indians . . .

prepared themselves for the chase illustrates very well the state
of mind and discipline the Indians upon the reservation are in.
It shows in what light they are beginning to view such conduct,
and by adopting the white man's course toward the murder, they
will induct themselves into the right feeling on such matters—the
surest guarantee to their own behavior.[15]

Between 1857–1858, Texans organized their own "ranging" companies to
protect themselves from raids. According to Barry, the Comanches knew the
terrain and "darted in, rounded up stock . . . and drove them away before
the settlers were aware that the foe was in their midst." The native men then
easily outdistanced the "awkward chargers" on their lithe mustangs. The
"Rangers" established a camp on Hubbard Creek near the reservation, hoping
to inhibit stock thefts by the reservation natives and prevent non-reservation
Indians from driving stolen stock through the land. In an attempt to keep
natives on the reservations the government provided monthly beef rations
to the reservation inhabitants. White settlers and rangers sometimes attacked
reservation residents hunting outside their prescribed lands, contending that
the natives were just out stealing livestock. Many Texans believed that Indian
agents were corrupt and protected their charges from legitimate persecution
for theft and murder. Several disgruntled settlers living near the reservations
circulated a petition to remove the allegedly unscrupulous agents, including
Neighbors.[16]

Both a report by a select committee of the Texas Senate and letters from
Neighbors refuted the allegations against the residents of the Brazos River
Reservation and the appointed Indian agents. According to the legislative
report, the natives that "roam the borders of Texas are not friendly disposed,
and a large portion of Comanches continue to raid within the state. Comanches
of the reservation pass and repass through the country." Concerning the
population of the Brazos River Reservation, the report commented that they
"are applauded for their good faith and friendship; and reports are made that
those Indians are not concerned in the outrages . . . and that the mischief is
done by Indians beyond their control, or by the white men." In several letters
Neighbors emphasized that investigations confirmed that no traces of "any

connection between these depredatory bands and the Indians settled on the reserves" existed. He pointed out that the Tonkawas and other "friendly" Indians had done all they could "in protecting the frontier against those outside bands, who have been engaged in the latter depredations."[17]

On January 21, 1858, Neighbors sent an editorial to *The Texas Sentinel* rebutting the citizens' letters concerning atrocities. According to Neighbors, the citizens' letters contained a "complete misrepresentation of the facts," and the citizens had damaged the reputations of both himself and the reservation Indians. Defending his charges, he reminded the public that many natives, including Tonkawas, regularly served as guides for settlers "engaged in lawful expeditions" tracking down stolen property. Neighbors reiterated that "the [reservation] Indians were always willing to go [as scouts], and the Kickapoos [and other non-reservation Indians] had been the ones committing offenses." Neighbors realized the danger of an impending frontier war, stating: "Unless measures are adopted . . . to relieve our frontier from forays of deprecating bands, it will be impossible to prevent people of Texas from making indiscriminate war upon the Indians that will endanger the peace of our whole frontier."[18]

To ascertain the veracity of the conflicting reports from citizens and agents, the Department of Interior sent Thomas T. Hawkins to investigate the discord surrounding the Texas Indian reservations. Hawkins concluded that the reservation natives and their agents were innocent of any allegations, with most of the accusers refusing to come forward to present their evidence. Hawkins nevertheless suggested that removing the reservation population to a location further away would eventually be necessary. Indians living on the reservations could not venture off their lands to hunt food or gather their wandering livestock without danger of an attack from bigoted farmers and ranchers. The solution, it seemed to Hawkins, was to again remove the Indians further from white settlements.[19]

Recollections by Charles Goodnight, noted stockman and Indian fighter, exemplified the diametric attitudes of frontier Texans toward the Tonkawa people. Goodnight first met members of the Tonkawa tribe shortly after they arrived on the Brazos River Reservation. He described them as "a harmless, inoffensive, rather lazy, dirty bunch of Indians . . . being hated by all other tribes they stayed along the frontier and mixed with the frontier people." Goodnight recalled that the men of the tribe supplied their families with the plentiful game in the area, but the tribe "had a habit of begging roasting ears and all the dead cattle they could find." According to Goodnight, the Tonkawas "were always ready and anxious to help us trail and fight other Indians . . . They were splendid trailers and excellent fighters."[20]

Living up to Goodnight's comments, Tonkawa warriors from the Brazos River Reservation continued their practice of joining white settlers in punitive expeditions against other "hostile" tribes, especially the Comanches. In December 1857, fifteen or twenty Tonkawas scouted for a detachment of the Seventh U.S. Infantry through land occupied by Kickapoos. The next April Plácido, "the faithful and implicitly trusted friend of the whites," led his warriors on a major campaign against Comanches raiding frontier settlements.[21]

In Spring 1858, Texas Gov. Hardin R. Runnels ordered state troops to strike Comanche villages north of the Red River before the summer raiding season. Runnels promoted Capt. John Salmon "Rip" Ford to the rank of major and placed him in command of a force of 103 Texas Rangers. Indian Agent Shapley Ross gathered 113 reservation Indians, including Plácido and several Tonkawa warriors, to act as scouts and guides for the expedition into the "immemorial home of the Comanches." The two commands joined at Cottonwood Springs in Spring County and rode toward the Comanche camps in the breaks of the Canadian River. On May 11, 1858, after a "Toilsome march of several days," Tonkawa scouts led Ford to an overlook where he could view Comanches chasing buffalo through "his glass." As daylight waned Ross, "having every confidence in the trustworthiness of his faithful Tonkawas," sent a party to positively locate the Comanche camps and ascertain the number of warriors in each camp. Documents in the Ross Family Papers stated that one of the Tonkawas, "disguised as a Comanche," entered the main camp on the Rio Negro, or false Wichita River, and returned with the information he and the other scouts had gleaned.[22]

"Moving like wraiths" through the shadowy jumble of trees and brush, the Tonkawa scouts located one of several camps belonging to a band led by renowned Chief Pohebits Quasho, or Iron Jacket. The chief acquired his sobriquet from a shirt of scaled mail that he wore, perhaps a remnant of a fallen Spanish explorer from the previous century. Iron Jacket became a powerful prophet because of his alleged invulnerability to rifle balls and arrows afforded by the armor. The Comanche chieftain claimed "by a puff of his breath" he could divert enemy missiles away from his body.[23]

Before sunrise on May 12, 1858, the Texans and their Indian scouts prepared to charge into an engagement known as the Battle of Antelope Hills. Each of the Indian scouts tied on a white armband to distinguish themselves from the Comanches during the attack. Plácido claimed for his Tonkawas the "privilege of wreaking vengeance on their hereditary enemies." The combined force rode to a rise overlooking a small camp on the banks of a branch of the Canadian River. Ford gave the signal to charge and the Tonkawa warriors rode into the encampment, scattering the inhabitants and killing every Comanche warrior they spied. A lone warrior escaped to ride across the river and warn the main Comanche camp of the onrushing enemy.[24]

Warned of the danger, the surprised Comanches leaped to their tethered war ponies and soon both forces were arrayed in line and prepared for battle, with the reservation Indians deployed on Ford's right flank. Iron Jacket, festooned with "gaudy ornaments" including "red flannel streamers" trailing from his feathered headdress, and "besmeared in warpaint" dashed along his line "exhorting his warriors to battle." Iron Jacket led several charges against the Texans, who ineffectually fired at the famous chief. Many of the Texans began to wonder if indeed the powerful Comanche did not lead a charmed life.[25]

As Iron Jacket led a foray toward the Tonkawa scouts, Jim Pockmark, a scout with "steely nerve" and "unerring eye," took careful aim with his rifle and "brought the Big Medicine to the dust." When Iron Jacket fell mortally wounded, Ford's line erupted with a blast of rifle and revolver fire, and with "yells and war whoops," his entire command charged into the disorganized Comanche warriors. Confronted by the hard-riding Texans and their native allies, the Comanches fought a determined retrograde action through the brush and thickets, attempting to protect their women and children. The resulting running fight lasted for several hours as the combatants dispersed through the rugged terrain.[26]

About one o'clock in the afternoon, Ford's men straggled back to the destroyed camp and, on lathered and weary horses, faced an attack from another group of Comanche warriors led by Peta Nacona. The Tonkawas herded about four hundred captured horses away from danger and returned ready for battle. With Peta Nacona ready "to spring like a lion" to "swoop down and annihilate the enemy," the two sides faced off for more than an hour. The Comanches, "mounted on gaily comparisoned [sic] and prancing steeds" and "flaunting feathers in all gorgeous display of intersavage pomp," rode out between the lines and challenged the Texas Indians to individual combat. Several of the warriors fighting for Ford who accepted challenges fell dead or wounded to the "expert" Comanche horsemen. Ford recalled that the individual combats stirred visions of "plumed knights . . . and exhibitions of gallantry" and "feats of horsemanship splendid." Ford remembered that Indians of both sides applied their lances and shields "with great dexterity."[27]

An angry Plácido led his Tonkawas in a charge toward the Comanche line, which worked as a ruse to lure the Comanches into an abortive counter-charge. When Ford ordered the Tonkawas back because they had removed their distinguishing white armbands, Peta Nacona led an attack toward what he believed to be a retreating enemy. A group of Rangers led by a Lieutenant Nelson struck the Comanches' exposed flank and the Indians broke before a "concentrated and well directed fire," and a disorganized running fight ensued in which one Tonkawa and one Ranger were wounded. The Texans claimed several Comanches killed and wounded, but their exhausted horses forced an end to the fray. Although he left his dead and wounded warriors on the battlefield, Peta Nacona brilliantly covered the escape of most of the women and children. The chief's white captive wife, Cynthia Ann Parker, and her children escaped with the other women.[28]

Ford later wrote of the battle that Plácido and all his warriors "fought like so many demons . . . it was difficult to restrain them, so anxious were they to wreak havoc upon the Comanches." The Texans reckoned that they faced more than three hundred Comanches, killed seventy-five warriors, and captured eighteen women and children, with the loss of two Rangers killed and six wounded.[29]

In Fall 1858, responding to outcries from enraged settlers, Gen. David E. Twiggs, Commander of the Department of Texas, ordered Capt. Earl Van Dorn, Second U.S. Cavalry, to conduct an offensive strike against Comanches and Kiowas reportedly gathering north of the Red River. Van Dorn organized an expedition composed of four companies of the Second U.S. Cavalry and one company of the Fifth U.S. Infantry, and sallied forth against the Comanche Nation. Acknowledging the expertise and dedication of Indian scouts, Van Dorn employed a number of Brazos River Reservation Indians, including Plácido and his Tonkawas, as scouts and guides. Lawrence "Sul" Ross, son of S. P. Ross, gathered 135 Waco, "Tehuacano," Tonkawa, and Caddo warriors to guide Van Dorn's cavalry from Fort Belknap into Indian Territory.[30]

Scouting ahead of the cavalry column, Ross' Indian guides discovered Comanche Chief Buffalo Hump and his band "trading and gambling" with other Indians at Wichita Village on the Red River. After stealing two Comanche ponies the scouts returned to Ross and imparted the information from their reconnaissance. Ross convinced Van Dorn of the scouts' reliability and persuaded the army officer to strike out for the village with his entire command.[31]

Van Dorn's Indian scouts located Buffalo Hump's main camp on Rush Creek and, at sunrise on October 1, his entire force "struck as a whirlwind." The cavalry and Indian scouts charged through the sleeping Comanches, shooting and yelling, almost "destroying that entire band of the Comanches." Prior to the attack, Tonkawa scouts located Buffalo Hump's horse herd and drove the ponies away, forcing many of the Comanches to fight on foot. Although the surprised Comanches fought determinedly from a series of brushy ravines, allowing most of their women and children to escape, Van Dorn's command captured more than three hundred of the Comanche horses, a large supply of jerked buffalo and pemmican, and burned 120 tipis. The Tonkawas plundered much of the lower camp and "counted coup" on many of their traditional enemies. Van Dorn awarded the native scouts the captured horses and "all the plunder they could carry." Eighty Comanche warriors, including Subchief Arickarosap (White Deer), died in the fighting, while their attackers lost four soldiers killed and at least twelve others wounded, including Van

Dorn and Ross. The Tonkawas suffered no casualties and considered their "medicine" very strong. U.S. Army Lt. William Burnett said of the Indian scouts, "If it had not been for them [scouts] Major Van Dorn would not have seen a Comanche."[32]

The next Spring, Tonkawa scouts again led Van Dorn on a successful strike against a band of Comanches. In May, while on an extended patrol, Plácido and several other Tonkawas guided the U.S. Cavalry across the Kansas border to a Comanche village located on Crooked Creek, a branch of the Cimarron River. Although asked to keep out of the fight, the scouts refused and tied on white headbands for identification. The entire detachment attacked the unsuspecting Comanches, destroying their village. The jubilant Tonkawas returned to Texas with the captured horse herd.[33]

While Tonkawa warriors faithfully served as scouts for the Texas Rangers and United States Army, a growing movement among white settlers called for the expulsion of all Indians from Texas, or failing that, an extermination of the Indians on reservations. In December 1858, under Baylor's influence, frontiersmen formed companies to ride down and kill any native discovered off the reservations. The year before, Neighbors dismissed Baylor as the Comanche Agent due to malfeasance. As the two men advocated very different points of view, white settlers were left divided on which policy to pursue regarding the reservation Indians. Some on the frontier doubted Baylor's accusations about the members of the reservations, while many others took up Baylor's cause. Buck Barry sided with Baylor, stating the Indians were "never to come among us on any pretensions whatever."[34]

Any Indians that left the reservation did so under threat of a "war of extermination." In January 1859, a force of at least two hundred white settlers gathered to oust all Indians from the Brazos River Reservation. When the Texans galloped onto the reservation they met a large group of Indian warriors painted for war, and supported by a company of U.S. cavalry from Fort Belknap. The Texans left the reservation, but "milled about" near the boundary for two months before going home. During this time, older native children carried bows and arrows to protect themselves and the smaller children.[35]

Overdue federal annuities and inadequate government support exacerbated the problems that Indian agents encountered while caring for the Brazos River Reservation members. Neighbors frequently complained about the condition of various commodities sent to the agency, writing: "The goods are of an inferior quality . . . [and] if the goods were purchased as per contract price of last year, the Indians have been badly cheated." Agent Matthew Leeper also reported to Fort Belknap that the government had led the Indians to believe that their agent would receive "assistance and cooperation" from the U.S. Army "in sustaining them." Unfortunately, according to Leeper, "at a time when support was needed . . . the Troops were removed off the Reserve."[36]

From the perspective of the Indian agents, removal of the reservation natives seemed the only solution. Neighbors himself counseled such an answer a year previously, but the government took no action. Neighbors concluded that the reservations were not maintainable in Texas and should be abandoned to the "lawless bands of white barbarians who now infest that portion of our state." Responding to a petition for removal of the reservation Indians by Texas citizens, Texas Governor Runnels appointed George B. Erath, Richard Coke, J. M. Smith, J. M. Steiner, and John Henry Brown to a commission that agreed that removal was the only way to maintain peace on the frontier, and that "once removed, every Indian found south of Red River should be regarded as hostile." Erath said that killing reservation Indians was "a natural consequence" because the Texas frontiersmen "could not distinguish one tribe from another." Brown, the Ranger captain responsible for keeping the peace around the reservation, later said that "the whole issue was more or less distorted for political effect." With "many exaggerated and false statements [condemning the Reservation Indians]."[37]

Determined to remove all Indians from Texas, by force if necessary, Baylor recruited another large group of vigilantes to drive the Indians across the Red River. On May 23, 1859, about 250 men from several frontier counties advanced onto the Comanche reservation, intent on destroying the buildings and driving the Comanches into Indian Territory. In a single skirmish "three citizens and seven or eight Indians were killed," causing the rest of the Comanches to flee to the other reservation, or to their relatives on the plains.[38]

Indian Agent Robert S. Neighbors and his wife. Courtesy of
The Center for American History, The University of Texas at Austin.

Moving on to the Brazos River Reservation, the unruly group found
themselves confronted by a large number of armed "friendly" Indians
painted for war and supported by a company of U.S. infantry. Outnumbered
by a determined foe, Baylor decided to fall back to Palo Pinto where
reinforcements continued to arrive. Baylor sent surveillance groups around
the reservation to determine the cavalry's intent and to keep the Indians
"bottled up" to prevent any food resupply. Barry rode onto the reservation
and demanded that the Indian agents and U.S. Army soldiers move the
natives north of the Red River, but the commander of the U.S. troops vowed
to follow his orders and fight to protect the Indians if necessary. He also

promised that he "would do all he could do" to move the Indians if Baylor's men "would hold off entering [the] reservations." After a few days, the frontier mob lost interest and "melted away," but they had made their point. In June, both state and federal governments made arrangements to break up the Texas reservations and relocate the Indians to Indian Territory.[39]

On August 1, 1859, Neighbors, Samuel A. Blain, Ross, and Leeper, escorted by Maj. George Thomas commanding four companies of the Second U.S. Cavalry, led approximately 1,500 Brazos River Reservation Indians north into Indian Territory. Due to the vigilantes' threats, many native families departed the reservation without all their possessions, leaving behind large numbers of horses and mules that had wandered across the reservation boundaries. Exacerbating their pathetic condition, the U.S. government failed to provide promised supplies to the Indians until December, when reports stated their condition as "destitute and hungry." Only by allowing the Tonkawas to hunt nearby buffalo herds did the agents prevent starvation among the tribes. The 109 Tonkawa men, 136 women, and an undetermined number of children moved onto the Wichita Reservation near Fort Cobb, on the north bank of the Washita River west of present-day Anadarko, Oklahoma. Neighbors left Blain in charge of the Indians and returned to Texas with Leeper and Ross. At the small village near Fort Belknap, Edward Cornett, firing a shotgun from ambush, killed Neighbors, probably because of Neighbor's undaunted support of the reservation Indians.[40]

Ironically, by February 1860, several settlers, including Barry, claimed that raids increased after the removal of the Brazos River Reservation Indians. The incidents became more violent as raiders moved from simple livestock theft to massacre. Ranging companies joined with army troops in combating the marauders, but the combined forces could not suppress the general uprising along the entire frontier.[41]

# 6  THE C.S.A., MASSACRE, AND RETURN TO TEXAS, 1860–1867

False accusations resulted in the Tonkawa tribe's removal to Indian Territory, their massacre by antagonistic tribes, and their eventual return to Texas. In mid-August 1859, the Tonkawa tribe arrived along the banks of the Washita River, west of present-day Anadarko, Oklahoma. Officially established on August 16, 1859, the reserve became the home of the Wichita, Caddo, Tonkawa, and Penateka Comanche tribes. On September 1, Samuel A. Blain assumed the duties of principal Indian Agent of the Washita Reservation. Maj. George H. Thomas and his troops returned to Texas and, not until October 1, did the army provide any protection for the Indians, when Maj. William H. Emory established the military post of Fort Cobb near the Washita River at the north base of the Wichita Mountains. Two companies of the First Cavalry and one company of the First Infantry Regiment garrisoned the fort. A company of Texas Rangers also moved into the post for about a year, employing several Tonkawa warriors as scouts on their patrols along the Red River.[1]

When Robert Neighbors left for Texas in September he commented, "I made my last talk [to the Tonkawas] yesterday—Old Placido cried like a child at the thought of my leaving, and if it was put to a vote there is not one [Tonkawa] that would agree with me to leave." The Tonkawas trusted that as long as Neighbors remained their agent he would protect them from assaults by other tribes, but without their trusted friend they faced a volatile future. Plácido boasted an especially close relationship with Neighbors, always confident that Neighbors did his utmost to ensure the best for the Tonkawas no matter the consequences. Neighbors support also guaranteed Plácido's leadership. Without the old man the tribe might split and join other bands, which might lead to intertribal bloodshed. Plácido had no indication that Neighbor's friendship and support would cost the agent his life.[2]

While most of the Tonkawas remained on the Washita Reservation, some went back to Texas to continue their role as scouts. In March 1860, Col. Middleton Tate Johnson from Fort Belknap utilized Tonkawa warriors to scout out Comanche stock thieves badgering the local citizenry. During a patrol north of the Red River, Plácido and several Tonkawa scouts tracked down and killed eleven Comanche and two Kiowa warriors. On July 1, 1860, Capt. Fulkerson Ross organized "an Indian Spy Company" to scout for Col. William C. Dalrymple's six companies of Texas Rangers. The thirty-five Indians in this company, mostly Tonkawas, scouted for the Texas Rangers, and later Confederate soldiers combating Indian raids along the northwestern Texas frontier.[3]

In Fall 1860, Gov. Sam Houston commissioned Lawrence S. "Sul" Ross as a Ranger captain and stationed his company near Fort Belknap. In late November a Comanche war party rode into northern Parker County, "committed serious depredations," and fled toward the northwest. The raid prompted Ross to again call on the Tonkawas expertise as trackers, and twenty-five Tonkawas volunteered to guide Ross in pursuit of the Comanches. Ross gathered his forty-man company, twenty-one U.S. cavalrymen provided by Capt. N. G. Evans, Commanding Officer at Camp Cooper, and seventy volunteer citizens from Palo Pinto County under Capt. Jack Curington. The Tonkawas tracked the Comanches to a temporary village hidden in the cedar brakes of the Pease River. Early on the morning of December 18, realizing the Indians were preparing to leave, Ross deployed his command for an attack. Curington's men had fallen behind during the march and followed

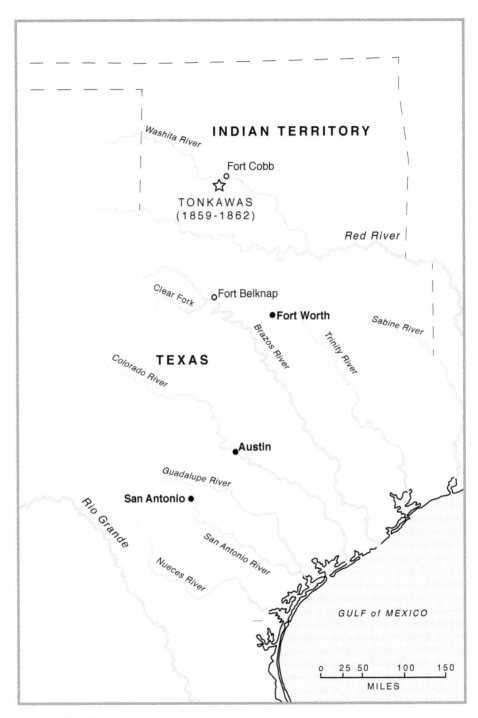

Map by Donald S. Frazier.

along leading their broken-down horses. The rough country offered no grass and, because the men did not bring sufficient grain, the horses were forced to survive on bits of bark and sprigs of young cottonwood trees.[4]

Acting with alacrity, Ross arrayed his men on line and slapped spurs to his horse. Yelling and shooting, the cavalry, Tonkawas, and twenty Rangers charged into the surprised camp. Most of the Comanches fled before their hard-riding attackers and, in less than half an hour, the pursuers captured the camp and 350 head of horses. Pushing his tired mount to the limit Ross caught up to and killed Mohee, chief of the little band. Lt. Thomas Killiher captured an escaping white woman and her two-and-a-half-year-old daughter. Another lieutenant named Sublett captured a young Indian boy. When the command returned to the settlements Issac Parker confirmed Ross' suspicions about the white woman. She was, indeed, Cynthia Ann Parker who had been captured by raiding Comanches some twenty-four years previously. Wife of Peta Nocona, Cynthia Ann's two sons were with another band and not captured. According to Ross, her years with the Comanches transformed her "as perfectly an Indian in habit as if she had been so born." Pining away for her Comanche family, Cynthia Ann died ten years later shortly after the death of her daughter Topusana or Prairie Flower. Some say she died of a broken heart. One son, Quanah Parker, survived to become a "popular and trustworthy" chief of the Quahadi Comanche.[5]

After the Civil War began in April 1861, U.S. troops abandoned Forts Cobb, Arbuckle, and Washita, but the Confederate government kept the reservation near Fort Cobb open. Matthew Leeper succeeded Blain as agent under the Confederate government, which promised to supply the needs of the Indians at the Wichita Agency and protect them from tribes loyal to the United States. On August 12, 1861, Gen. Albert Pike, C.S.A., finalized a treaty with the Comanche and several other Indian bands. Not all tribes residing on the reservation attended the signing, however, and remained loyal to the United States, many fleeing to Kansas. The Tonkawas pledged their loyalty to their Texas friends, thus allying themselves with the Confederacy.[6]

There were many reasons why the Tonkawas allied with the Confederacy, but the greatest factor that influenced the tribe's decision was their close tie with their Texas friends. Always faithful and loyal to Texas, the Tonkawas aided the Rangers, especially in tracking down the Comanches. Perhaps the Tonkawas also hoped that the Confederacy might fulfill the treaty obligations promised by the United States, but never satisfied. Other reasons, such as the fear of the Kiowas and Comanches, added to their decision. One other matter probably indirectly influenced the Tonkawas: the Confederate government considered any tribes who failed to ally with the Confederacy as Union allies. This policy, also used to coerce neutral bands, included attack and assumption of control by force if necessary.[7]

During the summer and fall of 1861, while most of the Tonkawa tribe lived quietly on the reservation near Fort Cobb, several tribal warriors continued scouting for the Texans, who now wore Confederate grey. In June, Col. Henry E. McCulloch, commander of the First Texas Mounted Rifles, C.S.A., journeyed to Indian Territory and signed peace treaties with several tribes on the Fort Cobb Reservation, including the Tonkawas. McCulloch and Maj. Edward Burleson of the First Texas Mounted Rifles, escorted by five companies of the regiment and Tonkawa scouts, rode westward in search of several Comanche and Kiowa bands hoping to sign peace treaties with the warlike Indians. Although the Texans managed a peaceful face-to-face meeting with Comanche Chiefs Red Bear and Eagle Chief, and prominent Kiowa leaders Lone Wolf, Satank, and Satanta, the Indians refused to sign any treaties with the Texans.[8]

Later that summer, McCulloch employed Tonkawa scouts in several patrols searching out Comanche and Kiowa marauders who raided West Texas frontier settlements, then bolted back to their refuges in Indian Territory or the rough canyons of the Llano Estacado. McCulloch and Burleson, determined to end the persistent raids, enlisted several Tonkawas to act as scouts for cavalry sweeps into the Comanche sanctuaries. The Texans provided the Tonkawas with ammunition and rations, as well as promises of any horses and plunder captured from Comanche and Kiowa villages. Although the Tonkawas led McCulloch's men to several large Comanche encampments, one with more than a thousand horses, both the Texans and Tonkawas rode south without any plunder. On August 9, Confederate Indian Agent Albert Pike supplied the roving tribes with letters of protection because several chiefs had promised to bring their tribes into the reservations "someday." Extant records did not indicate that any Tonkawa scouts participated in any of the later bloody battles fought between McCulloch's regiment and the Comanches.[9]

The year 1862 aptly demonstrated the animosity other tribes held for the Tonkawas. Any enmity remained inconspicuous in January, however, when Mathew Leeper reported to Superintendent of Indian Affairs Elias Rector that "the Tonkawa have warm, comfortable houses, made of poles and grass, such as they had in Texas." Leeper added that he built Plácido "a big double log house with chimneys to each room, and a hall or passage in the center."[10]

War sympathies of the white settlers exacerbated the friction between the reservation Indians, who Pike described as a "motly hoard." Pike himself expressed some concern about the disharmony among the tribes and requested Confederate troops at Fort Cobb. The discord commenced during the spring and summer of 1862 when renegade Cherokees and Shawnees sympathetic to the Union drifted onto the agency demanding food and voicing complaints against the Tonkawas, as well as joining Comanches in making threats against Leeper and his family. Fearing for their safety, Leeper bundled up his family and took them back to Texas. During the summer a few skirmishes ensued between the resident Indians and these newcomers. In July, the Tonkawa still received rations from the Confederate government for their assistance as scouts and guides. Indians demonstrating any support for the Union, however, received the bare essentials—and sometimes not even that.[11]

Long distances, and the war, aggravated miscommunication between Richmond, Virginia, and Indian Territory. In August, shortly after Confederate troops abandoned Fort Cobb, Confederate President Jefferson Davis reported that the Indian tribes which had signed the Treaty of 1861 remained faithful to the treaty "despite delays in aid and money." In actuality, Plácido and his Tonkawas were the only tribe that proclaimed total loyalty to the Confederacy, remaining near the agency except for short hunting expeditions.[12]

In September, disregarding Comanche warnings of dire consequences, Leeper returned from Texas, touching off simmering resentments. On the afternoon of October 23, rancor against the Tonkawas and Leeper erupted into open warfare. A combined force of Delaware, Shawnee, Kickapoo, Seminoles, Cherokees, and a few Comanches, armed with rifles supplied by federal troops in Kansas, attacked the agency. The attacking Indians killed the agency clerk and his two assistants as they sat before a fire in the main building. They then ransacked the store and commissary and torched all the agency structures. Agency interpreter Horace P. Jones, awakened by the first rifle shots, ran from his nearby house, leapt onto a horse, and galloped off to warn Leeper of the attack. A companion of Jones fell to the Indians as he rode toward Texas. Leeper lay concealed in the brush until morning, when a band of "friendly Comanches" discovered his hideout.[13]

Infuriated by a rumor that the Tonkawa had killed and dismembered a Caddo boy, the Indians attacking the agency vowed to continue their violence at the Tonkawa camp. When the Tonkawas received word of the attack on the agency, they decamped for Fort Arbuckle and the protection of the Confederate garrison recently stationed there, but the group moved too slowly. At dawn on October 24, just south of present-day Anadarko, in what is known as Tonkawa Valley, the mixed group of Indians attacked the Tonkawa camp with maniacal fervor. Still in their tipis and caught off guard, the 306 Tonkawas stood little chance against the superior numbers and heavy firepower of their attackers. Sometime before the attack, many young Tonkawa men departed camp on a buffalo hunt, taking most of the tribe's firearms and leaving the majority of the remaining Tokawas armed with mostly bows and arrows. The aggressors were mounted and carried rifles of "the newest pattern" supplied by the federal army in Kansas. When the firing ended, 137 men, women, and children lay in the smoldering ruins of the Tonkawa village. The attackers rode away leaving the Tonkawa bodies for the coyotes. Six years later, bones and skulls of the slain Tonkawas still lay bleaching in the sun around the old camp.[14]

Leeper's return, the killing of two Shawnees by the Tonkawas, and the rumors of the death of the Caddo youth supposedly precipitated the attack, but hidden motives prevailed. The Indians prosecuting the attack, especially the Comanches, hated the Tonkawas primarily for their alliance with Texans against the Plains tribes, but also for cultural differences. During the 1850s, Randolph Marcy called the Tonkawas "renegades and alien from all social intercourse with the other tribes." John S. Ford noted that the tribe was "the black beasts" of the Brazos River Reservation, blamed by other tribes for causing "various unfortunate occurances" through "sorcery." These accounts most likely refer to the Tonkawa practice of cannibalism, a custom that other native tribes had long used as a point of demarcation. Using Leeper's "machinations," the Civil War, the Tonkawas agreement to work as scouts for the white man, cultural differences, and any other pretext, the Comanches instigated the attack on the Tonkawas as retribution for past grievances. Union troops in Kansas further provoked the assault by providing rifles and ammunition to any native groups who promised to attack Confederate soldiers or their Indian allies.[15]

"Old Placido" died defending his people during the melee, supposedly in hand-to-hand combat. The aged chieftain may well have fallen in the grips of an adversary. One retelling of the massacre attested that Plácido and a chief named Blackfoot fatally wounded one another in a knife fight. According to this rendition, Plácido lived long enough to cut off his antagonist's hand and send it to Shapley Ross in Texas as a memento of friendship. The withered hand still resides in a collection of Tonkawa memorabilia at Baylor University.[16]

After his death several noted Texans testified as to the bravery, fidelity, and the debt owed to Plácido. Charles Goodnight reported that in 1860 Plácido's body held twelve wounds from "lance, arrow, and gunshot . . . [which] attested the valor of [a] real warrior." The rancher wrote that Texans owed much to this "wary old man." John Henry Brown later wrote that Plácido embodied a "soul of honor" and "never betrayed a trust." He was "brave to the upmost." Texans who rode with Plácido "implicedly trusted" him, and the chieftain "rendered invaluable services on the behalf of early Texan pioneers . . . in recognition of which, he never received any reward of a material nature, beyond a few paltry pounds of gunpowder and salt." Several frontier Texans thought a monument should be erected to the Tonkawa chief.[17]

Fearing complete annihilation, "a pitiful remnant" of the tribe—approximately 170 men, women, and children—fled, first to Fort Arbuckle and then back to Texas, arriving near Fort Belknap and Jacksboro in early winter. A Fort Belknap soldier described the tribe as suffering from "poverty and a demoralizing life." The Tonkawas continued to serve the Confederacy with a company of forty-five Tonkawa scouts under Chief Castile mustered into the First Frontier District of Texas, armed with only four rifles as "bows and arrows served the rest." State officials, however, demurred from "arming so large a body of Indians and allowing them to roam over the country . . . and may be productive of bad results."[18]

Conversely, many citizens on the Texas frontier reversed their previous attitudes and welcomed the Tonkawas back, including John R. Baylor and James B. "Buck" Barry, two of the most prominent voices in expelling the Tonkawas from Texas. Baylor utilized several Tonkawa warriors as scouts for his frontier defense company, while Barry was instrumental in locating a portion of the tribe near Belknap, where he led an effort to provide subsistence for the destitute Tonkawas. Barry later called Chief Castile "my friend and clever scout." Barry and several others considered settling the tribe in Callahan County along Deep Creek where ample water, good grass, and "plenty of buffalo" abounded. The Tonkawas, however, fearing an onslaught by increasingly aggressive Comanches chose to remain near Belknap, with a few drifting farther south to Camp Colorado. Barry wrote that despite their travails the Tonkawas were "yet willing to do all they can for Texas."[19]

In December 1863, the Texas Legislature appropriated $20,000 to provision the tribe. Gov. Pendleton Murrah applauded the action saying, "they [Tonkawas] are in our midst, they are friendly . . . are willing to fight for us. They are desolate and without a home." The governor reminded the people of Texas that the Tonkawas "were induced to come by promises held out to them of a home and military service in Texas . . . they have been subsisted by the officers of this [Frontier] Regiment . . . [and] have been friendly and true to the White man for years," and "entertain the most bitter hostility towards their Comanche foes and are eager to be employed in war against them [Comanches]."[20]

When Gen. James W. Throckmorton assumed command of the northwestern Texas frontier, he initiated several measures to feed, clothe, and arm the Tonkawa tribe. He sent them thirty muskets, a keg of powder, ammunition, and percussion caps to arm Castile's company. He also provided the Tonkawas with cooking utensils and several bolts of grey cloth produced at the state penitentiary. In June 1864, Capt. Y. A. Isbell became the acting state agent for the Tonkawa tribe. Isbell's major duty consisted of coordinating beef and flour rations and other supplies for the Tonkawas through Gen. Sam Bell Maxey in Indian Territory, Barry from Belknap, McCulloch from the Northern District of Texas, and the individual commanders of the First Frontier District. Isbell also managed to procure a few rifles and more shirts for the Tonkawa warriors scouting for Texas troops. Later, as governor after the Civil War, Throckmorton provided the Tonkawas with a league of land and appointed John L. Lovejoy as their agent.[21]

In January 1865, four Tonkawa scouts participated in one of the last and most lamentable events in Civil War Texas. In late 1864 more than six hundred men, women, and children of the Kickapoo tribe fled Kansas and Indian Territory because of persecutions by other Indians. The Kickapoos planned to join their kinsmen who had settled in Northern Mexico some fifteen years earlier. On December 9, 1864, a frontier defense company intersected the Kickapoos about thirty miles west of the old post of Fort Phantom Hill. Believing the large contingent of Indians "hostile," frontier commanders began to raise a large force of Texans to attack the Indians. The Second Frontier District supplied nearly three hundred men, with the Frontier Battalion providing another 161, making the combined force of Texas and Confederate troops more than four hundred mounted men strong. Both contingents followed the Kickapoo trail, the Texas troops guided by four Tonkawa scouts. On January 7, the Texas and Confederate forces located the Kickapoos on Dove Creek, a tributary of the Middle Concho River. About 9 a.m. on January 8, the two groups joined for an attack with an effective force of 380 men. The Texans estimated the total number of Indians at about one thousand in a large camp well suited for defense.[22]

The Texans' hurriedly contrived a plan of attack which called for the Texas militia to position themselves for a dismounted assault from the north while Confederate troops moved in from the southwest, driving off the Indians' horses and continuing a mounted charge through the village. About 10 a.m. the attack commenced, but was no surprise. Warned by the camp's lookouts, the Kickapoos took cover in the heavy brush and ravines that cut through their camp. When the Texans approached the Kickapoos blasted them with a withering fire. Many of the Indians had modern Enfield rifles and used the weapons with great proficiency. While the Texas troops retreated before a hail of bullets, the Confederate cavalry—including the four Tonkawas—drove off about one thousand horses while approximately seventy-five troops continued toward the village. These men soon felt the brunt of the Indian's accurate fire. The Kickapoos maintained an "unrelenting fire" until about 5 p.m. when the Texas force began a general retreat.[23]

A group of Kickapoo warriors arranged a hasty ambush and a counter-charge that threw the Confederate force into confusion, allowing the Kickapoos to recapture most of their ponies. The battered Texans moved off about three miles to count their dead, which numbered twenty-six, and tend their twenty-three wounded. The Texans thought they killed at least a hundred Kickapoos, but the tribe, after reaching Mexico, reported only eleven killed and seven wounded. The Texans plodded north through a storm which dropped two feet of snow, forcing them to eat several of their horses. The Tonkawa scouts recovered the pack train which had been abandoned by the Texans. The Kickapoos continued an uninterrupted journey to Mexico.[24]

After the Civil War the disheartened Tonkawas failed to fend for themselves, begging food and generally annoying the local citizenry. As Texas governor, Throckmorton requested that the federal government provide the Tonkawas with beef, flour, clothing, as well as plows and seeds, but the tribe received almost no support from Washington bureaucrats. In 1867, Maj. Samuel Starr, commander at newly established Fort Richardson, called the Tonkawa tribe "a lazy vagabond race." Starr asserted that if the Tonkawas could get enough to eat from another source they would not hunt. Growing disgusted with the Tonkawas, Throckmorton wrote Col. James Oakes, commanding U.S. troops in Texas, that according to Lovejoy, the Tonkawa's "behavior has been so bad that I have determined to let them shift for themselves." Throckmorton wanted the military to move the "demoralized" tribe to Indian Territory, or at least, to the frontier "where they cannot get whiskey."[25]

The Texas governor's office contacted President Andrew Johnson, seeking federal assistance in caring for the Indians in Texas that had no recognized U.S. agent. The Texans argued that the Indians "had no means of obtaining a livelihood." Many Texans argued that destitution led the Indians to commit atrocities on Texas' western frontier, which aroused the settlers' ire, resulting in more frequent complaints to the governor. In 1866 Texas sent a delegation to alert the national government of the conditions along the frontier. In response, the U.S. Congress signed the Treaty of Washington with the Cherokee Nation, which allowed the government to settle other tribes on the "Cherokee Outlet" between the 96th and 100th meridians. Throckmorton believed returning the Tonkawas to Indian Territory a mistake and, on September 20, 1866, sent a letter to United States Indian Commissioner Dennis N. Cooley requesting that the Tonkawas not be forced back into Indian Territory because of the 1862 massacre. Throckmorton did not want the Tonkawas relocated among their enemies who once tried to annihilate the tribe. The governor reminded Cooley that the Tonkawas were innocent of recent crimes on the frontier and that they had always been "peaceful and honest."[26]

On November 1, 1866, the Texas legislature preempted federal action by appropriating funds to support the Tonkawas and authorizing the governor to appoint an agent for the tribe. This act allowed the Tonkawas to remain in Texas, but did not halt Throckmorton's attempts to secure federal assistance for the tribe. He bombarded the Bureau of Indian Affairs with letters requesting federal support for the tribe and permanent settlement near a frontier post to guarantee the Tonkawas' protection from their enemies. In March 1867, Throckmorton succeeded when the War Department ordered the commander at Fort Richardson to assume responsibility for the Tonkawa tribe. On April 18, 1867, 103 Tonkawa men, women, and children arrived at Jacksboro bearing a letter from the U.S. Indian Commissioner requiring the military to issue any food supplies required by the tribe. Unofficially, for a time at least, the Tonkawas became the "far ranging eyes" of the Sixth U.S. Cavalry stationed at Fort Richardson. Soon the four "stock" English phrases of the Tonkawa scouts became part of the military jargon of the post. Officers and men alike mimicked the Tonkawas' "Maybeso yes, Maybeso no, Maybeso catchum, and Maybeso no catchum."[27]

For many Tonkawas, often to their detriment, ranchers' beeves seemed a more readily available food source than government rations, buffalo, or deer. In 1867, a rancher named Wallace discovered five Tonkawa warriors camped near the head of the Guadalupe River. The Indians had killed a "fat maverick steer" that Wallace claimed as his and "set in for general jollification." Smelling meat roasting over coals, Wallace and three of his cowboys followed the aroma to the Indians' camp. The drovers dismounted and crept up on the unsuspecting Tonkawas. Wallace described one warrior as "about 6 2 or 6 feet 3 inches tall," and "turning the meat on spits." At a command all the cowboys' rifles "cracked at once," killing two Tonkawas and wounding another. The three living Tonkawas escaped into the brush, but the white men captured all their "bows arrows and a flintlock rifle." Reportedly, the large Tonkawa man who was killed had "about 20 pounds of brass rings on his arms."[28]

Strife between those seeking to supplant Plácido as chief caused the Tonkawas other problems after their return to Texas. Campos, survivor of the Anadarko massacre, became the tribe's most noteworthy medicine man. The major contenders for leadership of the tribe arose between the old chief's son Charley and Castile. Charlie first succeeded as the tribal leader, but his drinking and ineptitude resulted in his replacement by Castile, known among the whites as "a fighter of distinction."[29]

Some discord continued among the Tonkawas as Charley attempted to regain his position of power. When Castile's daughter sickened and died after treatment by a lesser medicine man, the enraged chief shot and killed the medicine man who had performed his incantations over the girl. In hopes of regaining the position of chief, Charley managed to get Castile tried under Tonkawa law. Instead of a death sentence as Charley hoped, Castile received an unusual sentence for his crime. The tribal council ordered Castile to lead all charges against the Comanches. According to Goodnight, "If he [Castile] ever flinched or wavered, he was to be shot immediately by his own people."[30]

Notwithstanding the discord among the Tonkawas, several Tonkawa men continued to serve as scouts for the U.S. Army and Texas Rangers. In 1867, a band of Comanches led by "a large Negro" killed a man named Hazelwood on the road north of San Antonio. A detachment of cavalry, with "ten or twelve Tonkawa guides," tracked down and attacked the Comanches. During a running fight the Tonkawas overtook and killed a wounded Comanche warrior and the cavalry took a Mexican in the party prisoner. When the soldiers turned back, the Tonkawas killed and scalped the Mexican captive because he was allied with their enemies.[31]

Apparently many of the Tonkawas wandered away from Belknap and visited some of their old environs to the south. In Summer 1866, Jeff Maltby reported that fifteen Tonkawas, "accompanied by a white man," visited several ranches in Burnet County begging watermelons. Tonkawas visited Bell, Coryell, Mills, and McClendon Counties as well. On a visit to Valley Mills the Tonkawas warned several farmers not to build homes and a mill in the flood plain. Unfortunately, the white settlers did not listen and in the late 1860s a flood devastated the area, killing livestock, and washing away the flour mill. Local citizens finally heeded the Tonkawas' advice and moved the mill and settlement to the present location of Valley Mills.[32]

During the late 1860s, responding to intensified conflicts between westward moving pioneers and Plains Indians, the U.S. War Department established a string of new forts from Montana to the Rio Grande. On July 29, 1867, Lt. Col. Samuel J. Sturgis led Companies I, K, and L, Sixth U.S. Cavalry, to a high point in Shackleford County overlooking the Clear Fork of the Brazos where the soldiers established a post soon to be known as Fort Griffin. On August 4, 1868, the War Department resettled 143 destitute and poorly armed Tonkawas and Lipan Apaches, "suffering from the want of attention and supplies," to Fort Griffin from the vicinity of Jacksboro and Fort Belknap, which the Sixth Cavalry had reoccupied the previous year. The army promised to provide a refuge for the tribe and employ at least twenty-five Tonkawas as scouts and guides to pursue "hostiles" that swooped down out of the Texas Panhandle and Indian Territory to plunder isolated frontier cabins. To protect themselves from these same Comanche and Kiowa raiders, the Tonkawas established their camp below "government hill" near the fort. After a short visit to the new Tonkawa-Lipan encampment the post surgeon displayed the growing attitude of many Eastern reformers toward all Indians by bemoaning the "frightful hygenic [sic] condition" of the indigent Tonkawas' village.[33]

# 7  U.S. ARMY SCOUTS AND GUIDES, 1867–1872

U nder their new Chief Castile (which the soldiers pronounced "Cast Steel") and medicine man Campos, the reinvigorated Tonkawa tribe superbly demonstrated their expertise as warriors and trackers. In a "mutually advantageous" agreement, the U.S. War Department officially enrolled twenty-five Tonkawa warriors as scouts and guides. In return for their services the army not only paid the Indian scouts a monthly salary, but furnished each of them with a .50 caliber Spencer repeating carbine, ammunition, and a mount. Later, after they captured several Comanche and Kiowa war ponies, the War Department reimbursed the Tonkawas at a rate of $.40 per day if the men rode their own horses and provided their own tack. Additionally, the army issued the scouts with great coats, flannel shirts, blankets, ponchos, and boots, but deducted tobacco and other incidentals from their pay. The government also provided rations of beef, flour, coffee, salt, and sugar for the assemblage of Tonkawas and Lipan Apaches living near Fort Griffin.[1]

The Tonkawa's abilities soon earned them a position as a valuable asset to army patrols. Capt. John Lee, commanding officer at Fort Griffin in 1869, considered the

Tonkawa scouts "a great acquisition" because of their knowledge of the country and tracking expertise. Capt. Robert G. Carter, Fourth U.S. Cavalry, noted that the Tonkawas were "very valuable as scouts," coming from "a powerful and warlike tribe . . . implacable enemies of the Comanches." Another officer, requesting authorization to re-enlist a number of Tonkawa scouts, wrote that the Tonkawa scouts were "always anxious to accompany scouting parties . . . and are almost as serviceable without being enlisted." The officer's comments referred to the fact that several Tonkawa warriors accompanied army patrols as scouts even though the Indians were not among the twenty-five Tonkawas officially mustered into the army.[2]

Mounted on fresh horses, painted for war, sporting blue uniform jackets, and brandishing their Spencer carbines, the Tonkawa scouts epitomized the Western image of a proud warrior. For ten years the scouts' admirable performance, along with the accolades they earned, reinforced the tribe's self-esteem. Army officers, however, failed to understand that performing any type of menial labor was beneath the dignity of a Tonkawa warrior. When Lt. Col. S. H. Starr asked Tonkawa Charley, Plácido's son, "Why don't you and your tribe take up a lot of this land, go to work, plant corn, build yourselves houses, and try to live like men?" Charley asked Starr, "Why you no plant corn?" Starr replied that as an officer and soldier he was not expected to work. Charley adroitly turned the tables on the officer when he proudly slapped his chest and replied, "Me warrior me no work!"[3]

Army officers and civilian scouts alike described the Tonkawas as "superior trailers" that could follow "a dim trail at a gallop." One officer declared that the "great success of scouting parties is owing to a great measure to having them [Tonkawas] as trailers." Another officer recalled that "It is wonderful to what extent the trailing instinct had been developed in these Indians . . . I have seen them going at top speed, spread for a lost trail, with their heads so near the ground that their hair swept the grass" and the one who picked up the trail "screamed like the lead hound in a flying pack." Richard Henry Pratt, who commanded the Tonkawa scouts at Fort Griffin in 1874, commented that when seeking minuscule signs of a trail the Tonkawa warriors scattered out in a ragged line, riding with their heads almost on the ground. When

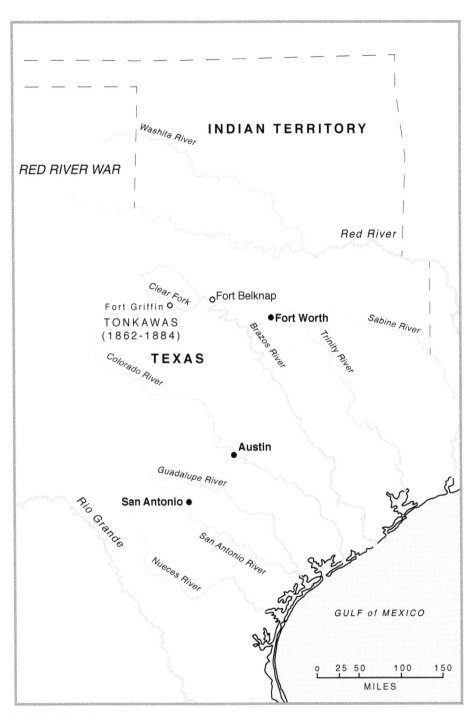

Map by Donald S. Frazier.

one detected a sign of their quarry, he howled "like a wolf" and led his companions off in hot pursuit. Charles Goodnight claimed that he had an internal compass and was never lost on the plains, and that the only better tracker and scout than he was a Tonkawa "who had keener senses than I and his eyesight could carry farther than mine."[4]

On January 15, 1868, George A. Otis, curator of the Army Medical Museum, set events in motion that preserved a number of Tonkawa ethnological materials. Otis sent a letter to the chief medical officer for the District of Texas requesting that post surgeons assist in expanding the museum's "collection of Indian crania, and also of Indian weapons, and implements." Otis requested that army surgeons in "Indian country" collect "bows and arrows, war clubs and spears, implements of the chase, etc" adding that the museum wanted "stone arrowheads, axes, and such like memorials" of the "fast disappearing tribes." Otis also made arrangements to provide medical officers copies of George Bibbs' *Instructions for Research Relative to the Ethnology and Philology of America* to guide the officers' efforts. At Fort Griffin, Assistant Surgeon D. Henry McElgerry began collecting artifacts from within his area. On June 8, 1868, Otis acknowledged a letter from McElgerry delineating the contents of two boxes of specimens sent to the museum from Fort Griffin. In August, Otis recorded that McElgerry sent several Tonkawa pieces, along with a few Comanche items "captured at Paint Creek, Texas." Soon after the items arrived Joseph Henry, secretary of the Smithsonian Institution, opened negotiations to have the Tonkawa, and several other Indian collections, transferred to the Smithsonian. On January 21, 1869, the surgeon general of the army authorized the transfer of 309 specimens "illustrative of the manners and customs of the Indian of North America" to be exchanged with the Smithsonian for items relating to "the human anatomy." Included in the Smithsonian collection are sixty-eight Tonkawa items sent by McElgerry. Two items from the McElgerry collection, a dressed and painted buffalo hide and some ceremonial laurel berries called Owwah-cholic by the Tonkawas, disappeared before a January 1968 inventory. A "girdle," which army accession documents recorded as made of "tanned skin of a Comanche Indian" generated some particular interest.

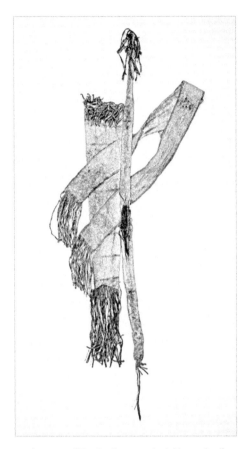

Tonkawa hide quiver and bow case with two small leather bags attached, blue and yellow decoration, before 1874. Texas. Mrs. Starr Hayes Collection. Photo by Carmelo Guadagno. Courtesy, National Museum of the American Indian, Smithsonian Institution.

Subsequent analysis of the girdle failed to conclusively determine the source of the skin, but did indicate the girdle exhibited "characteristics of human skin."[5]

Maj. William H. Wood, commanding officer of the Sixth U.S. Cavalry, believed that with enough men—and the service of Tonkawa scouts—he could prevent the Comanches and Kiowas ranging western Indian Territory and the Texas Panhandle from raiding into West Texas. As part of his plan, Wood established patrol bases along the road between Forts Griffin and Concho at old Fort Phantom Hill and Mountain Pass, known locally as Buffalo Gap. A company of infantry, five mounted cavalrymen, and two Tonkawa scouts occupied these small posts, scouting and providing escorts for the mail and travelers.[6]

In Spring 1868, the Tonkawas more than proved their worth as scouts. In the midst of a late "Norther" a group of cowboys rounding up cattle collided with a Comanche raiding party along Battle Creek in Callahan County. The cowboys un-holstered their six-shooters and repeating carbines and, in a running fight, drove a superior number of Comanches off toward the northwest. While searching for several comrades and scattered stock the riders discovered the body of George Hazelwood, with a number of empty cartridges and unusual black arrows littering the area around his body. They also found a dead Comanche nearby and evidence that Hazelwood had wounded at least two other Indians in a desperate fight in a grove of oak trees. As the Indians continued northwest they decided to revenge their losses against a number of settlers at the Ledbetter Salt Works in Shackelford County. Again, superior firepower saved the frontiersmen. The settlers killed four warriors and drove off the remaining Comanches. As the Indians turned away from his two blockhouses, Ledbetter rammed the kingpin from a wagon tongue down the barrel of his "six pounder" and fired a parting shot at the retreating warriors.[7]

After the Comanches departed two settlers from the group at the salt works walked ten miles to Fort Griffin where they recounted their harrowing experience to Capt. Adna R. Chaffee, who ordered out a detachment of ten troopers from the Sixth Cavalry guided by Tonkawa scouts. Several stockmen joined the command and the combined party rode out in pursuit of the fleeing Comanches. For two days the Tonkawas easily trailed the Comanches, who were encumbered by three wounded warriors on travois dragged behind their horses. About eight miles south of present-day Haskell, the Tonkawas spotted the Comanches encamped on the banks of Paint Creek. The pursuers spent a long cold night in a dry camp awaiting dawn to attack the Comanches.[8]

Before dawn the Tonkawas, "like spectres in the dim starlight," led the soldiers and cowboys to the Comanche camp. As the first light of dawn filtered through the trees of March 6, 1868, "Like an avenging nemesis, riding on the wings of swift destruction," the command charged into the Comanche camp. In the short and sanguinary melee the party rode down and killed several Comanches, while others rallied around a large swarthy man. The Tonkawas ferociously attacked this group of Comanches with guns and knives. Tonkawas Cloud and Charley ignored the defenders' "heavy fire," rode near the circle of warriors, and as "their pistols blazed," ended the career of Cato, a renegade black soldier whom the Tonkawas hated. At least twelve Comanches died during the fight, with only two of the attackers wounded. General Orders Number 19, Headquarters, Fort Griffin, dated March 10, 1868, commended Chaffee for his "short and decisive campaign," which resulted in killing several "hostile Indians, with their Mexican and mulatto leaders." Tonkawa Johnson, leader of the scouts, reportedly left the fray with seven fresh scalps "hanging from his belt."[9]

Tonkawas likewise scouted for the Buffalo Soldiers of the Ninth U.S. Cavalry stationed at Fort Concho. In the summer and fall of 1869 large parties of Kiowas and Comanches carried out several bloody raids along the San Saba and Concho Rivers. Col. Edward Hatch resolved to drive the "hostels" out of the region north and west of Fort Concho. He placed Capt. John Bacon in command of a cavalry detachment cobbled together from six companies of the Ninth Cavalry. On October 10, Bacon led his unit out of Fort Concho and headed for the Clear Fork and the old Fort at Phantom Hill. At the old post a detachment of the Fourth U.S. Cavalry and twenty Tonkawa scouts augmented Bacon's command, increasing its strength to 198 soldiers and scouts.[10]

Bacon moved upriver searching for the illusory Plains Indians, but found none. A large party of Comanches and Kiowas saved the captain from further search. At sunrise on October 28, an estimated five hundred warriors attacked the cavalry encampment from all sides. At a cry of alarm from the guards the black soldiers and their Tonkawa allies grabbed their Spencer carbines and deployed to defend themselves. The Comanche and Kiowa warriors soon

Charley, Tonkawa Indian Chief, c. 1867. Courtesy of the Texas State Library & Archives Commission.

"found themselves in a hornet's nest" of fire from the repeating carbines. In a bitter, and sometime hand-to-hand battle, the Buffalo Soldiers and Tonkawas drove off a far superior attacking force. Bacon organized his troops and sent the Tonkawas to trail the retreating hostiles. At mid-afternoon the next day the Tonkawas led Bacon's men to a large camp and in a "fierce charge" the cavalry scattered the Comanches and Kiowas "in all directions." Bacon destroyed the camp and claimed forty warriors killed and seven women captured. His men rounded up fifty-one Indian ponies after the fray. Bacon reported eight men wounded, but none fatally. The number of Comanches and Kiowas killed or wounded when they attacked the soldiers' bivouac remained undetermined.[11]

Frequently Tonkawa warriors demonstrated their adeptness at protecting cavalry mounts from would-be horse thieves. In April 1870 near Fort Phantom Hill a band of forty Comanches attempted to steal a herd of cavalry horses over which several Tonkawas stood guard. The Tonkawas fell on the would be thieves with such ferocity that they almost wiped out the Comanches and captured thirty ponies to boot.[12]

In July, Kiowa Chief Ton-ne-un-co (or Tene-angopte), Kicking Bird or Striking Eagle, led a band of more than one hundred Kiowa warriors off the Fort Sill Reservation, beginning a series of raids along the northwestern Texas frontier. Normally a "peace chief," Kicking Bird led the raid to sustain his position as chief. On July 5, several of Kicking Bird's warriors, unbidden by the chief, attacked a mail stage at Rock Station on the Salt Creek Prairie, sixteen miles from Fort Richardson. The Sixth U.S. Cavalry responded with a fifty-seven-man patrol commanded by Capt. Curwen B. McClellan, who followed scattered sign left by the Kiowas to the banks of the north fork of the Little Wichita River. About 10 a.m. on the July 12, McClellan's lead elements believed they located Kicking Bird's main camp near present-day Seymour.[13]

McClellan ordered his troopers to draw their sabers and led them forward at a trot toward the Kiowas. As the cavalry approached a gathering line of Indians, two more groups of mounted Kiowas appeared on each of McClellan's flanks, threatening to cut his command in two. McClellan ordered his men to open fire and the Kiowas charged across the prairie "with bells tinkling and feathers streaming." Subjected to a "galling fire" the cavalry began a six-hour retreat before the implacable Kiowa warriors. Shortly before dark the cavalry fought their way back across the south fork of the Little Wichita and Kicking Bird decided to break off the action. McClellan lost three men killed and twelve wounded, but five men of his command received Medals of Honor for heroism during the engagement. Had Tonkawa scouts accompanied McClellan they might have detected Kicking Bird's carefully laid ambush, possibly saving him from an ignoble defeat.[14]

In October, five Tonkawa scouts working with Capt. William A. Rafferty and twenty troopers of the Sixth U.S. Cavalry intercepted an Indian raiding party along the north fork of the Little Wichita River, not far from the scene of McClellan's defeat. The Indians drove a large herd of stolen homesteader's stock before them, planning a circuitous return to Indian Territory. When the cavalry charged, the raiding party scattered, but in a running fight covering more than eight miles the troopers rode down and killed two warriors, wounded at least one more, and recovered eighteen stolen horses. Suffering no losses in his command Rafferty discovered that one of the dead Indians was Keech-quash, chief of the Kichai. When searching the chief's body the Tonkawas found a hunting pass, bolstering the settler's contentions that most of the raiding Indians came from the reservations north of the Red River.[15]

The next month two Tonkawa scouts led Chaffee and Lt. Henry M. Kendall, with the post guide and twenty troopers of Company I, Sixth Cavalry, along the trail of another band of Indian stock raiders from north of the Red River. About twenty miles north of Fort Richardson the Tonkawas brought the cavalry up to the stock thieves. In a fight covering some fifteen miles, Chaffee's men managed to recapture seven stolen horses, but were easily outdistanced by the Indian's swift ponies.[16]

On May 18, 1871, an estimated war party of one hundred Kiowa, Kiowa-Apache, and Southern Cheyenne warriors led by Satanta (Set'tainte or White Bear), Satank (Set-Angia or Sitting Bear), Big Tree (Ado-eete), and noted medicine man The Sky Walker (maman-ti) attacked Henry Warren's "corn train" on Salt Creek Prairie on the old Butterfield Trail between Forts Richardson and Griffin. The Indians killed seven and wounded most of the other twelve teamsters who managed to escape through the brush. The Indian raiders ransacked the wagons, scalped and mutilated the corpses, and roasted Samuel Elliot over a slow fire. General in Chief of the United States Army William T. Sherman, who happened to be visiting the Texas frontier posts at the time, ordered Col. Ranald Slidell Mackenzie, whose tough Fourth U.S. Cavalry Regiment replaced the Sixth U.S. Cavalry at Fort Richardson in April 1871, to pursue the perpetrators with "extreme vigor" and "attack any party of Indians there found." Revolted by the massacre, Sherman believed "that the numerous robberies and murders on this frontier have been done by the Fort Sill Reservation Indians," and directed Mackenzie toward that post. Mackenzie, at the head of 193 of his troops and led by sixteen Tonkawa scouts, tracked the raiding party into Indian Territory and onto Fort Sill where Col. Benjamin F. Grierson's Tenth U.S. Cavalry, another regiment of Buffalo Soldiers, had arrested the Kiowa chiefs.[17]

Portrait of Col. Ranald S. Mackenzie. Courtesy of West Point Museum Collection, United States Military Academy Museum.

On June 8, a detachment of cavalrymen from the Fourth U.S. Cavalry loaded the handcuffed and leg-ironed Kiowas into two wagons and drove off toward Jacksboro, where the chieftains were to be tried for murder. Lt. George A. Thurston commanded the escort composed of several of his troopers and a party of Tonkawa scouts. The Tonkawas, led by McCord, rode along the flanks of the wagons. At least two guards, cradling loaded carbines, rode along in each wagon with the driver and prisoners. As soon as the drivers headed their horses southward Satank began singing his "wild, weird death chant."[18]

When the wagons neared Cache Creek Satank made his move. Surreptitiously removing his handcuffs, he threw off the blanket covering his body, pulled a large "scalping knife" from his leggings, and slashed at Cpl. George Robinson, who was in charge of the wagon. Satank hastily scooped up the corporal's fallen carbine and leveled the Spencer at the nearest guard. Thurston immediately ordered his men to fire. Cpl. John B. Charlton, riding in the second wagon, reacted almost instantly and shot Satank with his own Spencer.[19]

Satank went down but was not finished. The wounded Kiowa, "with the vitality of a grizzly bear," sat up in the wagon bed, frantically working the lever of the carbine, which mercifully for the nearest trooper had jammed. A fusillade from the outriding Tonkawas and Charlton slammed into the Kiowa, one bullet passing through Satank's body and slightly wounding the teamster riding the "near wheel mule." Riddled with multiple gunshot wounds Satank, who Indian Agent Laurie Tatum called "the worst Indian of the Fort Sill Reservation," fell dead. According to Captain Carter, the Tonkawa scouts leapt off their horses and immediately scalped the Kiowa chief, adding "a rich prize" to their "much valued war trophies." The seventy-year-old Satank supposedly told a Tonkawa before the trip that "you may have my scalp. The hair is poor, it isn't worth much but you may have it."[20]

Satank's people later buried him at Fort Sill. Satanta and Big Tree eventually arrived in Jacksboro, were tried for murder, found guilty, and sentenced to hang. In 1873, Texas Gov. Edmund J. Davis first commuted their sentences to life imprisonment, and then in October paroled the pair, allowing the two

Kiowas to return to Fort Sill, from where both sallied out to participate in the Red River Wars in 1874–1875. Infuriated, Sherman wrote Davis that he believed that Satanta and Big Tree would return to their old ways, and that "if they are to have scalps, that yours is the first that should be taken."[21]

During Spring 1871, Comanches, Kiowas, and Kiowa-Apaches left their reservations and stepped-up their raids all along the northwestern Texas frontier, causing local settlers to inundate Washington, D.C., with letters of complaints. As a result of these grievances, substantiated by notarized affidavits presented to Sherman personally, Gen. Joseph J. Reynolds, commander of the Department of Texas, assented to Mackenzie's suggestion to commence a campaign to force the hostile Indians off the South Plains and onto reservations in Indian Territory. Sherman also approached Secretary of War William Belknap and received permission to allow the U.S. Army "a free hand" in pursuing Indians into Indian Territory if necessary to arrest raiders and retrieve stolen livestock.[22]

In July, even before the end of Satanta and Big Tree's trial, Mackenzie began to organize his command for a campaign against the Indians raiding from their sanctuaries in Indian Territory. He ordered all ten companies of the Fourth U.S. Cavalry to assemble at a forward supply base on Gilbert's Creek near where it flowed into the Red River. On the night of August 2, Lt. Peter M. Boehm, easily identified by the "white sombrero hat" that Mackenzie authorized him to wear as commander of scouts, and his detachment of Tonkawa scouts rode into the regimental bivouac. As soon as his regiment joined, Mackenzie led it north and west for several days through a country "entirely devoid of grass . . . The ground dry, parched and baked." The Tonkawas, nonetheless, kept Mackenzie's mess furnished with deer and wild turkeys. After crossing the Red River into Indian Territory, Tonkawa hunters liberally supplied the command with buffalo and antelope meat.[23]

On August 9, Mackenzie's regiment joined Colonel Grierson's Tenth U.S. Cavalry on the banks of Otter Creek in Indian Territory. After a brief conference the two colonels organized their units and, on August 17, departed in a two-pronged search for Kicking Bird's village. Matthew Leeper and Horace P. Jones accompanied Mackenzie and Grierson as interpreters.

Tonkawa scouts rode with both commands as guides through the "wild country" of the upper Red River drainage. During the next ten days the majority of Mackenzie's command succumbed to the intense heat and "vile" water of the "Texas gypsum belt," becoming "heap sick" and disabled with "violent cramps and purging."[24]

One of Mackenzie's dyspeptic soldiers caused a stampede of C Company's mounts, adding more work for the Tonkawa scouts. The soldier put on a white night shirt and, when the "nocturnal ghostly apparition" wandered too close to the horses, they stampeded. Lt. Boehm and the Tonkawas leapt on their barebacked ponies and began to roundup the scattered mounts. Boehm's horse saved his life when it came to a sliding halt just before running off a high gypsum cliff. The next morning while searching for lost mounts the Tonkawas and a detachment of cavalry almost ran headlong into a war party of Kiowas "fantastically dressed . . . painted and ornamented with beads and feathers."[25]

Lashing their horses into a run the Tonkawas pursued the fleeing Kiowas until the Kiowas stopped and requested a parlay. The Kiowas refused to divulge any information concerning Kicking Bird's village, and Mackenzie later allowed the Kiowas to go free, much to the "utter disgust of the loyal Tonkaways," who considered the Kiowas enemy prisoners. The Tonkawa scouts expected scalps and plunder, unaware that higher headquarters had ordered Mackenzie to not attack the recalcitrant Kiowas. Mackenzie decided to elude the Kiowas spying on his command by executing a night march. He used one Tonkawa to lead his men, while the other scouts guarded the flanks and reconnoitered ahead of his column.[26]

Turning up the north fork of the Red River the Tonkawa scouts discovered several small pools of rainwater, showing the soldiers how to dig in the sandy arroyos for water. Despite fresh Indian signs throughout the area, the Tonkawas almost lost their ponies to a band of Kiowas. While digging themselves, the Tonkawas allowed the Kiowas to approach near enough to stampede their horses. With a cry of alarm, a Tonkawa spotted their enemies and they all leapt on their mounts to give chase. The Tonkawas lost the Kiowas in the breaks of the river, and had no luck discovering any trails in the area once a thunderstorm washed out all fresh tracks.[27]

The soldiers' luck changed about two days later when the Tonkawas guided the command to Sweetwater Creek. After refreshing their mounts with plenty of fresh water, Boehm and the scouts cast about for a fresh trail. When asked about the frequent smoke columns seen during the day McCord, a Tonkawa scout, replied that the "smokes" were Kiowa signals warning of the cavalry's approach to their village. Late in the day the Tonkawas spied a "hostile" Indian and, "Whooping and yelling," ran down and captured the Indian, who proved to be a Lipan. Tonkawa Johnson said that the Lipan was a member of Kicking Bird's band, and mistook the Tonkawas for members of his hunting party, allowing the Tonkawas to come close enough to capture him. Johnson said that the captured Indian indicated that the Kiowa village was nearby, but a short search before dark produced no positive results.[28]

Captain Carter reported that the night after the capture "we had quite a reception" of the Tonkawas "about our campfire." According to Carter, the Tonkawas' "dusky faces" shown in the flickering firelight as they smoked their hand-rolled cigarettes in a circle around the captive. Johnson and McCord attempted to converse with the captive through both spoken and sign language. Johnson, whose mother was a Lipan, professed to be fluent in the language, but several cavalry officers doubted his claim. Whether mislead by the captured Lipan or disillusioned by his orders, Mackenzie directed his men to strike out down the Sweetwater Creek. If he had marched up the creek, Mackenzie and his men would have found Kicking Bird's camp in "two or three hours." No one ever discovered why Mackenzie ordered his men in that direction, or why he dismounted and commanded his men not to shoot at the abundant game they encountered.[29]

At least one Tonkawa scout either failed to hear, or completely ignored, Mackenzie's no shooting order. When a rifle boomed across the plains Mackenzie ordered his adjutant to "bring in the culprit." The adjutant attributed the shot to "Old Tonkaway Henry" and "in Injun jargon" tried to convince the scout to accompany him to Mackenzie's location. The Tonkawa refused and the officer grabbed Henry's bridle. The scout reached for his carbine and the officer for his six shooter. Carter intervened and, "spurring his powerful horse, and seizing Henry by the shoulders, and plying the 'quirt' to his [Henry's] pony," managed to drive Henry back to the column. Once there, Henry's "woebegone face" provoked loud guffaws and Mackenzie decided against any punishment. Carter remembered that "Henry was good after that."[30]

On August 28, Mackenzie ordered a series of short marches back to his supply base, and eventually Texas. During the return trip several horses and mules broke down from heat exhaustion and lack of forage and were abandoned. Mackenzie sent Boehm and the Tonkawa scouts ahead to bring back supplies to the staggering column. When the column finally reached the Tenth U.S. Cavalry supply base on Otter Creek on September 1, Mackenzie discovered that Grierson had contacted Kicking Bird and convinced the chief to take his band to Fort Sill. Grierson had, Mackenzie evermore alleged, kept the chief informed of Mackenzie's movements, thus allowing the Kiowas to elude the Fourth U.S. Cavalry. "Bitterly disappointed," Mackenzie ordered his regiment back to Texas, never forgiving Grierson for his actions.[31]

During the Fourth U.S. Cavalry's short stay at Otter Creek, McCord complained to Mackenzie about short rations of sugar, coffee, bacon, and flour. Mackenzie sent for Boehm to explain how his chief of scouts allotted rations to the Tonkawas. Boehm explained that he issued three days of rations at a time but the Tonkawas might eat the entire ration for breakfast, depending on their skill to kill a buffalo, deer, or antelope later in the day. McCord did not grasp that three days' rations must not be consumed at one meal and angrily commented about Boehm, "He heap Lie. He heap go to hell. He heap damned." Mackenzie then explained again to McCord that the rations must last three days. The Tonkawas so trusted "Big Chief" Mackenzie and his promises that McCord stood up, smiled, shook hands all around, and "stalked off to his camp perfectly satisfied and contented."[32]

On September 19, 1871, only six days after Mackenzie's lead elements returned to Richardson, and before men and horses of the Fourth U.S. Cavalry completely recovered from their last patrol, Mackenzie received a warning order to prepare his regiment for an extensive fall campaign against the "wild Comanches of the Staked Plains." On October 3, Mackenzie with approximately six hundred troopers and twenty Tonkawa scouts from Forts Richardson, Concho, and Griffin set out on a large-scale expedition to drive several Comanche bands off the Panhandle and onto reservations.

With Tonkawa scouts riding point and flank guard to prevent surprise attacks, the cavalry left old Camp Cooper on the Clear Fork heading toward the headwaters of the Double Mountain Fork of the Brazos River. On October 7, Mackenzie established a supply camp on Duck Creek near present-day Spur, intending on traveling farther northwest in search of suspected Indian sanctuaries.[33]

That night Mackenzie ordered the Tonkawas to conduct a search for a Kwahadi Comanche band he believed to be in the area. The Tonkawas expressed some concern about leaving the main column without a soldier escort, troubled that the soldiers might mistake the scouts for Comanches when they rejoined the command. Without waiting for the scouts' report, Mackenzie ordered the campfires left burning to deceive the Comanches and commenced a night march to follow a dim trail discovered by one of his officers. Without the Tonkawa scouts leading, Mackenzie's entire command stumbled into a craggy box canyon, forcing the group to establish a cold, dry camp. Late the next day the Tonkawa scouts returned from their foray, men and horses drained from a scrap with a small band of Comanche warriors. When the tired Tonkawas informed Mackenzie that they had cut a trail leading to a Comanche village Mackenzie ordered his command into the saddle to follow the trail.[34]

The troopers made little progress, however, when on the night of October 10 a group of Quahadis raided the cavalry's horse herd. Encamped at the mouth of Blanco Canyon, the soldiers both sidelined (tied one fore-foot to the opposite hind foot) and picketed their mounts, but a rush of whooping Comanches waving buffalo robes and the resulting shooting and shouting stampeded several horses. The Comanches succeeded in capturing sixty-six cavalry mounts, including Mackenzie's "fine grey pacer."[35]

At dawn a detachment of three officers and eleven cavalrymen rode in pursuit of about a dozen Comanches attempting to steal even more horses. A small group of soldiers rode up over a steep bluff and unexpectedly clashed with as many as one hundred of Quanah Parker's Quahadi Comanches. The hard-used cavalry mounts dictated a slow withdrawal, covered by a steady fire from the troops' Spencer carbines. Capt. E. M. Heyl turned tail and left Carter with about five men to face the onrushing Comanches, and only the fortuitous arrival of Boehm and the Tonkawas saved Carter from annihilation. The Tonkawas, in a long-distance firefight, and by making several false charges, kept the Comanches at bay until Mackenzie appeared with the bulk of his command, scattering the Comanches. During the fray Carter lost one man killed, in addition to the stolen horses.[36]

Carter left a narration of his impression of the combat between the Tonkawa scouts and the Quahadi Comanches. According to the captain the Comanche warriors "heartily" responded to the "shouts and war-whoops of our scouts, sometimes interluded with most emphatic and old-fashioned round cursing." Carter continued with the events "peculiar to an Indian fight," a "grand, but rather dangerous circus." The Indians faced off in an irregular line of battle, always in "constant motion, every individual warrior fighting for himself." Warriors from both sides rode about "whooping or yelling and brandishing his arms." The Indians, however, "At no time . . . approach close rifle distance." Periodically a Tonkawa and Comanche dashed toward one another, "both apparently bent on meeting in personal combat or a duel." Carter remembered that "as we breathlessly watched, expecting every moment to see the collision, they whirled and delivered their fire strongly reinforced by untranslatable Indian language, which we took to be serius [sic] name calling." After the warriors delivered their epithets and long-range fire, "they darted back to their places in the ever-changing line." The Tonkawas continued in their feints until Mackenzie arrived and the Comanches retreated.[37]

For two days the Tonkawas followed the arduous, twisting trail of the Comanches onto the Llano Estacado and, on October 12, drew close enough to force the villagers to abandon lodge poles, buffalo robes, stone axes, and puppies too young to sustain the demanding pace. Warriors appeared in an attempt to draw the main body of the cavalrymen away from their village. Late in the afternoon, just as Mackenzie's point caught sight of the travois moving the Comanche village, an early season Texas "norther" blew in, pelting pursuer and pursued with rain, sleet, and snow. When darkness fell, "Like a great black curtain," Mackenzie ordered his men into a defensive circle, preparing for "a cold, bitter, night." Comanche warriors sporadically fired into the camp throughout the night. When a detachment of cavalry sent out into the "black blizzard" to "chastise" the Comanches became lost within less than five-hundred yards of the main body, the Tonkawas inside Mackenzie's perimeter guided those with the patrol back to safety utilizing "a peculiar yell rarely used by Indians except when lost." The next day dawned clear and cold, but after a few hours of a vain search, it became apparent that the Comanches had vanished through the snowstorm. Disgruntled, Mackenzie returned to winter quarters and began preparing for a major campaign the next spring.[38]

On the return trip to the supply camp on Duck Creek Mackenzie learned a valuable lesson when he allowed his impatience to override good judgement. Several Tonkawa scouts spotted two Comanche warriors and quickly drove them into hiding among the ledges and brush at the edge of the Llano Estacado. Mackenzie stood behind the scouts chafing at what he perceived as unnecessary caution and delay. Moving even closer to direct the Tonkawas assault, his impatience cost him a Comanche arrow through the fleshy part of his right thigh. "In their own good time," the Tonkawas stole through the rocks and killed both Comanches. The Tonkawas then scalped their enemies, cut off their ears, and peeled a small strip of skin from their breast. The rest of the bodies they left for the wolves.[39]

Carter recalled that before the Tonkawas descended the high bluffs to dispatch the Comanches, the scouts gave the soldiers "one of the finest circus acts" ever seen. The scouts performed "lofty tumbling, somersaults, vaulting, standing on their heads, etc." Carter wrote that the acrobatics were the best "ever our good fortune to see in an Indian country."[40]

Carter also depicted the Tonkawa preparations for battle during Mackenzie's 1871 fall campaign. He recollected that the scouts pulled out "A small piece of looking-glass," spat into "the hollow of the hand," and mixed "much green, red, and yellow, and black, and ochre paint" which the Tonkawas "applied in reeking dobs." To their "cream claybank dun or white poney [sic]," the scouts "plentifully striped." To complete their battle ensemble, the Tonkawas donned "headdresses, horns, and much red flannel, and bright[ly] color[ed] feathers." As battle neared "[o]ur gallant allies then pranced alongside the column, posturing, moving their heads from side to side, brandishing their carbines and, evidently, feeling all the pride of conquering monarchs. So self-conscious were they of the dignity which all this display of paint, feathers, and gee-gaws, etc., gave them."[41]

Mackenzie's regiment returned to its posts by late November and settled in for a reasonably quiet winter. During the spring and summer of 1872, Tonkawa scouts and the U.S. Cavalry, posted at Forts Griffin and Richardson, reacted to several Comanche and Kiowa raids along the frontier. On April 21, local citizens reported that a small band of Comanche horse raiders had stolen several horses and fled northwest. A forty-man detachment from Company F, commanded by Capt. Wirt Davis and guided by two Tonkawa scouts, cut the trail of five unshod Comanche ponies driving several shod horses. The cavalry took up the chase and pursued the thieves at a trot for several miles. When the cavalry detachment closed on the Comanches, the men scattered and the Tonkawas lost the Comanches' trail in a maze of tracks left by herds of buffalo and mustangs. The command cast about for the lost trail but to no avail, riding more than three hundred miles in eight days.[42]

In May, Mackenzie sent eleven patrols out of Fort Richardson, but only two made contact with hostile raiders. On May 18 a small patrol led by Lt. John McKinney, along with Henry Strong as chief of scouts, engaged about twenty native men near present-day Wichita Falls. The Indians managed to escape, but with at least three of their number wounded and tied to their ponies. On May 23, a detachment from Companies A and B, led by Captain Heyl, bivouacked about fifteen miles from Richardson when a large party of Comanches attacked the cavalry encampment. Despite a reported "overwhelming number of hostiles," Heyl suffered only one trooper mortally wounded, but his entire command was driven back to Richardson.[43]

About 5 p.m. on June 9 a Kiowa war party, led by White Horse, attacked the homestead of Able Johnson Lee, some sixteen miles down the Clear Fork from Fort Griffin. The Indians killed or took prisoner Lee's entire family. Colonel Wood, now commanding Fort Griffin, sent Lt. E. C. Gilbreath with a patrol of ten men and two Tonkawa scouts to ascertain the facts of the raid. Gilbreath reported that the Lee massacre was "one of exceeding brutality."[44]

According to the evidence discovered by the Tonkawa scouts, Able and his wife Lilly, along with daughters Frances (age eight), Cordellia (age fifteen), Susanna (age seventeen), their son John Able Lee (age six), and a man

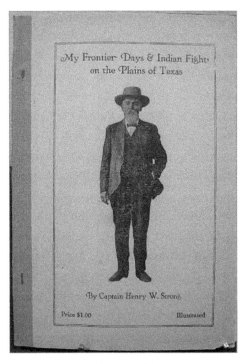

My Frontier Days & Indian Fights
on the Plains of Texas

By Captain Henry W. Strong

Price $1.00                    Illustrated

In his later years, scout Henry W. Strong published his recollections
of his time scouting for the U.S. Army in *My Frontier Days &
Indian Fights on the Plains of Texas* (Dallas, Texas, 1926).

named McCarthy were at the Lee home when the raid took place. Able and
Lilly died inside the house, and Frances was killed running away from the
homestead. All died of arrow wounds and were scalped. Gilbreath reported
that "every particle of skin upon which the hair grew was removed from
the head." The Kiowas also cut off Mrs. Lee's ears and mutilated all the
bodies. The raiders took Cordellia, Susanna, and John Able prisoner and
rode off to the northwest. Wood ordered two additional patrols to search
for the captives, but extant records provided no clue as to any success in
recovering the remnants of the Lee family. Rainy weather and high water
prevented the Tonkawa scouts from successfully following any trails. When
the Kiowas learned of the pursuit they hurriedly returned to the safety of
Indian Territory.[45]

In reaction to the numerous Comanche and Kiowa raids along the northern frontier Brig. Gen. Christopher C. Auger, who replaced Reynolds as commander of all U.S. troops in Texas, observed, "I fear more extensive operations will have to be undertaken against these Indians before they will remain peaceable." The hostile bands used Mexico and reservations in Indian Territory "as places of refuge and security for themselves and their plunder, the present defense system will not effect much." Coinciding with Auger's comments, on June 14 Mackenzie ordered even more aggressive patrols launched from Forts Richardson and Griffin, hoping to curtail Indian raids along the North Texas frontier. Mackenzie himself assembled ten companies of cavalry, and with twenty Tonkawa scouts, rode out of Griffin on an extended patrol up the Double Mountain Fork of the Brazos River, across the Llano Estacado, to Fort Sumner in New Mexico Territory and back to Puerta Luna on the Pecos River.[46]

From July 2–14, Capt. Napoleon Bonaparte McLaughen led Companies D and I, Fourth U.S. Cavalry, on a long, dry patrol from Fort Griffin to the Mucha Qua (Mushaway) Valley, between Gale and Snyder, and on to the "Staked Plains," casting about for signs of stock thieves. Tonkawa scouts struck several trails of Comanche bands roving the area. One trail indicated that as many as sixty Comanches headed toward the Colorado River, and another trail marked the passage of thirty shod horses and mules driven northwest. An isolated thunderstorm obliterated much of the available sign, but the Tonkawa scouts managed to follow the stolen stock over the hot, dusty plains with "poor grass" for two days. On July 8, the troopers gave chase to a single Indian, but failed to catch their elusive quarry as the cavalry mounts had been without water for more than thirty hours. McLaughen turned his command back toward Fort Griffin with little success.[47]

On September 2, Mackenzie's Fourth U.S. Cavalry, after riding about 640 miles without contacting any Comanches or Comancheros, returned to the Duck Creek supply base. On September 21, after repairing their equipment and shoeing their mounts, Mackenzie's troopers and Tonkawa scouts rode into the Texas Panhandle. The Tonkawa scouts soon discovered the trails of several "large parties" of Indians. The Tonkawas trailed the Comanches along the rim of the Palo Duro Canyon, possibly the first time Mackenzie heard of this Comanche winter haven. The Tonkawas reported that the canyon contained "good water and grass" and that the canyon drainage led to the Red River Valley.[48]

On September 29, the Tonkawa scouts discovered a trail running along McClelland's Creek, a tributary of the north fork of the Red River. The tracks on the trail indicated that a number of Indians had used a mule to carry a load of grapes picked from the plentiful vines along the creek. The nine Tonkawas followed the trail for about twelve miles until they came upon the village of Chief Mo-way. Several scouts rode back to report the Comanche's dispositions, while others remained to observe the camp.[49]

Mackenzie organized his men into a column of fours, uncased his flag and guidons, and at 4 p.m., two hundred cavalrymen and scouts thundered down on Mo-way's surprised village. Comanche warriors snatched up their weapons and sprinted for their tethered war ponies. About eighty warriors congregated at the edge of the river and "put up a desperate stand," but a troop of cavalry outflanked them and the Indians fled, dumping their dead in a deep pool to prevent the Tonkawas from scalping and mutilating the bodies. In a "brisk fight of about half an hour," the cavalry killed at least twenty-four Comanche warriors and captured 124 women and children. Mackenzie reported that seven of the female prisoners were Mexicans who "had become Indians." After the short but furious battle, the troopers burned 262 tipis and destroyed a "large amount of property." Mackenzie lost one man killed, two mortally wounded, and two others wounded less severely.[50]

Short of supplies Mackenzie's hungry troops gorged themselves on Comanche pemmican and jerky as they ransacked the village. Sgt. John B. Charlton sampled "a nice piece of lighter colored meat," which he was unable to identify. He asked McCord what the meat might be. With innate rascality the Tonkawa replied "Maybe so him white man." Charlton immediately lost his dinner and any further curiosity about Comanche vittles.[51]

Burning the Comanches' tipis and their contents robbed the Tonkawas of any "plunder," creating some disfavor with Mackenzie. According to Strong, Mackenzie's civilian chief of scouts, the Tonkawas "were having a good time scalping and plunging their knives into the bodies [of the dead Comanches]." When Mackenzie undertook to halt the mutilations, Tonkawa Henry said "some very uncomplimentary things" to Mackenzie. Strong recalled that the Tonkawas hated all Comanches and "thought no indignity was too great for a dead one."[52]

When the Tonkawas rode away from the sacked camp, they drove a large herd of captured horses, estimates ranged from eight hundred to as many as three thousand, along with them. Mackenzie awarded the animals to the scouts to compensate them for a lack of booty and to replace several ponies wounded or killed in the recent engagement. On the night of October 11, Bull Bear and 120 Comanche warriors attacked the Tonkawa camp. Badly outnumbered the twenty Tonkawas broke before the onslaught, allowing the Comanches to stampede the horses. Bull Bear's warriors recaptured nearly all of their horses, in addition to most of the Tonkawas' ponies. The lack of support from the soldiers, and Mackenzie's criticism of the incident afterwards, led several Tonkawas to resent their white allies. Mackenzie provided the Tonkawas with remounts from the few remaining captured ponies, further wounding the men's pride.[53]

By the end of 1872, dogged by Mackenzie's soldiers and the Tonkawa scouts, many free roaming Comanche and Kiowa bands moved onto the reservations in Indian Territory. Some of these groups surrendered large quantities of stolen goods and livestock to U.S. and Texas officials, providing proof that they had been the culprits raiding Texas settlements. With the reduced requirements for army patrols on the northern Texas frontier, Auger ordered Mackenzie to turn his attention to the Rio Grande where Kickapoo Indians and Mexican bandidos crossed the river to raid isolated ranches in South Texas.[54]

# 8 FRONTIER SCOUTS AND THE RED RIVER WARS, 1873–1875

Between January and March 1873, correspondence between the commanding officer at Fort Griffin and the Department of Texas negotiated re-enlisting at least twenty-five Tonkawa scouts to be stationed at Griffin. In April, Ranald S. Mackenzie headquartered his regiment and a contingent of these Tonkawa scouts at Fort Clark near Bracketville and prepared to conduct aggressive operations against the Mexican banditos and Kickapoos that frequently crossed the Rio Grande to raid isolated Texas ranches. By many accounts, Gen. William T. Sherman verbally ordered Mackenzie to take whatever measures necessary to halt the raids along the Rio Grande, including, if necessary, crossing into Mexico and destroying the Kickapoo village. On May 23, 1873, Mackenzie led two companies of his Fourth U.S. Cavalry Regiment out of Fort Clark searching for the Kickapoo miscreants. Two Tonkawas accompanied his command as scouts. Although the cavalry made no con-tact with the elusive Kickapoos, the Tonkawa scouts warned Mackenzie that Fort Clark could expect an attack practi-cally anytime. To preclude such an attack, Mackenzie sent Tonkawa scouts Castile and Johnson to warn Kickapoo

Chief Costilietos that Mackenzie would follow any raiders back into Mexico, kill all the men, take the women and children prisoner, and destroy the Indians' village.[1]

On May 28, Mackenzie lived up to his promise. The previous day Mackenzie crossed the Rio Grande with four hundred troopers and twenty-seven Tonkawa and Seminole scouts. In a lightening attack Mackenzie's men charged into the village, killed nineteen natives, and before riding away from the burning village captured the chief, forty women and children, and sixty head of horses. Mackenzie lost one man killed and two wounded in the action. In thirty-two hours the cavalry and scouts completed a grueling 120 mile ride, fought a major engagement, and splashed back across the Rio Grande early on the May 29. Mackenzie sent all the prisoners to San Antonio for confinement.[2]

In early 1873 an incident occurred that caused a rift between the Tonkawas and Fort Griffin soldiers. The previous October five Tonkawa scouts led out on an expedition guiding Captain Heyl and his detachment of cavalry assigned to protect a crew from the Texas and Pacific Railroad surveying a route from Fort Worth to El Paso. After arriving at El Paso, Tonkawa scout William allegedly went on a bender, remaining drunk for several days, and the young warrior's subsequent death led to the controversy. According to Heyl's official account, on February 9 Sergeant Enwright reported that William was drunk and creating a disturbance. Enwright ordered Sergeant Lane to arrest William and throw him in the guardhouse. When Lane attempted to arrest William the Tonkawa ran to his tent, grabbed his Spencer, and loaded a round into the chamber in an attempt to shoot Lane.[3]

According to Heyl, Enwright forcibly subdued William, which caused the young warrior to later flee the encampment. Heyl stated that the sergeant ran up and snatched the carbine away from William, and was "compelled to use force" in order to confine the drunken Tonkawa. About midnight, using the ruse of "answering a call of nature," William slipped out of the stables and eluded the corporal of the guard. On February 12 a very ill William returned to camp. Heyl attributed the Indian's illness to "sleeping out nights with nothing but a thin shirt, leggings, and moccasins on," continual drinking, and wading the Rio Grande, which was "full of ice."[4]

On the morning of February 13 Heyl sent all of the Tonkawas with a detachment of cavalry heading for Hueco Tanks east of El Paso. On February 16 the men brought back the body of William, who had died at the tanks. Heyl explained that he had sent along medicine for William, but the Tonkawa died anyway. Doctors Gale and Lewis, assistant surgeons at Fort Bliss, stated that William died of "pluro pneumonia."[5]

The Tonkawas, however, vehemently disagreed with Heyl's version of events. According to the scouts, Sergeant Ainwright, Company K, Fourth Cavalry, kicked William in the chest five times and "broke his ribs or breast bone." The sergeant also kicked William in the head and dragged him "60 or 75 yards by the hair." Ainwright then tied William to a tree. The Tonkawas stated that the weather was very cold, with snow on the ground. Around midnight some sympathetic soldiers cut William loose and he ran off to El Paso. The next morning a very sick William returned to camp and the next day Heyl ordered William out with a party of guides to Hueco Tanks. The Tonkawas agreed that William was sick and died just as the detachment reached Hueco Tanks. The Tonkawas said that, "All the soldiers told us that sergeant Ainwright killed William." He died as a consequence of the "kicking and other bad treatment. We all think so too." All the scouts believed William's treatment was carried out under the sanction, if not the direct orders, of Heyl.[6]

An El Paso civil court indicted the sergeant for "killing William, a Tonkawa Indian," who died from "broken ribs and other bodily injuries inflicted by Sgt Enwright." The court exhumed William's body and "a Doctor Oliver . . . after a careful examination of the body" reported that all the Indian's ribs were intact, and he could not discern any bodily injuries. The doctor's statements corroborated the army's official account and the court acquitted Enwright.[7]

Reports of William's death filtered back to Castile at Fort Griffin and, "in an excited and enraged state," the chief stormed into Col. George P. Buell's office demanding "satisfaction." Buell called the incident a "great outrage" and promised to investigate the circumstances of William's death. After the detachment returned Buell took statements from the Tonkawas, supposedly tending to believe their version and hoping to find other witnesses to substantiate the scouts' allegations against Enwright. Extant records, however, contained no results of Buell's investigation, nor any punishment of soldiers for William's death.[8]

Instead of assuaging the Tonkawas' rancor Buell only increased their resentment. First he ordered a Protestant pastor to conduct funeral services for several Tonkawa children who had died from the flu. Campos argued with the minister and accused him of trying to "bewitch" the tribe. The shaman blamed two additional deaths on Buell and the pastor's interference. Next Buell told the tribe that their beef rations would be reduced, but he had petitioned the Bureau of Indian Affairs to provide a herd of sheep to replace the beef rations, and that he would "give his personal attention to the matter." The insulted Tonkawa chiefs angrily informed Buell that they were warriors and would not deign to become herders, a task they associated as women's work. When the sheep arrived the Tonkawa men gave the animals to their women and children to shepherd.[9]

During the same summer, the army and Tonkawas reached another impasse. The War Department adopted the new single-shot Springfield carbine for the U.S. Cavalry and wanted the Tonkawas to exchange their repeating Spencer carbines for single-shot Sharps carbines. A board of army officers had decided that no repeater could stand up to the rugged treatment of military service, and according to the board, repeaters tempted troops to waste ammunition. Wiser than those in Washington in the ways of firepower the Tonkawa scouts refused to give up their Spencer carbines. In September, Castile met with Richard Henry Pratt, the new commander of scouts at Fort Griffin, and offered to buy Winchester rifles for the scouts if the army would provide the ammunition for the new rifles. Pratt forwarded the proposition through channels, in part writing:

> the scouts under my charge are very much dissatisfied with the proposed exchange of their Spencer carbines for the Sharps, which is an arm they have a great dislike for. They have each proposed to supply themselves with a Winchester rifle or carbine provided they can be furnished with ammunition and they will dispense with the use of the government arm. As the expense

will be lessened, and I believe their satisfaction and usefulness will be greater, I respectfully request . . . I be authorized to make this arrangement and furnished [the Tonkawa scouts] with ammunition for the Winchester gun.

Wisely, Brig. Gen. Christopher C. Auger, commander of the Department of Texas, at least partially agreed with Pratt and allowed the Tonkawas to retain their Spencers.[10]

Disgusted with the recalcitrant Tonkawas Buell considered moving them to New Mexico Territory. He went so far as to open a study of costs and routes to relocate the Tonkawas and Lipans at Fort Griffin to either the Mescalero or Jicarilla Apache Reservation near Fort Staunton. Renewed Indian raids along both the Rio Grande and northern Texas frontier, however, ended any deliberation concerning moving the scouts. The army required the Tonkawas' exceptional tracking skills to locate the hideouts of the illusive Comanches and Kiowas who had begun another spate of raids in the fall and winter of 1873.[11]

In November, Tau-ankia (son of prominent Kiowa Chief Lone Wolf) led a band of Kiowa warriors off the Fort Sill Reservation to raid Texas ranches. The party swept down the Nueces River, killing several ranchers, and on into Mexico where they killed at least fourteen Mexicans and stole 150 horses before returning to Texas. On December 9, Tonkawa scouts led Lt. C. L. Hudson and forty-one troopers of the Fourth U.S. Cavalry to Kickapoo Spring in Edwards County, where Tau-ankia's party camped. In an early morning attack the cavalry and Tonkawas scattered the Kiowas into the brush around the spring. The troopers chased several individual warriors through the brush, killing nine, including Tau-ankia and Gui-tain, Lone Wolf's nephew. For their services the Tonkawas received all the captured weapons and thirty ponies belonging to the Kiowas. Lone Wolf vowed revenge on both the Tonkawas and white soldiers for his son's death.[12]

During the winter of 1873 a band of Comanches rode in ahead of a "Norther" and drove off all the horses from Wallace Brown's Ranch. A "company" of Rangers and nine soldiers from Heret's Creek camp saddled up and pursued the Indians through a gathering storm. The Rangers and soldiers went into camp on Mulberry Creek and the Comanches, well aware of their pursuers, slipped in through the falling snow, cut the hobbles, and led off the Rangers' horses. Luckily the soldiers had picketed their mounts in a different location and the Comanches missed them. Buell, afield with other troops, heard of the thefts and ordered the Tonkawa scouts to track down the horse thieves. The Tonkawas followed the Comanches' trail and led Turner, with a few troops, to the hidden camp. In a dawn surprise attack Turner's men and the Tonkawas charged into the camp, shooting down all the Comanches. Due to the Tonkawas' efforts the rancher and the Rangers recovered all their purloined mounts. Joseph Matthews paid the Tonkawa scouts $3 per head for returning the horses to the abashed Rangers.[13]

In late January 1874, citizens reported to Buell that Comanches had raided several ranches near Fort Griffin and probably headed the stolen livestock west toward the Double Mountain Fork of the Brazos. Buell quickly responded and rode out of Fort Griffin with Capt. P. L. Lee and fifty-five Buffalo Soldiers of D and G Companies, Tenth U.S. Cavalry. Pratt and eighteen Tonkawa scouts fanned out in front of the column to ferret out the Comanches' trail. On February 5 the scouts caught up to their quarry in the valley of the Double Mountain Fork of the Brazos. In a chaotic running fight, the Buffalo Soldiers and Tonkawas rode down and killed eleven warriors and recovered sixty-five stolen animals. The following June, Johnson's Tonkawas, guiding two troops of the Fourth U.S. Cavalry, chased a band of Comanches into Blanco Canyon, where the Comanches managed to elude their pursuers. From the winter of 1873 to the spring of 1874, at least thirty Comanches and Kiowas died during raids into Texas. As a result of these deaths, hundreds of Kiowa and Comanche warriors vowed to join Lone Wolf in his revenge against the Tonkawa scouts for guiding the soldiers.[14]

In early 1874, Comanche medicine man Isa-Tai incited a major Indian uprising on the South Plains. Isa-Tai promised "strong medicine" to destroy all whites on the plains, especially the hunters decimating the buffalo herds. To prove his power, he supposedly vomited up a wagon load of cartridges. Isa-Tai assured all that followed him of their invulnerability to soldiers' guns. Quanah Parker and several other noted Comanches, Kiowas, and Southern Cheyennes joined Isa-Tai's confederation. The medicine man also proposed attacks on the Tonkawas because they aided white soldiers against other tribes. Horseback, a Comanche peace chief, warned the commander at Fort Sill about the plan to exterminate the Tonkawa tribe. When Buell was notified of the danger he offered the Tonkawas the protection of Fort Griffin. Accepting his offer, the Tonkawas shifted their camp into the "shadow of fort buildings."[15]

On June 27, a combined force of Comanches, Kiowas, and Southern Cheyennes, estimated to number about seven hundred warriors, opened a crusade to wipe the plains clean of white interlopers. The Indians first struck an assemblage of buffalo hunters camped at Adobe Walls on the South Canadian River in present-day Hutchinson County. The hunters' ably defended themselves with their long-range Sharps rifles and the thirteen to fifteen casualties they inflicted on their attackers caused Isa-Tai's dismissal as a false prophet. Without a strong leader the coalition dissolved and the warriors disappeared into the barrancas of the high plains, only to reappear throughout the summer to steal horses and confront the cavalry and Texas Rangers.[16]

In July, disgusted that the "Quaker Agents" could not restrain the Comanches and Kiowas from leaving their reservations and raiding south of the Red River, Secretary of War William Belknap authorized a major campaign against the defiant Plains Indians, "to punish them for recent depredations along the Kansas and Texas frontiers." Col. Nelson A. Miles' Fifth Infantry Regiment marched out of Fort Dodge on August 14. Miles led his column southwest toward the upper reaches of the Texas Panhandle to entrap the Southern Cheyennes, Comanches, and Kiowas between several other columns moving up from the south and west. Buell commanded a force of six companies of cavalry from the Ninth and Tenth U.S. Cavalry Regiments and two of infantry to guard thirty supply wagons. In late September, guided by thirty Tonkawa scouts, Buell's command made its way up the Salt Fork of the Red River by way of Fort Griffin and Fort Sill. With his supply base also at Fort Sill, Lt. Col. John W. Davidson received orders to operate independently with the six remaining companies of the Tenth U.S. Cavalry, three companies of the Eleventh U.S. Infantry, and a contingent of Tonkawa scouts. From Fort Bascom, New Mexico Territory, Maj. William R.

Price led four companies of the Eighth U.S. Cavalry toward the morning sun. Each column was "At liberty to follow the Indians wherever they go, even to the agencies," but their orders instructed all the commanders to "act in concert if possible."[17]

In compliance with his instructions Mackenzie ordered eight companies of his Fourth U.S. Cavalry, four companies of the Tenth U.S. Infantry, and one company of the Eleventh U.S. Infantry to rendezvous at Fort Concho. The scouts included six white soldiers and civilians, thirteen Black Seminole soldiers, twelve Tonkawas, and "some Lipans." Lt. William A. Thompson commanded the scouts, assisted by Sgt. John Charlton and civilian guide Strong. The Tonkawas included Johnson, chief of scouts, John William, Anderson, Cooper, Old Henry, McCord, and Wildcat. Johnson, veteran of several campaigns and a one-time Comanchero, possessed invaluable knowledge of the routes in and out of the barren, featureless Llano Estacado.[18]

On September 18, before Mackenzie departed his supply camp on the Fresh Water Fork of the Brazos, an additional seven Tonkawa scouts arrived to reinforce his reconnaissance corps. Military and civilian personnel alike knew the value of native scouts. A reporter wrote that the Tonkawas were "used as advanced scouts and trailers and are quite necessary to an expedition of this kind."[19]

After his experience the three previous years, Mackenzie followed Gen. George Crook's advice to junior officers concerning utilization and treatment of Indian scouts. Crook wrote, "The first principle is to show them that we trust them. They are quick to note any lack of confidence. They . . . know how best to do their work. They understand this business better than we do." Directing the scouts in details will "merely disgust them," making them "time servers." Crook cautioned his officers that misuse of native scouts would induce them to work in the presence of a white officer, but "loaf" when not under direct supervision. Crook advised, "explain to them what you expect . . . and let them do their work in their own way, . . . [the scouts] know better how to obtain the information which is needed, . . . and should be allowed to use their own methods in getting it. We cannot expect them to act automatically as drilled soldiers do. Their best quality is their individuality," and if "destroyed their efficiency goes with it."[20]

On September 20, in a "sharp fight," four Tonkawas clashed with a party of twenty-five Comanches. When the Comanches downed a Tonkawa's horse he nimbly leapt onto "another old animal," and all the Tonkawas "ran for their lives." Fighting a running battle, the four Tonkawas arrived safely back at the Seminole-Tonkawa camp. Unfortunately, the pursuing Comanches discovered the scouts' horse herd and ran off about a hundred ponies. McLaughin and several of his troopers pursued the Comanches and recovered "a few" of the scouts' horses.[21]

During the latter stages of September, as Mackenzie's column pushed northwest toward the Panhandle, thunderstorms and rain pelted the soldiers, resulting in almost no advance toward the Comanche haunts. On the night of September 21 a thunderstorm with lightening "like sheets of flame" and torrents of rain struck the camp and mired the column in mud. On September 24 a cold, wet "Norther" blew in, further bogging down the cavalry's advance, but Thompson and Strong reported that their Tonkawa scouts had discovered several trails of Indians driving herds of horses away from Mackenzie's line of march. Unfortunately, the scouts lost the signs in the darkness and then inclement weather completely obliterated the trail.[22]

Mackenzie continued up and over the Caprock, well aware that several Comanche bands knew of his movements. Cognizant of the need to protect his mounts, he ordered extra measures to guard his horses and camps during the march north. Prior to the campaign General Augur cautioned Mackenzie that, "A commander [campaigning] against hostile Indians is never in such imminent danger as when fully satisfied that no Indians can possibly be near him." Despite all the precautions the Comanches snaked near the cavalry's picketed horses and attempted to make off with several mounts.[23]

As daylight faded on September 26 the troops hobbled their mounts and settled down in a skirmish line for the night. A bright moon rose and Lt. Charles Hatfield remembered that he "could read a newspaper by [the] moonlight." About 10:15 p.m. a Comanche raiding party attacked the main camp. The Comanches tried to break through the skirmish line to the picketed horses, but a concentrated fire from Company A broke the attack. When reinforcements arrived to support Company A, the attackers retreated about three hundred yards into some broken ravines, from where they maintained a continuous fire into Mackenzie's camp all night.[24]

After daybreak the Indians continued their sporadic long range fire from high points around the soldiers' camp, and Mackenzie sent Boehme's Company E and several Indian scouts to drive the Comanches from their hiding places. The cavalry charged into the Comanche positions and a running fight followed that covered more than three miles. Forty years later Hatfield reminisced, "The sun rising in our rear seemed to light up the entire line of hostiles and their full dress of gaudy paint and feathers, as they turned in their saddles to fire at us . . . Scurrying across the prairie in rapid flight." The lieutenant continued, "I recollect well saying to myself, now and look take it all in, for with the rapid advance of civilization and settlement on the frontier, the like of this I will never see again."[25]

Charging in from the flanks Thompson's scouts spotted a lone Comanche riding up a rugged arroyo and took chase. A Black Seminole reined in his plunging mount, leapt to the ground, carefully aimed his carbine, and downed the fleeing Comanche's war pony. A Tonkawa flashed past the Black Seminole, chased down the running Comanche, and shot him in the head. The Tonkawa rode up so near the dismounted warrior that the muzzle blast from his revolver left powder burns on the Comanche's skin. Hatfield remembered the Comanche as "a handsome fellow with a gorgeous headdress."[26]

The short battle ended and pursuit broke off when the Comanches disappeared "as completely as if the ground had swallowed them." Mackenzie's troops claimed that they killed at least fifteen warriors, but the fleeing Comanches recovered the bodies of their comrades. The cavalry suffered only three horses wounded during the night.[27]

Mackenzie immediately dispatched the scouts out to scour the countryside for any signs of the scattered Comanches, while the remainder of his column rested and awaited events. The scouts returned with word of a large trail heading away from Mackenzie's troops. About 3 p.m. Mackenzie ordered his bugler to sound "Boots and Saddles" and continued pursuing the Comanches. Despite their best efforts the scouts lost the large trail sometime after sunset.

At 2 a.m. Mackenzie halted his exhausted command for a rest as his scouts had neither eaten nor slept for more than twenty-four hours.[28]

After a short rest the Tonkawa scouts, led by Johnson, located another Comanche trail. Johnson, Sergeant Charlton, and Job, another Tonkawa, followed the smaller trail until it converged with several other trails. The trio then tracked the Comanches until the vast Palo Duro Canyon "opened before them." Charlton and Johnson dismounted, dropped to their hands and knees, and crept to the rim of the canyon, while Job remained with the horses. As the pair peered into the immense chasm they spied a "dark mass of hundreds of grazing horses and tipis . . . up and down the canyon as far as they could see."[29]

On September 28 the scouts returned to the main column and led the cavalry to a precipitous trail that wound down to the valley floor. The sight of an estimated 2,500 Indians camped along the canyon amazed most of the soldiers. At least one company of cavalry and several Tonkawas reached the valley floor before Comanche leader Red Warbonnet spotted the invaders and fired a warning shot before being cut down by the Tonkawas. When they saw the troopers descending the dim trail the Comanches set up a cry of alarm and scattered into the brush as the soldiers charged toward them.[30]

After reaching the canyon floor Company A and the Tonkawa scouts galloped up the valley to capture the Comanche horse herd. As more troopers reached the bottom of the canyon they charged through the Indian encampments, destroying at least five separate villages belonging to Cheyenne Chief Iron Shirt, Comanche Poor Buffalo, and Kiowa Chief Lone Wolf. In the disorganized skirmishing the soldiers killed at least five Comanches and wounded "eleven or twelve others." During the fighting the Tonkawa women accompanying their men plundered the Comanche villages, accumulating a hoard of bows and arrows, buffalo robes, shields, "new blankets just from the reservations, cooking implements of every description, the breech loading arms with plenty of metallic cartridges," lead and powder, "bales of calico in turkey red," sacks of mission and reservation flour, and "groceries in profusion." Mackenzie reported that he captured 1,406 "ponies, mules and colts," of which 1,048 he ordered shot, and the remainder distributed among the scouts and guides. The Tonkawas handpicked more than 350 of the best ponies before the cavalry troopers destroyed the herd. Mackenzie had learned a hard lesson two years previously when Bull Bear's Comanches regrouped after a fight and returned to recapture their horses.[31]

According to several sources Tonkawa women not only accompanied their husbands on forays, but fought beside them and performed scouting duties as well. Descriptions of Tonkawa women included being "strong physically and vindictive in disposition," which describes a legendary female Tonkawa scout. Those who knew her described Texas-the-Tonk as "fair skinned," 5' 3" in height, but "stout for her size." Although not listed on official U.S. Army muster rolls of the Tonkawa scouts, she was a wife of well-known Tonkawa Johnson and scouted for the Fourth, Ninth, and Tenth U.S. Cavalry Regiments during the early 1870s.[32]

Born near Victoria, Texas-the-Tonk reportedly was in her early twenties when the Tonkawas moved from the Brazos Agency to Indian Territory, and returned to Texas with the survivors of the 1862 massacre. In October 1869, Texas-the-Tonk scouted for Capt. John Bacon, Ninth U.S. Cavalry, and participated in the desperate battle on the banks of the Clear Fork of the Brazos River. In 1872, she rode along with Mackenzie's expedition into Mexico against the Kickapoo Indians. Her exploits included fighting in at least three other battles with Comanche and Kiowa warriors. Returning from a scouting expedition against the Comanches on the Staked Plains, probably in June 1872, Texas-the-Tonk failed to arrive at a rendezvous with Captain Faulk's company of the Tenth U.S. Cavalry. Johnson and the other Tonkawa scouts futilely searched for the missing woman, but failed to find any sign of Texas-the-Tonk.[33]

Another search party from Fort Griffin eventually discovered, and buried, her strangled corpse on King Creek about fifteen miles southeast of Fort Griffin. Described as having a "full face" and smiling disposition, Texas-the-Tonk died at the age of thirty-six, the mother of two sons and two daughters. When wolves dug up her body and "scattered her bones about," Lt. D. K. Taylor, commander of the Tonkawa scouts at Fort Griffin, ordered her remains retrieved and brought to the fort. A statement attributed to Taylor said that "Texas-the-Tonk . . . rendered great and invaluable service to the

Government and the people." On October 2, 1873, Taylor sent her remains to the U.S. Army Medical Museum in Washington, D.C. The army transferred the skeletal remains of Texas-the-Tonk to the Smithsonian Institution in 1898. Recently the National Museum of Natural History notified the Tonkawa tribe that her remains were prepared for repatriation, if the tribe could locate lineal descendants of Texas-the-Tonk.[34]

During the Palo Duro melee, Tonkawa scout Henry's carelessness offered a bit of entertainment to several troops. Henry dropped a running war pony from under a fleeing Comanche and, for whatever reason, hung his carbine back on his saddle. Neglecting to draw his revolver the scout rode up to the dazed warrior. Recovering his equilibrium, the Comanche leapt up and dragged Henry from his saddle and commenced to pummel Henry with his bow. "At every cut of the bow Henry leaped about three feet in the air, making frantic gestures towards the troops, and yelling 'Why no shoot? Why you no shoot?'" Guffawing at the shrieking scout, one of the soldiers finally shot the Comanche. Henry took the scalp "with great satisfaction . . . [but] nursed a grouch against the whole bunch" for several days.[35]

After the battle Mackenzie recorded that the scouts lacked adequate remounts and that booty of some type was required to compensate the Indians for their work. Shortly before the Palo Duro campaign Comanches stole a "large number" of horses from the Tonkawa herd near Fort Griffin, which Mackenzie replaced with ponies captured from the Palo Duro herd. He wrote that only a "promise of horses and booty can keep [the scouts] interested in scouting." He offered that poor pay and long patrols undermined the Tonkawas' spirits and spoils were the only way to "get such dangerous work" out of the scouts.[36]

Despite a paucity of horses and forage Mackenzie's Tonkawa scouts continued to successfully screen his column on the return from Palo Duro and, in the process, led the cavalrymen to additional Comanche encampments. Mackenzie wrote that he had lost more than forty horses to the rigors of combat and his remaining mounts were in "poor shape" because the army quartermaster had failed to deliver sufficient forage for his command. Nevertheless, on November 3, 1874, Tonkawa scouts guided a cavalry detachment to a Comanche village inhabited by eight families. The small unit immediately charged through the village, killing two warriors and capturing nineteen women and children. Two days later Thompson and nine scouts located a herd of Comanche horses and cut the Indians off from their ponies. In a running fight the Tonkawas killed one Comanche and his horse. Through interpreters the captured Comanche women stated that the Plains tribes were "much frightened" and most were "going to the reserve in a few days." On November 25, Mackenzie sent Johnson and four other Tonkawas to scout the areas around Canyon Blanco and Tule Canyon to ascertain if the native groups were actually forsaking their refuges on the Llano Estacado and decamping for Indian Territory.[37]

Mackenzie intended to follow the scouts with an extended patrol to the headwaters of the Red River and onto the Staked Plains and thence toward Fort Sumner, New Mexico Territory, but lack of supplies and weather forced a change in plans. His horses had traveled ten days on a single day's rations and he had only enough "sound mounts" for 260 men. The last week of November Mackenzie established a camp near present-day Floydada, in Floyd County, but rain, sleet, and snow forced him to abandon any thoughts of continuing his campaign to the northwest.[38]

Buell likewise experienced success in the Red River Wars, due primarily to the Tonkawa scouts. During the first week of October the Tonkawa scouts trailed a small party of Comanches, which managed to elude Buell's cavalry. The scouts, on the other hand, captured two of the Comanche's war ponies. Late in the afternoon of October 8 a Tonkawa scout rode into Buell's camp and reported that he had "shaken the hand of a Comanche some twenty miles to the South." Buell ordered his men to saddle and headed toward the reported enemy camp. Before dark the Tonkawa scouts discovered a Kiowa spying on the column and killed the warrior before he could divulge any information to his compatriots. The Tonkawas followed the trail to the Salt Fork of the Red River where, on the afternoon of October 9, Buell's point glimpsed a small party of Indians to their front.[39]

Capt. Ambrose Hooker and several troops of the Ninth U.S. Cavalry charged the Indians and killed one warrior before the rest vanished into the Salt Cedars. The soldiers soon discovered a camp of fifteen lodges, which they quickly destroyed. For two days the Tonkawas doggedly trailed the group of Comanches and Kiowas northwest "through rough terrain" to the edge of the Staked Plains. Here Buell found and destroyed an abandoned camp of seventy-five tipis. From the smoking ruins the Tonkawas followed the Indians to McClellan Creek, where the trail enlarged as more and more small parties joined the main band retreating before the Buffalo Soldiers. The Tonkawas and cavalry pressed the Comanches so hard that the Indians' trail was littered with "camp equipages and worn out ponies."[40]

Buell intended to overtake the fleeing Comanches or to drive them into either Mackenzie's or Miles' commands. In the afternoon of October 12 his troops rode into another village abandoned by the Comanches. Much larger, this encampment consisted of 475 lodges, which the soldiers and Tonkawas looted and burned. The Comanches turned for the Canadian River, but Buell hesitated to follow because he was short of supplies and his horses were "greatly fatigued." After a short conference Buell and his commanders decided to continue and dispatched couriers back to Fort Sill to request an emergency resupply of forty days rations. Twenty-five Comanche warriors drove the couriers back into camp. Buell then sent Private Williams of E Company, Tenth U.S. Cavalry, and a Tonkawa scout to evade the Comanches and ride to Fort Sill for supplies. At dark on October 14 Tonkawa scouts erroneously fired on a detachment from Miles' column, mistaking the soldiers for Comancheros. A howitzer shell "screeching over their heads informed them [Tonkawas] of [their] mistake."[41]

Buell learned that his troops had driven more than seven hundred Indians into Miles' column and now both commands rode in pursuit of the Comanches. On October 16 Buell's fatigued troopers finally arrived at the Canadian River, but with "horses so exhausted" that his men had to walk half of the time. The Comanches dispersed into the river breaks and Buell directed the Tonkawas to find their main camp. He ordered Captain Morrow to assemble "100 picked men and mounts," ready to attack any Indians reported by the Tonkawas. On October 24 Buell received a partial resupply from Miles and turned south to Sweetwater Creek where he discovered that he had driven a large party of Indians into Davidson's column, some thirty miles to his front. In three days, Davidson captured 314 Comanches, forty-five Kiowas, and more than two thousand horses. Davidson's Tonkawa scouts then led the Buffalo Soldiers to a Southern Cheyenne camp on McClellan Creek, where the black troopers destroyed seventy-five lodges.[42]

By the time the 1874–1875 winter blizzards struck the Southern Plains, several large bands of Indians were en route to Fort Sill and the Wichita Agency to surrender. Relentless pursuit by U.S. cavalry troops and winter storms forced many of the native bands to butcher their horses for food, and they had no place to go but to the reservations in order to survive the unrelenting cold. Satanta and Big Tree returned to Fort Sill in October. In February, Lone Wolf and 252 Kiowas surrendered at Fort Sill. The next month, about 1,600 Cheyennes returned to their reservation. In April, Moway led two hundred Comanches back to Fort Sill. In early June, 407 of the most intractable Quahadi Comanches staggered into Fort Sill, many afoot. The army rounded up the most defiant leaders of the tribes and shipped them off to confinement in Florida.[43]

During the spring and summer of 1875, even without incitement from the absent war chiefs, several small parties of Comanches and Kiowas slipped away from their reservations and returned to the Texas plains, intent on stealing horses and collecting a few fresh scalps. The Buffalo Soldiers of the Tenth U.S. Cavalry remained proactive against these "renegades" from north of the Red River, following their Tonkawa scouts, and attacking the raiders wherever found. On May 6 a patrol of Company A under Sgt. John Marshall intercepted and scattered eight raiders near Catfish Creek. The next day, Lt. Thad Jones' detachment of H Company and Tonkawa scouts overtook the party on the banks of the North Concho River and recaptured thirty-three head of stock.[43]

In late May 1875, Gen. Edward O. C. Ord ordered Lt. Col. William R. Shafter to Fort Concho to assemble a large force and "rid the area" of these persistent Comanche raiders. Shafter brought together six companies of the Tenth U.S. Cavalry, two companies of the Twenty-Fourth U.S. Infantry, and one company of the Twenty-Fifth U.S. Infantry for the expedition. Lt. John L. Bullis and C. R. Ward directed the Seminole and Tonkawa scouts. Shafter's logistical train consisted of sixty-five wagons, more than seven hundred mules to pull the wagons and pack supplies, and a beef herd driven along to provide fresh meat for the expected four-month campaign.[44]

On July 14, Shafter's column rode out of Fort Concho to establish a supply camp on the Fresh Water Fork of the Brazos River prior to conducting sweeps for the Indian marauders. On July 27, near Mustang Springs in present-day northwest Midland County, Tonkawa scouts struck the trail of a lone Indian pony. The scouts continued along the trail and discovered signs where several other Indians joined the first. Tracking the unshod ponies into the afternoon, the Tonkawas spotted a large body of Indians moving through the shimmering heat. The scouts signaled Capt. Nicholas Nolan, who brought up his troops with "all possible haste," but discovered only a small, deserted camp. Pressing onward the Tonkawas located a larger camp, which the Comanches had also abandoned, along with all their supplies. Nolan's cavalrymen destroyed "seventy-two lodges" and all the supplies in the larger camp, and then settled in for the night. A heavy early morning rainsquall washed out the Comanches' trail and, despite a diligent search, the Tonkawas could not re-establish contact with the fleeing Comanches.[45]

Disgusted with what he perceived as Nolans' inept pursuit, Shafter began his own extended hunt for the missing Comanches. On August 5, he sent the Tonkawa and Seminole scouts out ahead of his Tenth U.S. Cavalry to ferret out the elusive denizens of the Staked Plains. In order to travel more swiftly Shafter abandoned his wagons and utilized a mule pack train to carry his supplies. The alkali-encrusted cavalry mounts plodded west more than a hundred miles to a small lake called Casas Amarillas, but the red-rimmed eyes of the troopers failed to espy a single Comanche. Shafter then pointed his weary column southwest on a long, dry march. The Texas summer sun baked his men and dried up all the known water holes. Lack of water forced Shafter to swing back to Horsehead Crossing on the Pecos River. On September 5 the cavalry departed the Pecos and returned to Fort Concho without firing a shot at a single "hostile" Indian.[46]

Over time, Mackenzie and other officers learned to appreciate their native scouts. In army operations in Texas, mostly pursuits of Indian raiders or stock thieves, twenty-two percent of the time Indians acted as scouts and guides. Tonkawas represented the majority of these scouts, with Lipans, Seminoles, or Delawares constituting the remainder of the indigenous guides. In more than a quarter of the army's engagements scouts led the soldiers, initiating many of the actions themselves. Numerous reports and dispatches authored by army officers included laudatory comments for the scouts. During October 1874, in today's Greer County, Oklahoma, Buell's Tonkawa scouts struck a band of Kiowas and pursued them to their encampment. Buell brought up his troops and attacked the village to "destroy hundreds of lodges." Buell wrote that it afforded him "great pleasure" to commend "the services rendered by the Tonkawa Indian scout Jessie during the scout of the cavalry . . . and in guiding the column back to the present camp [Hill Creek, Indian Territory] so directly during stormy weather and in a severe norther." Buell rewarded Tonkawa Jessie with an immediate promotion to corporal.[47]

Tonkawa scouts also tracked down thieves who absconded with equipment belonging to the Tenth U.S. Cavalry, earning additional praise from their officers. Sometime during the winter of 1876, thieves broke into the ordnance room at Fort Griffin and stole "a large amount of ordnance." Tonkawa scouts tracked the culprits to the "place where the arms were secreted," and recovered forty-seven of the forty-nine revolvers taken from the post. 2nd Lt. George Evans commented that the weapons "otherwise would never have been found without their [Tonkawa scouts] aid." Evans wrote of the Tonkawas that they were "excellent as scouts," their discipline "ordinary," and maintained their arms and accouterments in "good" condition. The lieutenant lamented that the scouts' military appearance was "indifferent."[48]

Not all army officers, however, respected the Tonkawa's unique capabilities. Even Mackenzie berated twenty Tonkawas for losing a horse herd when they retreated before more than one hundred attacking Comanches. As early as 1870, Maj. William H. Wood, then commanding officer at Fort Griffin, sanctimoniously scorned the Tonkawas as scouts and attempted to get them relocated to Fort Concho, or failing that, offered the Indians' services to anyone who would relieve him of the responsibility of caring for the thirty-six men, sixty-three women, and thirty-one children of the Tonkawa tribe, whom he considered a nuisance. Delighted that the Tonkawa population had "rapidly diminished," Wood wrote that the tribe would soon become extinct and "no longer be a burden to the government or anyone else."[49]

In 1872, the post surgeon at Fort Griffin wrote of a "large camp" of Tonkawas that, "in their drunken brawls, kept the settlement in constant terror." Many lawless characters lived near the fort in "The Flats." Tonkawa men freely imbibed in the liquor themselves and lounged around their village when not involved with a scouting expedition. Local citizens did not understand why the women labored while their husbands just loafed around.[50]

When the Tonkawa scouts returned from a successful foray, the entire tribe turned out for a ritualistic celebration, which sometimes spilled over into the civilian community. D. A. Nance, a local storekeeper raised along the Clear Fork, remembers painted Tonkawa warriors parading down the streets of "The Flats." When the celebration included fresh Comanche scalps the festivities lasted throughout the night. Both men and women danced

Dutch Nance store, c. 1868. First store in Fort Griffin. Nance Collection.
Courtesy of The Old Jail Art Center, Albany, Texas.

around the "grisly prizes" adorning the tops of poles planted in the center of the dance circle. Soldiers, townspeople, and cowboys gathered to gape at the spectacle presented by the Tonkawas. Local resident J. J. Bragg recalled that a young Tonkawa and Comanche warrior killed one another in a bloody hand-to-hand knife fight over a slain deer. After the duel other Tonkawas cut the head and heart from the dead Comanche, one warrior suspending the severed head on one side of his war pony and the scalp on the other as he proudly rode into Fort Griffin. Other warriors brought the remains of the Comanche into their village where the women burned the torso over a fire during the traditional scalp dance. Bragg observed the "aged and infirm" Chief Campos "dressing the scalp," the hair, four to five feet in length, "nicely plaited" and "profusely set with silver ornaments."[51]

As with most frontier soldiers of the era, black or white, Tonkawa scouts resorted to alcohol and gambling to combat boredom when not on patrol. Fort Griffin soldiers' visited the saloons and brothels of "The Flats," while the Tonkawas sometimes visited the bordellos set up for the Buffalo Soldiers and bought bootlegged liquor from whiskey peddlers. Both white men and native men lost their army pay to the unscrupulous gamblers frequenting the saloons near the post. Well-known scout Johnson, reportedly smitten by Ida Creaton, imbibed copious amounts of cheap whiskey to assuage his heartaches when the white girl spurned his advances. A young woman recalled that Johnson, "in a drunken stupor," staggered toward the Creaton's house, where he was usually welcomed. On this occasion, the Tonkawa threatened Ida's brother John with a knife. Although more than six feet tall, Johnson was so inebriated that the young man easily disarmed the big warrior.[52]

As commander of the Tonkawa scouts, Pratt attempted to curb the influence of illegal whiskey on the scouts, presumably ending the Tonkawas' disruptive behavior. Previously counseled by the post commander for being drunk and disorderly, the Tonkawa scouts paid little heed to verbal chastisement, forcing Pratt to adopt "severe methods" to restrain drunkenness among the scouts.[53]

After a bout with rotgut whiskey, Chief Castile agreed with Pratt that whiskey was "bad" and the Tonkawas must stop drinking. Pratt warned Castile that the next time the chief got drunk he would spend seven days in the guardhouse and work with the prison detail pushing a wheelbarrow and picking up garbage. Pratt also told the Tonkawa that a soldier armed with a fixed bayonet would insure that the chief worked. If the chief continued to get drunk, Pratt promised him that he would remain in the guardhouse all the time "then I know you will not get drunk."[54]

Two weeks later, Castile was so inebriated that he could not rise from the ground, and Pratt discovered him with another Indian standing over the chief with a rock threatening to kill Castile. Pratt took the other Indian to the guardhouse, relieving the Tonkawa of a half quart of whiskey en route. The sergeant of the guard and his detail hauled Castile to the guardhouse. Pratt ordered the Tonkawa chief to work with a wheelbarrow for a week. Pratt recounted that the entire tribe was indignant and "old women wailed" near the post because their chief had to perform such demeaning labor. After his punishment, Castile told his people that they should stop drinking and warn Pratt when bootleggers were in camp. Soon after the Tonkawas informed Pratt that two men were in their village hawking whiskey. Leading a detail of cavalry troopers Pratt captured the peddlers, smashed their remaining stock on some rocks, and relieved the Tonkawas of some whiskey they had bought. Pratt remembered that his "whiskey problems were minimal after the incident." Forced inactivity, however, intensified the scouts' boredom, which led to even more immoderate behavior among the Tonkawas.[55]

## 9 DESTITUTION, A NEW RESERVATION, AND A NEW CENTURY

With the removal of the last major Comanche and Kiowa bands to Indian Territory, thus virtually ending the Indian Wars on the South Plains, the army seldom required the services of Tonkawa scouts. Without their government salaries and subsidies, the tribe became destitute and powerless. Broken promises and harsh treatment destroyed their old way of life and several manifested a growing hostility toward white settlers. Secretary of War William W. Belknap insisted that officers follow War Department General Order #54, 1872, which prevented army commissary officers from issuing foodstuffs to Indians not enrolled as army scouts. While Belknap refused to continue allocating rations to the tribe, Secretary of the Interior Columbus Delano refused responsibility for the Tonkawas because the tribe did not reside on a recognized reservation. Gen. Edward O. C. Ord commented on the irony of former hostiles "loaded down with presents," while the "loyal Tonkawas" were starving.[1]

Many Texans, as well as some U.S. officials, lamented that the Bureau of Indian Affairs lavished food and clothing on the Comanches and Kiowas, while the Tonkawas received no support whatever, surviving on the largesse of a few army officers. In 1876 the *Dallas Daily Herald* reminded its readers of the Tonkawas' service to Texas and urged the state to come to the aid of the tribe, which "has nearly been exterminated on her [Texas] behalf." In an attempt to assist the Tonkawas and Lipans the U.S. government assembled the remainder of both tribes living in Texas at Fort Griffin under control of Capt. J. B. Irvine, Twenty-Second U.S. Infantry, who officially petitioned the federal government in 1879 for more assistance for his charges stating, "they had always been friendly to the white man and had been of great service to the US Army in the Indian Wars."[2]

Not unlike others who find themselves in hard times, the Tonkawas turned to alcohol to ameliorate their depression and increasingly debased

Left: Tonkawa Johnson the Scout, Fort Griffin, Texas, c. 1877. Right: Tonkawa Minnie, an Indian squaw, also of the Tonkawa camp at Fort Griffin, c. 1877. Original pictures bought by Mrs. A. A. Clarke in Fort Griffin in 1877. Courtesy of The Old Jail Art Center, Albany, Texas.

perception of self-worth. Unfortunately, cheap whiskey only exacerbated the tribe's poverty and confirmed local citizens' image of the "loathsome" and "filthy" Tonkawas. One stated that, "It becomes a frequent sight to see these Indians . . . in a state of beastly intoxication." In late 1879 the Fort Griffin Echo reported that "Monday a number of Tonks managed to get hold of some whisky and soon the town was full of half-drunk Indians." The Tonkawas' behavior grew so boisterous that the Griffin constable arrested seven of them to "sober off" in jail. The next day the constable released the Tonkawas, but members of the tribe had grown accustomed to such treatment. Jack, a Tonkawa man, when forced to pick up garbage for shooting arrows across a busy street, reportedly complained, "What for me do that? Me no drunk."[3]

Cleanliness of the tribe also provoked some discord among the locals. One local resident remembered that "squaws did their wash" by wading into the Clear Fork and then hanging their clothes on nearby trees to dry. Citizens reported that the tribe never cleaned up their camp, they "just moved to a new one." An 1877 article in the Daily Democrat called the Tonkawas "noted thieves as well as beggars." Conversely, a man who had considerable experience with the Tonkawas offered a very different opinion of the tribe. Henry Strong, chief of scouts for Ranald S. Mackenzie, recalled that not all Tonkawas lived in squalid conditions, nor wandered about in filthy rags. He wrote that Tonkawa Johnson's wife was "always the neatest looking and cleanest looking of any squaw I ever saw on the plains."[4]

Vague insinuations sullied the Tonkawas' reputation and these innuendoes pervaded white attitudes, including those who came to Texas for the first time. An army wife's comments served as a perfect illustration. In 1874, Col. George L. Andrews, who commanded the Twenty-Fifth U.S. Infantry Regiment at Fort Davis, decided to move his wife Emily and her daughter Maude to Texas. The family traveled west toward Fort Davis along the San Antonio-El Paso military road. Somewhere near Rock Springs Station a patrol of Texas Rangers with two "Tonqua" scouts crossed the road while the travelers rested. Curiosity prompted Emily to walk forward in order to "view the brave Red Man," but "knowing their desire for light haired scalps, I kept at a good distance from them."[5]

Periodically denizens of the Fort Griffin area participated in Tonkawa tribal dances and celebrations. On several occasions cowboys "liberally lubricated with whiskey" joined in with the native dancers. The Tonkawas tolerated the exuberant cowboys that clomped around their dance circle. According to one drover's reminiscence several Tonkawa warriors even "provided feathers and painted our faces."[6]

Despite the myriad of unsavory comments leveled at the Tonkawas, many Texans remembered the tribe's contributions to the white community and overlooked their transgressions. Parson Ralph Riley, who ministered to the tribe, commented that he found the "Indians generous and thoroughly reliable, if you treated them right." Riley spent much of his time and money aiding the Tonkawas "who were neglected by their government." Most townspeople enjoyed watching Tonkawa horsemen race their ponies on the outskirts of town. Several local townspeople and cowboys frequently participated in Tonkawa ceremonies as spectators, with the tribe promising a few favored storekeepers a revered place in the "unbroken wilderness" of the Tonkawa afterlife. D. A. Nance reported that the Tonkawa promise rested on the light raisins, called nil-itch honn, which the Tonkawas particularly favored and could acquire only from the white storekeepers.[7]

In Spring 1877, on one of the army patrols guided by the Tonkawas, several scouts led Capt. P. L. Lee's Buffalo Soldiers and a group of buffalo hunters on a retaliatory raid against the band of Comanche Chief Nigger Horse. Previously the Comanches had slipped off the Fort Sill Reservation and raided Rath City, a trading center for buffalo hunters in present-day Stonewall County. The Comanches had also repulsed an attack by a group of hunters who followed the Indians to their village in Yellow House Canyon near the Caprock. The Tonkawas guided Lee's troopers to the enemy encampment, where the combined command swept down on the unsuspecting Comanches. In a brief firefight the white hunters, black soldiers, and Tonkawa scouts captured all the women and children in the village, while killing several warriors, including Chief Nigger Horse.[8]

Tonkawa warriors sometimes accompanied sheriffs' posses and local ranchers in pursuit of stock thieves. The fighters received acclaim for returning stolen stock to ranchers from as far afield as the Colorado River drainage. At least one rancher asserted, however, that when discovered with stolen livestock, the Tonkawas claimed that they had "just now" recovered the animals from the Comanches.[9]

The Tonkawas well knew that natives did not commit all the thefts of livestock near Fort Griffin. Often, when asked about the signs left by thieves, they said "maybe so white men." As proof of their speculations, they presented cigarette papers and other evidence to whomever captained the pursuing party. When a large herd of both horses and cattle disappeared near Fort Griffin the sheriff asked for help in rounding up the culprits. Tonkawa scouts led Lt. Richard H. Pratt and twenty Buffalo Soldiers to a group of "corrals out on the buffalo range." The party arrested nine white men at two camps and recovered "1000 cattle and 40 horses." According to Pratt the gang planned to steal the cattle, drive them north through the buffalo range, and then sell them at the railhead in Kansas.[10]

In addition to serving as unofficial scouts, several Tonkawas guided white men on hunting expeditions. In 1879 a group of Tonkawa men led Joe Matthews and W. P. Vandervert on a West Texas bear hunt. In fact, the 1880 U.S. Census recorded twenty-three Tonkawa families, consisting of 115 Tonkawas, in which all but two heads of households listed their occupation as "scout" or "hunter." The two exceptions, Sam Houston considered himself "Big Chief," and Wolf a "medicine man." During one hunting expedition a Tonkawa hunter frightened Theodore Roosevelt's brother when the native man boldly walked into Roosevelt's camp, announcing that he was a "Tonk," and freely helped himself to the stew bubbling in a pot over the campfire.[11]

The Tonkawa "Wolf Culture" prohibited the warriors from tilling the soil and participating in other tasks deemed menial, but did not prevent the women from performing such work. Tonkawa women maintained the major sense of community in the tribe. Tonkawa women cultivated small garden plots of beans, corn, and tomatoes near their village to feed their hungry families. They tanned the buffalo and deer hides the hunters brought in and scoured "The Flats" for rags and pieces of cloth to make garments for the tribe. Sallie Matthews remembered that Tonkawa women fashioned "poncho style" blouses from brightly colored calico, so long that they "trailed the ground in back . . . and when the wind blew, it floated out behind like a sail."[12]

Tonkawa women also took on other chores in order to survive. Some worked as laundresses for local citizens. Known as expert tanners of hides, Tonkawa women made beaded moccasins, which gained a reputation for ruggedness and painstaking neatness. Many local citizens bought or traded for the reliable and decorative footwear. The Tonkawas also made leather dolls for their own children, and favored white youngsters. A pair of these dolls presented to the Matthews family presently resides in the The Old Jail Art Center in Albany, Texas.[13]

Tonkawa women, from most reports, enjoyed holding and playing with babies, whether their own or from white families. According to Nance the Tonkawas named his infant daughter Lula (Wifwam or Little One), and visited his store often to see the baby. Nance remembered that Tonkawa warriors would stand around the baby's cradle and laugh with the little girl. Etta Soules recalled that her mother allowed Tonkawa women to sit on the Soules front porch in a rocking chair and hold the "freshly bathed and dressed infant sister." After the Tonkawas departed, however, Mrs. Soules immediately bathed and redressed her infant daughter.[14]

Supposedly restricted to the vicinity of their village, the Tonkawas freely roamed the area around Fort Griffin. Most Tonkawas spoke English, but when speaking to a stranger, they "spoke scarce a word above a breath." They were, however, not shy among their white friends. Nance, raised along the Clear Fork and whom the Tonkawas called "Notch," spoke the Tonkawa language and knew many of the tribe personally. The Indians visited Nance's store almost daily, purchasing raisins and marveling at the plethora of goods in his establishment.[15]

Nance and other frontier folk described the Tonkawas as very stealthy. A person at work might look up and a Tonkawa would be standing near him; when the person looked up again, the Tonkawa would be gone with no indication of the Indian's coming or going. Around Fort Griffin Tonkawas suddenly appeared at windows and walked into homes without knocking.

The unexpected appearance of a Tonkawa, in a land where raids were still a threat, upset many citizens. "Comes in like a Tonk" became a colloquial term for a stealthy person. The Tonkawas so frequently visited the mess house and kitchen at Fort Griffin that Col. George P. Buell issued an order prohibiting the Tonkawas from entering government buildings at will.[16]

As early as May 1875 the commanding officer at Fort Griffin recommended a reservation for the Tonkawas in Indian Territory. That November, Secretary of War Belknap "earnestly requested" that the Interior Department take some action with a view of placing the tribe on a reservation. A month later, Commissioner of Indian Affairs E. P. Smith suggested a home among the Kickapoos or removal to the Jicarilla or Mescalero Apache Reservations in New Mexico Territory, but there were no funds for such a transfer. Although the Indian Appropriation Acts of 1876–1878 provided $2,000 to $2,500 annually for the benefit of the Tonkawa tribe, the acts prohibited using any funds to remove the tribe from the vicinity of Fort Griffin. The Indian Appropriation Acts from 1879–1883 increased the annual Tonkawa subsidies from $3,000 to $4,800, but made no mention of any transfer to Indian Territory.[17]

On July 4, 1879, Irvine wrote the Bureau of Indian Affairs, reminding the commissioner that the Tonkawas had "no land or reservation." Irvine proposed that the first step in "encouraging them [Tonkawas] in the arts of civilization" was to provide the tribe with land and a home of their own. Acting Commissioner E. J. Brooks deemed it inadvisable to provide "any permanent abode" for the Tonkawas anywhere other than Indian Territory. Tonkawa chiefs feared moving to Indian Territory, however, because of Comanches and other Indians at "whose hands they had severely suffered." On January 23, 1880, after a suggestion from Irvine, Commissioner E. A. Hayt instructed Irvine to take "not more than five" Tonkawas to a location "recently selected by the Poncas and Nez Perces at a point on the Salt Fork near its junction with the Arkansas River."[18]

Hayt suggested that a reservation bounded by the northern border of the Ponca Reservation and eastern boundary of the Oakland Reservation, occupied by the Nez Perce from the northwestern Untied States, be explored as a "permanent reservation" for the Tonkawa tribe. In February, Lt. R. N.

Getty, Johnson, and four other Tonkawa men examined the country from Kansas to the Ponca Reservation. Getty opined that the "soil, timber, water and climate, of this tract" would make "an excellent location for the Tonkawas." Only one Tonkawa, however, seemed impressed with the land. The other Tonkawa representatives expressed misgivings about larger nearby tribes and an epidemic, possibly pneumonia, among the Nez Perce. The "coldness of the climate and the scarcity of game" also worried the Tonkawas, who were afraid that they would be killed off one by one while hunting and "no one would know who killed them." The Tonkawas wanted to remain in Texas where they felt safe from attack.[19]

The despondent Tonkawas clung to a futile hope that the Texas government would eventually "donate them land" on which they could live permanently. Texas would not authorize a reservation, but the United States government, however slowly, began to seek a permanent home for the tribe. In April 1880, the Interior Department issued a statement that, at that time, no further steps would be taken toward relocating the Tonkawa tribe. In 1882, Acting Agent Lt. Elias Chandler reported that the Tonkawas still had no reservation and "were dependent to a great extent upon the whims of the landowners in the vicinity of Fort Griffin." Chandler continued, at least partially mistaken, that the Tonkawas "were well contented and apparently had a horror of the idea of being removed to the Indian Territory." The same year a small band of disheartened Tonkawas rode away from "Uncle Joe" Matthews' Ranch near Fort Griffin where they had resided for several years. For several days the Tonkawas rode south toward Matagorda Bay, riding and hunting over their ancestral lands for the last time.[20]

During the preceding five years the Tonkawas rejoiced in only three births, while burying four of their dwindling numbers. The people were starving and tribal medicine men provided their only health care. In December 1882, with the Indian Bureau pressing for a permanent solution, the Interior Department finally concluded that the Tonkawas should be removed if the tribe could be located on a reservation "remote from the Comanches and Kiowas and near to a military post." On March 29, 1883, commissioners suggested that the Tonkawas might locate west of the Sac and Fox Reservations, in the vicinity of the Ponca, Pawnee, and Otoe Reservations.[21]

In 1883 President Chester A. Arthur, by executive order, assigned a tract of land to the Iowa Indians, later deciding to settle the Tonkawas on part of the "Iowa Reserve." The Department of the Interior, however, changed the plan and for a year it appeared that the Tonkawas were destined to live on the Quapaw Reservation. In December, Agent Daniel B. Dyer reported that the Quapaw tribe was willing to sell the Interior Department "2 or 3 thousand acres" of land for a Tonkawa reservation. In 1884 Tonkawa chiefs signed an agreement to move to Indian Territory "as soon as it should be the pleasure of the government to complete its preparations for their removal."[22]

On July 4, 1884, Congress passed an Indian Appropriation Act which provided $10,000 for the Tonkawas' "support, civilization, and instruction," as well as the removal of the surviving seventy-eight Tonkawas and their nineteen Lipan Apache allies from Shackelford County to a reservation in Indian Territory. On August 21, the Acting Secretary of the Interior granted approval for the Tonkawas removal to the Quapaw Reservation, but his decision was cancelled when the Quapaw tribe radically altered their stance and refused to allow the Tonkawas to reside on their reservation.[23]

In September, the Department of the Interior and Bureau of Indian Affairs agreed that the Tonkawas should be removed to the Iowa Reservation in Indian Territory. The Iowa tribe, however, also vociferously opposed relocating the Tonkawas onto their reservation. On October 16, Iowa Agent Isaac A. Taylor reported that if the Tonkawas were settled on any part of the Iowa Reservation, the main contingent of the Iowa tribe would refuse to move from their Nebraska lands to Indian Territory. Taylor also believed that those Iowas already in Indian Territory would leave the reservation if the Tonkawas moved there. According to the Executive Order setting aside reservation land in Oklahoma Territory, the Tonkawas held the same rights to government lands as the Iowa, or any other tribe. Nonetheless, and the Interior Department ordered the Tonkawas relocated from Texas.[24]

Army troops from Fort Clark herded the Tonkawas and Lipan Apaches onto rail cars parked on sidings in Albany for the journey to Cisco, Texas. En route to Cisco a Tonkawa woman gave birth to a son who the tribe named Railroad Cisco. While in Cisco a local woman remembered seeing the Indians on the railcars and the "squaws . . . picking the lice out of their children's hair." From Cisco the Tonkawas and Lipans journeyed to the Sac-Fox Agency. One of these, a fourteen-year-old orphaned boy named John Rush Buffalo, later provided researchers with much of what remains of the Tonkawa language. He died at the age of seventy-four in Tonkawa, Oklahoma, in February 1943.[25]

On October 22, 1884, ninety-two Tonkawas arrived at the Sac and Fox Reservation, near present-day Stroud, Oklahoma, and ten more reached the Iowa Reservation, "located so as not to interfere with the comfort and convenience" of the Iowas already there. The Iowa tribe resented the relocation of the Tonkawas to their reservation, sending a letter of complaint to the Interior Department. Dated October 27, the letter said in part, the relocation "was done without our consent and we were not even informed of their [Tonkawas] coming until we saw them . . . [on] our reservation. We regard this as an injustice to us and earnestly protest against those Indians being located on our land." The Iowas considered it an injustice "to thrust

John Rush (Tonkawa), Photograph by Frank A. Rinehart, found in the American Indians 1898 photo album, Trans-Mississippi International Exposition website.

into our midst and upon our land a tribe of strange Indians." The Iowa tribe demanded that "as soon as practicable they [the Tonkawas] may be removed from our Land."[26]

The Tonkawas and Lipans suffered through the winter short of food and satisfactory shelter. Most of their horses starved to death during the harsh winter. The winter of 1884–1885 was known as the "Big Die Off" in the western cattle industry. On March 3, 1885, Congress passed an act which authorized the President to issue a patent to the Iowa tribe that their reservation be held in trust by the U.S. government for "their [Iowa] sole use and benefit." In June the Tonkawas packed up their belongings again and, on

Portrait of Standing Buffalo (Tonkawa), c. 1894. Oklahoma? Frederick Starr Collection.
Courtesy, National Museum of the American Indian, Smithsonian Institution.

Tipi belonging to George Miles (Tonkawa), c. 1894. Oakland Ponca Agency, Oklahoma. Frederick Starr Collection. Courtesy, National Museum of the American Indian, Smithsonian Institution.

Sherman Miles (Tonkawa), Photograph by Frank A. Rinehart, found in the American Indians 1898 photo album, Trans-Mississippi International Exposition website.

June 30, 1885, the ninety-eight remaining Tonkawas and Lipans left their temporary homes and moved onto the 91,000-acre Oakland Reservation located in present-day Kay County, Oklahoma. Situated on the banks of the Salt Fork of the Arkansas River, approximately thirty miles northeast of present-day Enid, Oklahoma, the reservation soon became known as the Tonkawa Reservation. The Tonkawas refer to the trip from Texas to the Oakland Agency as their own "Trail of Tears."[27]

After permanent settlement on their 140 square-mile reservation, the Tonkawas, following their "Wolf Culture," initially hunted for subsistence, but soon attempted an agrarian lifestyle. Cultivating the land earned praise from government officials as establishing the Indians as subsistence farmers was a major goal of acculturation. In 1886 the Tonkawa Indian Agent reported from the Oakland Agency that the Tonkawas had improved their lot somewhat by limited farming. In fact, the tribe had "excellent crops" on a small thirty-five-acre plot of cultivated land. The Tonkawa farming equipment consisted of "four old horses, two or three plows, and some hoes."[28]

Barely had the Tonkawa tribe settled onto its new reservation before the "People of the Wolf" suffered another injustice, partly engendered by white lust for Indian lands. Passed on February 8, 1887, the Dawes Severalty Act allowed the government to break up Indian reservation lands of any tribe which the President determined "sufficiently advanced to benefit from the change." After the government pressured all Indians living in Indian Territory to accept allotment of their lands, the Tonkawa tribe only received 11,274 acres of their original 89,600-acre grant. On April 22, 1889, the federal government conducted the first "Oklahoma land rush," which allowed white settlers an opportunity to scramble for lands previously allotted to Indian tribes. In October 1891, heads of seventy-three Tonkawa households met at the Ponca Agency and received their 160-acre parcels; Congress ratified the agreements on March 3, 1893.[29]

On October 21, 1891, the Cherokee Commission reached an agreement with the Tonkawas whereby the tribe would cede the approximate 79,000 unallotted acres of reservation lands to the U.S. government for $30,000. On August 19, 1893, President Grover Cleveland issued an executive order that opened the lands of the Cherokee Outlet to homesteaders. At noon on

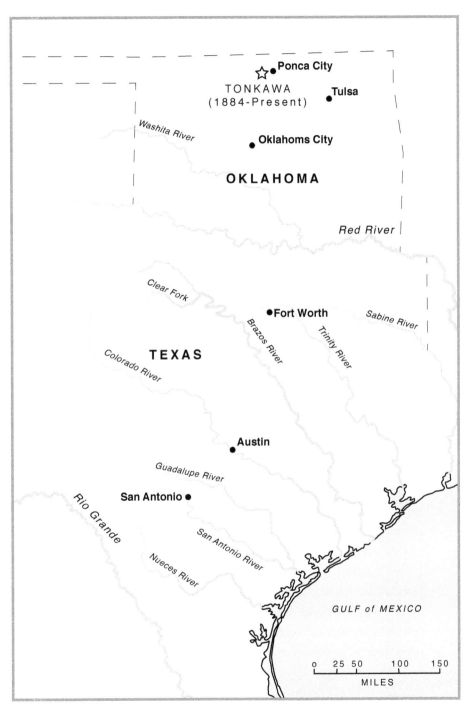

Ponca City

TONKAWA
(1884–Present)

Tulsa

Washita River

Oklahoms City

OKLAHOMA

Red River

Clear Fork

●Fort Worth

Sabine River

Brazos River

Trinity River

TEXAS

Colorado River

Austin

Guadalupe River

San Antonio ●

Rio Grande

San Antonio River

Nueces River

GULF of MEXICO

0   25 50        100        150

MILES

Map by Donald S. Frazier.

Portrait of Kitty Allen and Jennie Stevens (Tonkawa), c. 1894. Oklahoma? Frederick Starr
Collection. Courtesy, National Museum of the American Indian, Smithsonian Institution.

September 16, 1893, the government loosed about one hundred thousand
land-hungry white settlers to claim more than six million acres of land that
previously belonged to the Cherokee, Pawnee, Ponca, and Tonkawa tribes.
The "sooners" surrounded the Tonkawa land and established a town on
former reservation lands, which they named Tonkawa. For the next several
years the federal government repeatedly attempted to convert the Tonkawas
on the small Oakland Agency into dry land farmers by breaking up the
tribal government and repressing their customs and traditions. Some became
dependent on government subsidies to survive, but most Tonkawa families
became industrious enough to provide for themselves, resisting white
attempts to totally obliterate their culture and independence.[30]

*Left*: John Allen (Tonkawa), Photograph by Frank A. Rinehart, found in the American Indians 1898 photo album, Trans-Mississippi International Exposition website.
*Right*: Will Stevens (Tonkawa), Photograph by Frank A. Rinehart, found in the American Indians 1898 photo album, Trans-Mississippi International Exposition website.

The peyote religion, which evolved into the Native American Church, remains an excellent example of the Tonkawas' success in preserving at least part of their ancient culture. Long before they moved to the Oklahoma reservation the Tonkawas and Lipan Apaches practiced a religion that became the foundation of the Native American Church. As early as 1688, Spanish friars reported Lipan Apache and Tonkawa clans participating in peyote ceremonies. Jean Louis Berlandier's 1828 journal noted that "the Tancahues [Tonkawas] . . . still use the intoxicating plant in their feasts." Beginning in the 1880s the Comanches, Kiowas, Kiowa-Apaches, Caddos, Wichitas, Cheyennes, and Arapahos adopted the peyote religion as their own. Herbert E. Bolton claimed that the Tonkawas first imparted knowledge of peyote to other tribes during the 1850s confinement to the Brazos River Reservation. When the Tonkawas reached the Oakland Agency in 1884 they taught the Ponca, Oto, and Sac tribes, who lived on adjoining reservations, the peyote rituals. Members of the Osage, Quapaw, Pawnee, Kaw, Potawatomi, and Iowa tribes soon embraced the religion as well.[31]

The religious ceremonies, or mitote, involved consuming indeterminate quantities of peyote, a small, virtually spineless cactus native to the Rio Grande region of the Southwest. When chewed the bean, or button, of the plant produced a sort of "delirious exhilaration," which led to its nickname "dry whiskey." Known for its intoxicating and hallucinogenic qualities, users of peyote sometimes combined the buttons with tizwin, or other fermented native drinks, to render the peyote even more potent. Observers of the peyote culture commented that the natives consumed from four to forty of the buttons a night, "seeing or imagining all kinds of things."[32]

Disciples of the religion believed the peyote conveyed visions directly to them "from the Great Spirit." They also credited the plant with assisting priests to foretell the future, protecting all from "evil witchcraft." Herman Lehmann, a white captive who spent several years among the Lipan and Mescalero Apaches, said after eating hoosh (peyote), "we all felt so light and happy that we loved everybody and wanted to fly away." E. L. Clark, who lived among the Comanches, reported that the Comanches held meetings during which they ate "those poison roots," which "throws them into sort of a dream." After recovering the Comanches believed they had experienced "a Devine [sic] revelation."[33]

The culture and ceremonies of peyotism differed south and north of the Rio Grande. South of the river, natives and Mexicans incorporated a dance into their peyote rituals. North of the river, however, the peyote religion entailed only "ceremonious prayer and quiet contemplation." Initially only men participated in the ceremony, while the women prepared a "sacred feast" to be consumed by all after the rituals concluded. The men gathered in a tipi erected especially for the purpose. As many as possible sat in concentric circles around a ritual fire burning in a crescent-shaped mound in the center of the tipi. Next to the fire a ceremonial alter held the peyote. The senior priest opened the liturgy with a prayer, after which each participant received at least four peyote buttons. After chewing and swallowing the buttons the

Cyanotype of men in regalia dancing under an arbor, 1899. Oklahoma. E. M. Roff Collection.
Courtesy, National Museum of the American Indian, Smithsonian Institution.

men began to sing the sacred songs accompanied by a drum and rattles. Each man sang four songs in turn, interspersed with periods of prayer and distribution of more peyote.[34]

Practitioners of the religion reported that the drug in peyote induced a "sort of spiritual exultation" and well-being which sometimes lasted for days. Frequently practitioners of the religion brought ailing family members into the tipi, where the congregation prayed for a rapid return to health. At daylight the men sang the "Morning Star Song" and the women brought in the sacred meal. After eating all sang the "Meat Song." Depending on the number of peyote buttons consumed, the Indians remained under the influence of peyote from a single night to as long as four days. When the ritual concluded, families usually availed themselves of the opportunity to visit with each other before returning to their respective homes.[35]

As early as 1878 the Tonkawas practiced a form of peyotism that clearly incorporated Christian elements, but white Americans failed to understand the acculturated worship of the Tonkawa "peyote eaters." Many participants wore crucifixes, believing that Christ was "the Peyote Goddess," and that peyote was "given to use in the name of our Lord, Jesus Christ." In 1828, Berlandier noted that the Tonkawas and Lipans strung dried peyote "like a rosary." Most ceremonies also included a type of baptism, sprinkling of sacred water, at midnight. In 1888 agents in Indian Territory determined that "this hallucination is liable to assume a dangerous form" and issued orders forbidding the use of peyote in any form. Indian agents complained that peyote was an "impediment to civilizing" the Indians. Perhaps the agents misunderstood the ceremonies and linked peyote with the nascent ghost dance, which had erupted in significant violence on the Fort Apache Indian Reservation in 1880. The renowned Comanche Chief Quanah Parker, a leader of the peyote religion himself, managed a compromise which allowed the Indians to use peyote one night at each full moon for "three or four months."[36]

Despite restrictions on such trade, suppliers from around Laredo, Texas, continued to ship peyote to tribes in Indian Territory. In 1909, Chief Special Officer of the Bureau of Indian Affairs William E. Johnson, in a vain attempt to halt the trade, tried to buy and destroy an entire crop of peyote gathered north of Laredo by Hispanic peyoteros, harvesters and major suppliers of peyote for Indians north of the Rio Grande.[37]

In 1918 James Mooney, American ethnologist, persuaded American Indians who practiced the peyote religion to change the name of their religion to the Native American Church. Mooney used the name as a political strategy to protect American Indian ceremonies from oblivion. Mooney realized that, although Congress intended to suppress all native ceremonies, their Victorian attitudes toward religion would preclude congressional representatives from abolishing any church. As a result of Mooney's and others efforts, adherents of the peyote religion incorporated as the Native American Church in 1918. In 1944, members reincorporated the church as the Native American Church of the United States, and, when the religion spread to Canada in 1955, the Native American Church of North America.[38]

Although several states passed laws outlawing the use of peyote, and several native organizations oppose the church, the Native American Church continued to attract more members than any other organized religion, especially among the Navajo Nation. Many peyotists consider at least one journey to the "peyote gardens" of South Texas a mandatory religious experience. South Texas landowners locked their gates and refused entry to their property because of an invasion of individuals involved in "the drug culture" of the late 1960s and early 1970s, most of whom claimed to be members of the Native American Church. Although these transgressors almost disappeared by the mid-1980s, their actions led to a hefty price increase for peyote and restricted access for legitimate members of the Native American Church to their sacred gardens.[39]

The reservation system utilized by the United States government for the Tonkawas in both Texas and Indian Territory might have prevailed but for white greed and cultural preconceptions. The Tonkawas, and several other tribes, began a somewhat successful conversion to agricultural subsistence, evidenced by their harvested crops on both the Brazos River and Oakland Reservations. The Tonkawa reservation lands, especially in Indian Territory, were not overly crowded, allowing family groups to occupy their own small villages. Robert S. Neighbors appeared incorruptible and genuinely interested in helping the natives, but the United States government was unable to successfully settle the Tonkawas due to the antagonism of Indian-hating Texans and land-hungry farmers and ranchers. Often white settlers candidly expressed their jealousy of the reservation Indians, whom they considered "pampered wards." In most instances the Indian Bureau failed to aggressively enforce reservation policies, and oftentimes failed to uphold responsibilities regarding supplies and rations.[40]

Several individuals took initiatives to provide the tribe with a means to supplement the meager rations provided by the U.S. government. As early as 1873, Buell suggested to the Department of the Interior that each Tonkawa family receive a small flock of sheep, which he believed would provide both food and supplemental income to the Tonkawas. When the Bureau of Indian Affairs finally provided $700 for the sheep two years later, Buell described the Tonkawas' condition as "deplorable." Gen. Phillip Sheridan, no friend

Group portrait of Indian Congress participants, Tonkawa Delegates.
*Standing:* Winnie Richards, John Rush, Will Stevens, John Allen, Mary
Richards (Lipan); *seated:* John Williams, Chief Grant Richards, Sherman Miles.

Portrait of Indian Congress participants, Tonkawa
Delegates. Winnie Richards and Chief Grant
Richards. Photographs by Frank A. Rinehart,
found in the American Indians 1898 photo album,
Trans-Mississippi International Exposition website.

Portrait of Chief Grant Richards (Tonkawa), 1898. Omaha, Nebraska. David C. Vernon Collection. Presented by Laurence S. Rockefeller. Photo by Frank A. Rinehart. Courtesy, National Museum of the American Indian, Smithsonian Institution.

*Left*: Portrait of Winnie Richards (Tonkawa). Photograph by Frank A. Rinehart, found in the American Indians 1898 photo album, Trans-Mississippi International Exposition website. *Right*: Portrait of Mary Richards (Lipan-Tonkawa), 1898. Omaha, Nebraska. Photo by Frank A. Rinehart. Presented by Joseph A. Imhof. Courtesy, National Museum of the American Indian, Smithsonian Institution.

of indigenous peoples, endorsed Buell's actions by calling the Tonkawas "a most deserving people, probably the most so of any Indians we have." During the 1880s a young Scots immigrant attempted to teach the Tonkawas how to raise watermelons, but existing records indicated no success with cultivating watermelon patches.[41]

The major cause of agency failures in Texas remained the settlers' unremitting accusations against the reservation Indians for raiding local communities and then seeking shelter under army protection on the reservations. The settlers generally acted on emotion rather than fact, committing the same bloody atrocities with which they charged the Indians. No matter that the Tonkawas, over and over, proved themselves faithful allies of white settlers, they were Indians, and Indians could not be trusted for they constantly committed depredations against white persons.[42]

In Indian Territory, white lust for more land and a clash of cultures resulted in another broken promise. The Department of the Interior and eastern theologians attempted to eradicate Indian cultures, hoping to transform the

Portrait of John Williams (Tonkawa), 1898. Omaha, Nebraska.
Photo by Frank A. Rinehart. Presented by Joseph A. Imhof. Courtesy,
National Museum of the American Indian, Smithsonian Institution.

Tonkawas into Christian farmers. After losing most of their promised land,
the Tonkawas set about facing a new century on their small allotments.[43]

As the nineteenth century turned to the twentieth, the fifty-nine remaining Tonkawas at the Oakland Agency appeared content and somewhat af-
fluent. In 1905 their agents reported that the Tonkawas were "happy and
prosperous on their farms." The Tonkawa children attended a nearby government school, with a few sent to Chilocco, Kansas, to learn English.
According to the 1880 census, only Tonkawa Charley could read and write
English, although most of the tribe spoke the language with varying degrees
of fluency. The Methodist Church operated a mission on the Oakland Agency
to Christianize the tribe. In 1907 Oklahoma entered the Union as the forty-
sixth state and the Tonkawas became citizens of the new state, but not of
the United States. During the first years of the twentieth century, accepting

just about any price offered, most of the Tonkawas sold their land to white farmers and ranchers and moved to town. By 1910 so few Indians lived near the Oakland Agency that the Bureau of Indian Affairs closed the agency.[44]

During World War I and into the 1920s, the Tonkawas who still farmed or leased their allotments earned above average incomes for the area in which they lived. Tonkawa women regained their reputation as accomplished leather-crafters and saddle makers, selling their wares for top prices. The annual tribal powwows, festivals, and Christmas celebrations benefitted from the generosity of the tribe as the gatherings were always lavish and well attended. Regrettably, while most of America experienced a post-war boom, the Tonkawas saw their prosperity falter during the 1920s.[45]

# 10 TWENTIETH AND TWENTY-FIRST CENTURY TONKAWAS

Although many previous authors have dismissed the Tonkawa tribe as extinct since the early 1900s, the 483 people on tribal rolls in 1988 negate those erroneous assertions. The tribal population did decrease in the late nineteenth and early twentieth centuries. In 1880, 115 Tonkawa men, women, and children, ranging in age from two months to seventy years, lived near Fort Griffin. By 1900, only fifty-nine Tonkawas, most nearing middle age, resided on the Oakland Reservation. W. W. Newcomb stated that the Tonkawa tribe had virtually disappeared by 1944. Contradicting all assumptions, the United States government continued to recognize the Tonkawa people as a viable tribe and afforded them the same status and benefits as other, much larger tribes.[1]

Unfortunately, after World War I Tonkawa fortunes began to slide precipitously. Many of the old Tonkawa scouts died during the period between World War I and World War II. George Miles, an army scout and one of the last tribal chieftains, died in 1925. Johnson, renowned scout and always a colorful tribal figure, never completely gave up his native dress and was buried in ceremonial attire. Cochanna Rush, the last survivor of the 1862 massacre, died in 1935 at the age of 117.[2]

All the Spanish, Texian, and American attempts to transform the Tonkawa tribe into dry land farmers failed. Even though a few individual Tonkawas cultivated small plots of land and successfully raised a few crops, the tribe's culture was based on a hunting and gathering society, trailing wild game and harvesting pecans and berries from along the banks of rivers and creeks. The Tonkawa people never became true agriculturalists, cultivating the land as a mainstay of their diet. The Tonkawas remained too rooted in the Plains Indian warrior culture to daily toil in the soil.[3]

Laws enacted far from the Oklahoma Plains also adversely impacted the Tonkawas' future and prosperity. The 1887 Dawes Severalty Act deprived the Tonkawas of the vast majority of their promised 91,000-acre reservation. Under the provisions of the act heads of households received 160-acre plots of land, which the government held in trust for twenty years. Today very few Tonkawas retain deeds to their original grants. Their families grew too large to divide the small acreage among several children. Thus the Tonkawas sold off their small apportioned grants one-by-one. Of the thousands of acres once controlled by the Tonkawas, only 1,232.57 acres remain in their hands, with 994.33 acres tribally owned and 238.24 acres allotted to individuals.[4]

The Dawes Act also precluded the Tonkawas from receiving any of the large royalty checks paid to many Indians for their tribal mineral rights. During the Oklahoma oil booms of the early 1900s many Indians became wealthy, though some lost most of their cash to unscrupulous characters. In the early 1920s wildcatters opened the rich Three Sands oil field just south of Tonkawa, Oklahoma. Although the oil flowed from land previously encompassed by their reservation, the Tonkawas did not prosper from the crude extracted from the field as their land allotments lay north of the subterranean riches. Again white insatiable desire for Indian lands bilked the Tonkawa tribe out of a fiduciary cornerstone. A Mescalero Apache legend foretold the coming of the white man and the fate of most Indian tribes. "White men have filled up that which was the land of the Indian. The Indians [now] go the way of these white men . . . Indian men have cut their hair . . . wear only white men's clothing . . . Now those who were Indians cannot be distinguished [from] white." The legend concluded "Only white men with blue eyes will live in this country . . . now it has become so."[5]

On June 18, 1934, in an attempt to aid destitute Indians during the Depression, Congress passed the Indian Reorganization Act. The act provided funding for education, credit, employment, and authorized more traditional tribal organizations. This reversal of previous attempts to eradicate all remnants of tribal governments allowed tribes to organize councils which could administer local governmental affairs. Provisions of the act required each tribe to establish a council which drafted a constitution and submitted the final document to tribal members for approval. Under this act and the 1934 Oklahoma Welfare Act, Paul Allen, Walter Jefferson, and John Rush Buffalo certified the Tonkawa constitution on April 21, 1938. Since the adoption of the original constitution, and its amendments on April 2, 1977, and September 1, 1994, the Tonkawa govern themselves with a tribal council, headed by a president and vice president who are elected in April every two years. Although all adult Tonkawas are encouraged to participate in the democratic elections, most do not become involved in tribal council proceedings until they reach their late twenties or early thirties.[6]

Like most American Indians, the Tonkawa people live their lives controlled by a dominate Anglo-American culture. Many of the Texas Tonkawas spoke Spanish and English as well as the Tonkawa language, but American English currently dominates all native languages among the Tonkawas and their neighbors. Although several older tribal members continue to study Tonkawa culture and language, the tribe struggles to perpetuate their heritage and language. Some view the Tonkawa tongue as impractical as English is far too pervasive in today's society. Over the last century many Indian names have become Anglicized to something more palpable to English speakers (e.g., Eagle, Buffalohead, Running Wolf, CallsHim, and Littlewalker).[7]

Intermarriage with other tribes also reduced interest in Tonkawa customs and language. Intermarriage with the Lipan Apaches who accompanied the Tonkawas to Oklahoma in 1884 was common after the tribe first moved to Oklahoma, but marriages with nearby Poncas, Otoes, Osage, Pawnees, Kaws, Potawatomis, and Iowas became common thereafter. In 2001 even some astonished Comanches discovered that they have ancestors among their one-time enemies, the Tonkawa and Lipan Apache tribes. In 1961, of the sixty-two Tonkawas listed on tribal registers, only Joe Marcus Jesse, Paul Allen, and

Gertrude Martin were described as "full-blooded" Tonkawas. Many young natives in Oklahoma have blood from three, four, five, even up to eight tribes, but not enough to qualify as a full-blooded member of one particular tribe. To prove Tonkawa lineage, and qualify for tribal membership, a person must submit a birth certificate to the tribal council, which then certifies the document through a search of tribal and Bureau of Indian Affairs records.[8]

Present-day Tonkawa culture is dynamic and evolving, but certainly not the same as the romantic "noble savage" image of the nineteenth century. Modern Tonkawa, and most other indigenous cultures, are conglomerates of progressive native and Anglo-American cultures. Contemporary American culture surrounds Tonkawa members, and a technologically advanced media inundates them with what is considered today's American societal norms.[9]

During the 1920s, John Rush Buffalo recorded stories he heard as a young boy. He stated, "When they [adults] told these stories, I, being very young, was listening." The author interviewed one Tonkawa who vividly remembered his grandmother recounting a parody of the fable of the tortoise and the hare, but his sister can scarcely recall the story. Speaking fondly of his grandmother, he retold the tale using the Tonkawa words for turtle (mai-en) and rabbit (tan-musluc).[10]

In addition to members of the Native American Church, there are Baptists, Methodists, Catholics, Mormons, and others among the Tonkawa tribe. Older Tonkawas translated Bible stories into their own language. The aforesaid grandmother told a bedtime story about a man swallowed by a big fish, the Tonkawa version of "Jonah and the Whale."[11]

Although the Continental Oil Company (Conoco) constructed its national headquarters in Ponca City, less than fifteen miles away from the Tonkawa Reservation, few Tonkawas reap employment benefits from the oil company. In 2001 unemployment among the Tonkawa tribe remained at 21.9%, while Kay County, in which both the reservation and Ponca City are located, recorded an unemployment rate of just over five percent. In 2002 tribal records indicated a per capita income for the Tonkawas of $5,556. The Tonkawa tribal council employs a limited number of tribal members in its administrative offices and in the small gaming facility (casino) operated by the tribe on its small reservation. The Tonkawa Tribal Council channels income from the casino into the tribe's general fund. The tribe also administers federal funds allocated for education, job training, health/ diabetes care, transportation, and child care programs.[12]

Under Department of the Interior regulations the Bureau of Indian Affairs provides medical care for the Tonkawas through clinics established for other tribes, such as the Pawnee Clinic some thirty miles southeast of the Tonkawa Reservation. A major hospital is located in Ponca City.[13]

The majority of today's Tonkawas reside in a small reservation community. During the 1960s the government constructed 101 Housing units on the reservation, and the tribe owns fourteen more in the local area. Regional utilities provide electricity and natural gas service to the reservation. Tonkawa children attend Kay County public schools, with bus routes running through the reservation. Of the total tribal population in 2002, 61.5% received a high school diploma or higher, with 8.3% attaining a bachelor's degree or higher. A few tribal members attended a local community college. Numerous tribal members, however, reside across the United States. Brent Allen, for example, moved to Riverside, California, as a young boy and, until 2002, did not return to the reservation for thirty-five years.[14]

On special occasions Tonkawa dancers still perform the wolf dance, which commemorates the creation of the Tonkawa people. According to modern perceptions, Wolf acted as midwife to Mother Earth and Father Sky, who conceived the people. Wolf also became the primary teacher to the Tonkawas, by assuming responsibility of nurturing the untutored people. Wolf presented the tribe with bows and arrows, which symbolized the animal's ability to provide food, clothing, and shelter. The plains predator imparted to man the knowledge of how to hunt and provide for himself in a hostile environment. The Tonkawa called Wolf, or Hahtch-Sokona. Hahtch means earth or ground, and Sokona means to own, literally translated as "he owns the earth" or "owner of the earth."[15]

A modern Tonkawa powwow resembles a large family reunion, with all tribes invited to dance with their old enemies. Referring to white settlers, one Tonkawa stated that "If we had known who the real enemy was, we wouldn't have been fighting each other." Each tribe performs certain dances particular to their culture. For instance, the Tonkawas dance and sing a special song honoring the Lipan Apaches, old allies and no longer recognized as a tribe by the United States government. The Tonkawa, Mescalero Apache, and possibly Kiowa-Apache tribes absorbed the survivors of the scattered Lipan Apaches years ago. Most tribes perform a war dance, but the gourd dance is an agglutinate that binds all tribes together. Members of all tribes join in the gourd dance, no matter which tribe hosts the powwow.[16]

During powwows the Tonkawa tribe specifically recognizes veterans of the United States military. The scalp dance honors warriors, and today honors veterans on Memorial Day, Veterans Day, and other special occasions. Dancers who are veterans of the armed services festoon their ceremonial dress with such awards as the Combat Infantryman's Badge (CIB), paratrooper badges, awards for valor, service ribbons, and unit crests and patches. Many ceremonial costumes are red, white, and blue, resplendent with stars and stripes.

Mainstream America may have forgotten the Tonkawa tribe, but the Tonkawas remain staunch citizens proudly serving their country. The Tonkawa warrior culture pervades the tribe with men and women serving in all branches of the armed forces. On June 21, 2002, Felix Waldo Allen (Wa-Ki-The or Straight Shooter), died at the age of eighty-three. The oldest member of the Tonkawa tribe at the time of his death, Allen graduated from a rural school near Tonkawa, Oklahoma, and the University of Hawaii with a degree in Forward Directional Calculations. He enlisted in the U.S. Army in March 1941 and served in the Forty-Eighth Field Artillery Battalion in the Pacific Theater. One of Allen's sons, Donald Ah-Ta-hock, died during service in Vietnam. Felix Allen was the last of a generation with direct ties to Texas, with his father John AH-Ta-Hock, born in Texas and dying in Oklahoma.[17]

The Tonkawa scalp dance remains the tribe's war dance. Donald Patterson, tribal president in 2002, declared that "The enemy has changed and the battle is different. Now we battle alcohol & drugs, poverty, child abuse, spousal abuse, parental abuse, educational indifference, and all the social ills of modern American society." The scalp dance was divided into four major parts, with the most important sections traditionally performed by Tonkawa women intended to inspire the men in combat. The first phase consisted of a formal parade of dancers entering from the east, symbolizing the tribe gathering in a crescent for the ceremonial wolf dance. The tribe's crescent-shaped camps and villages opened to the east and Tonkawa warriors and hunters always returned to camp from that direction. In the second phase of the dance the men moved to form an outer ring as a female dancer led an inner procession, prancing with a long lance adorned with scalps and war trophies. Twelve other female dancers, representative of the twelve major recognized clans of the tribe, danced around the circle with a type of short lance, or "coup stick," each ornamented with additional trophies. The scalps and war trophies reminded warriors of prior successes in battle.[18]

In the third phase—the kick dance—the songs changed, with the drum beat and dance steps increasing in tempo. This sequence represented the men preparing themselves and their horses for battle. The men applied war paint and decorated their war ponies, tying up the horses' tails to prevent an enemy from using the tails to swing up behind the rider. Moving into the final phase, the "war journey," or "war expedition," the dance steps changed again, mimicking the excited prancing of a war pony as the warriors rode off to confront their enemies. The women shifted to dance shoulder-to-shoulder, symbolizing the men riding out and confronting their enemies together. The singers chant that the "enemy is calling" and the dancers move rapidly to do battle with their adversaries. Additionally, when the women moved into close proximity, they symbolize Tonkawa females joining together in order to survive in the absence of their men.[19]

The Tonkawa tribe practiced, then and now, a "give away" ceremony reminiscent of most Plains Indian cultures, whereby prosperous families distribute part of their wealth to other members of the tribe. Prior to a powwow, families collect money and gifts to give to friends and other tribal members who helped the family during difficult times, financial or emotional. During the dance ceremonies Tonkawas leave the dance circle and move to the selected individuals and formally present the gifts.[20]

The history of Tonkawa relationships with Euroamericans remained convoluted. Tonkawa leaders concentrated on tribal concerns, mainly survival, joining in alliances of convenience with other tribes, the Spanish, Mexicans, and Texians. In general, the United States government ignored the Tonkawas' plight and their faithful commitment to the Republic of

Texas, the Confederacy, and United States, with Indian tribes considered "hostile" receiving more government assistance than the allied Tonkawas. The expertise of native scouts, especially the Tonkawas, became the pivotal element that allowed both Texas Rangers and the U.S. Army to successfully contend with the Comanches, Kiowas, and other tribes inhabiting the South Plains. Unfortunately for the Tonkawas, their unwavering loyalty to the white settlers, along with their cannibalistic practices, cast them as pariahs among other tribes and resulted in an "inexorable decline," which increasingly forced the tribe to rely on government subsidies just to survive. The Tonkawas, like many other tribes, therefore, may well be considered used, abused, and forgotten.[21]

# NOTES

## PREFACE

1 George Klos, "'Our People Could Not Distinguish one Tribe from Another,' The 1859 Expulsion of the Reserve Indians from Texas," *Southwestern Historical Quarterly* 97, no. 4 (April 1994): 599–602.

2 Kelly F. Himmel, *The Conquest of the Karankawas and the Tonkawas, 1821–1859* (College Station, TX: Texas A&M University Press, 1999), 35–36.

## INTRODUCTION

1 Daniel J. Prikryl, "Fiction and Fact about the Titskanwatits, or Tonkawa, of East-central Texas," Institute of Texan Cultures, San Antonio, Texas, 1–9; Robert S. Weddle, *The San Sabá Mission: Spanish Pivot in Texas* (Austin, TX: The University of Texas Press, 1964), 73, 102–103, 114, 190; John R. Swanton, *The Indian Tribes of North America* (Washington, D.C.: Smithsonian Institution Press, 1952; rpt. 1969), 301; Dorman H. Winfrey and James M. Day, eds., *The Indian Papers of Texas and the Southwest, 1825–1916* (Austin, TX: Texas State Historical Association, 1995), I: 24, hereafter cited as *Indian Papers*; Paul H. Carlson, *The Plains Indians* (College Station, TX: Texas A&M University Press, 1998), 32.

2 Prikryl, "Fiction and Fact," 10–13; Swanton, *Indian Tribes*, 326-27; Jean Louis Berlandier, C. H. and Katherine K. Muller, eds., Sheila M. Ohlendorf, Josette M. Bigelow, and Mary M. Standifer, trans., *Journey to Mexico: During the Years 1826–1834*, Vol. II (Austin, TX: Texas State Historical Association and University of Texas Press, 1980), 306; Carlson, *Plains Indians*, 7.

3 Prikryl, "Fiction and Fact," 13–15; Berlandier, *Journey to Mexico*, II: 310–13; Jean Louis Berlandier and J. C. Ewer, eds., *The Indians of Texas in 1830* (Washington, D.C.: Smithsonian Institution Press, 1969), 51; Robert S. Weddle, "La Salle's Survivors," *Southwestern Historical Quarterly* 75, no. 4 (April 1972): 417–18.

4 Berlandier, *Journey to Mexico*, II: 311–13.

5 Ibid.; Carlson, *Plains Indians*, 31.

6 Berlandier, *Journey to Mexico*, II: 310–13, 384–85; Francis R. Lubbock, "An Account of the Tonkawa Indians as the Writer Remembers Them, 1884," November 12, 1884, Howard Collection, Dallas Historical Society, Dallas, Texas, 1–2; J. H. Kuykendall,

"Reminiscences of Early Texans," *Quarterly of the Texas State Historical Association* 7 (April 1903): 326–28; Edward A. Lukes, "DeWitt Colony of Texas" (PhD diss., Loyolla University, 1971), 153–59; Thomas F. Schilz, "People of the Cross-timbers: A History of the Tonkawa Indians" (PhD diss., Texas Christian University, 1983), 54, 73, 74.

[7]   Berlandier, *Journey to Mexico*, II: 379; Ernest Wallace and E. Adamson Hoebel, *The Comanches: Lords of the South Plains* (Norman, OK: University of Oklahoma Press, 1952), 70, 260, 287, 299; Kenneth F. Neighbors, "Tonkawa Scouts and Guides," *West Texas History Association Year Book* 49 (1973): 90–91; John C. Jacobs, "Robin Hood of the Tonkaways," *Frontier Times* 3 (November 1925): 36–38; Mary Maverick Green, ed., *Memoirs of Mary A. Maverick*, Arranged by Mary A. Maverick and her son, George Madison Maverick (San Antonio, TX: Alamo Printing Company, 1921), 18–19; Thomas W. Dunlay, *Gray Wolves for the Blue Soldiers: Indian Scouts and Auxiliaries with the United States Army, 1850–90* (Lincoln, NE: University of Nebraska Press, 1982), 23; Martin L. Crimmins, "The Tonkawe Tribe," *Frontier Times* 3 (June 1926): 43.

[8]   J. H. Kuykendall, "Reminiscences of Early Texans," *Quarterly of the Texas State Historical Association* 6 (January 1903): 252–53; Gregg Cantrell, *Stephen F. Austin: Emprassario of Texas* (New Haven, CT: Yale University Press, 1999), 136–40.

[9]   J. H. Kuykendall, "Reminiscences of Early Texans," *Quarterly of the Texas State Historical Association* 7 (July 1903): 29–30; Cantrell, *Stephen F. Austin*, 136–40; Lukes, "DeWitt Colony of Texas," 152–54, 156–59.

[10]  Winfrey and Day, *Indian Papers*, I: 28–30, 45–48.

[11]  Neighbors, "Tonkawa Scouts and Guides," 92–93; Winfrey and Day, *Indian Papers*, II: 150–51, 167–68, 211–12, 254, 261.

[12]  Winfrey and Day, *Indian Papers*, II: 197–98, 202–203, 205–206.

[13]  Deborah Lamont Newlin, *The Tonkawa People: A Tribal History from Earliest Times to 1893* (Lubbock, TX: West Texas Museum Association, 1982), 35–36.

[14]  Berta Hart Nance, "D. A. Nance and the Tonkawa Indians," *West Texas Historical Association Year Book* 28 (1952): 89; Noah Smithwick, *Evolution of a State, or Recollections of Old Texas Days* (H. P. N. Gammel, 1900; rpt., Austin, TX: University of Texas Press, 1983), 182–83.

[15]  A. R. Johnson, "The Battle of Antelope Hills," *Frontier Times* 1 (February 1924): 12–14, [excerpt from *Partisan Rangers* by Gen. A. R. Johnson]; Robert A. Hasskarl, Jr., "The Culture and history of the Tonkawa Indians," *Plains Anthropologist* 7 (November 1962): 224; Dunlay, *Gray Wolves*, 21–22; Schilz, "People of the Cross-Timbers," 169–71.

[16]  Neighbors, "Tonkawa Scouts and Guides," 93; Hasskarl, *Culture and History*, 225; Dunlay, *Gray Wolves*, 21; Schilz, "People of the Cross-timbers," 172–74.

[17]  Annie Heloise Abel, *The American Indian as Participant in the Civil War* (Cleveland, OH: The Arthur H. Clark Company, 1919), 181–86; Hasskarl, *Culture and history*, 225–26; Schilz, "People of the Cross-timbers," 175–76, 183–84; Neighbors, "Tonkawa Scouts and Guides," 96.

[18]  Neighbors, "Tonkawa Scouts and Guides," 96–101, 103–105, 108, 112; Richard H. Pratt, Robert M. Utley, ed., *Battlefield and Classroom: Four Decades with the American Indians, 1867–1904* (New Haven, CT: Yale University Press, 1964), 55–60; Ernest Wallace, ed., *Ranald S. Mackenzie's Official Correspondence Relating to Texas, 1871–1873* (Lubbock, TX: West Texas Museum Association, 1967), 24–25, 70–71, 76–77, 79; J. J. Bragg, "Days of Peril on the Clear Fork," *Frontier Times* 3 (April 1926): 44–46; Dunlay, *Gray Wolves*, 116–17; Charles M. Robinson, III, *Bad Hand: A Biography of General Ranald S. Mackenzie* (Austin, TX: State House Press, 1993), 147–48; John C. Ewers, "The Influence of Epidemics on the Indian Populations and Cultures of Texas," *Plains Anthropologist* 18, no. 60 (1973): 110–12.

19  Neighbors, "Tonkawa Scouts and Guides," 97; Pratt, *Battlefield and Classroom*, 55–56; Hasskarl, *Culture and History*, 226; Dunlay, *Gray Wolves*, 106, 117.

20  Report of the Commissioner of Indian Affairs for 1884, (Washington, Government Printing Office, 1884), 153F; Berlin B. Chapman, "Establishment of the Iowa Reservation," *Chronicles of Oklahoma* 21 (December 1943): 366–77; Nance, "D. A. Nance and the Tonkawa Indians," 94–95; Dunlay, *Gray Wolves*, 122–23; Oral history interviews, June 29–30, 2002, Donald Patterson, President, Tonkawa Tribe; Swanton, *Indian Tribes*, 304, 327; Neighbors, "Tonkawa Scouts and Guides," 112–13.

## CHAPTER 1

1  Robert A. Hasskarl, Jr., "The Culture and History of the Tonkawa Indians," *Plains Anthropologist*, 7, No. 18 (November 1962): 217–31; Daniel J. Prikryl, "Fiction and Fact about the Titskanwatits, or Tonkawa, of East–Central Texas" (San Antonio, TX: Institute of Texan Cultures), 1–9; John R. Swanton, *The Indian Tribes of North America* (Washington, D.C.: Smithsonian Institution Press, 1952, rpt. 1969), 301; W. W. Newcomb, Jr., "Historic Indians of Central Texas," *Bulletin of the Texas Archeological Society*, No. 64 (1993): 22–27; Paul H. Carlson, *The Plains Indians* (College Station, TX: Texas A&M University Press, 1998), 32; Deborah Lamont Newlin, *The Tonkawa People: A Tribal History from Earliest Times to 1893* (Lubbock, TX: West Texas Museum Association, 1982), 1–7; Mary Jourdan Atkinson, *The Texas Indians* (San Antonio, TX: The Naylor Company, 1935), 2, 211.

2  Herbert E. Bolton, "The Founding of the Missions on the San Gabriel River, 1745–1749," *Southwestern Historical Quarterly*, 17, No. 4 (April 1914): 328–31; Prikryl, "Fiction and Fact," 17–20; Mardith Keithly Schuetz, *The Indians of the San Antonio Missions, 1718–1821* (Austin, TX: The University of Texas Press, 1980), 7–8, 40–42, 47–48, 59–60; T. N. Campbell, "Ethnohistoric Notes on Indian Groups Associated with Three Spanish Missions at Guerrero, Coahuila, Archaeology and History of the San Juan Bautista Mission Area, Coahuila and Texas," Report No. 3, Center for Archaeological Research, University of Texas at San Antonio (1979): 13–15; Dorman H. Winfrey, et al., *Indian Tribes of Texas* (Waco, TX: Texian Press, 1971), 151–53.

3  Ibid.

4  Frederick W. Hodge, ed., "The Narrative of Álvar Núñez, Cabeza de Vaca," Frederick W. Hodge and Theodore H. Lewis, *Spanish Explorers in the Southern United States 1528–1543* (New York: Charles Scribner's Sons, 1907), 45–53; Morris Bishop, *The Odyssey of Cabeza de Vaca* (New York: Century Company, 1933), 94; Cleve Hallenbeck, *Álvar Núñez Cabeza de Vaca: The Journey and Route of the First European to Cross the Continent of North America 1534–1536* (Glendale, CA: The Arthur H. Clark Company, 1940), 31–103; Herbert E. Bolton, *Texas in the Middle Eighteenth Century: Studies in Spanish Colonial History and Administration* (Berkley, CA: University of California Press, 1915), 145–46.

5  Thomas F. Schilz, "People of the Cross-timbers: A History of the Tonkawa Indians" (PhD diss., Texas Christian University, 1983), 8–10, 18–19; Rudolph Charles Troike, "Tonkawa Prehistory: A Study in Method and Theory" (M.A. thesis, University of Texas, 1957), 26–27; Mariah Wade, "Go–between: The Roles of Native American Women and Álvar Núñez Cabeza de Vaca in Southern Texas in the 16th Century," *Journal of American Folklore*, 12, No. 445 (Summer 1999): 332–42; Prikryl, "Fiction and Fact," 8–10; Newlin, *The Tonkawa People*, 9–11; Winfrey, *Indian Tribes of Texas*, 151–52.

6   Schilz, "People of the Cross-timbers," 12–19; S. C. Vehik, "Oñate's Expedition to the Southern Plains: Routes, Destinations, and Implications for Late Prehistoric Cultural Adaptations," *Plains Anthropologist*, 111, No. 31 (1986): 13–20; Prikryl, "Fiction and Fact," 8–10.

7   Swanton, *The Indian Tribes of North America*, 301; Anna Lewis, "La Harpe's First Expedition in Oklahoma," *Chronicles of Oklahoma*, 2 (Winter 1924): 332; Prikryl, "Fiction and Fact," 2–4; Campbell, "Ethnohistoric Notes," 13–14; Troike, "Tonkawa Prehistory," 26–36; L. Johnson, Jr., and T. N. Campbell, "Sanan: Traces of a Previously Unknown Aboriginal Language in Colonial Coahuila and Texas," *Plains Anthropologist*, 140, No. 37 (1992): 185–212; L. Johnson, Jr., "The Reconstructed Crow Terminology of the Titskanwatits, or Tonkawas, with Inferred Social Correlates," *Plains Anthropologist*, 150, No. 39 (1994): 377–413; W. W. Newcomb, Jr., and T. N. Campbell, "Southern Plains Ethnohistory: A Re–Examination of the Escanjaques, Ahijados, and Cuitoas," *Pathways to Plains Prehistory: Anthropological Perspectives of Plains Natives and Their Pasts*, Don G. Wyckoff and Jack L. Hofman, eds., Memoir 3 (Duncan, OK: Oklahoma Anthropological Society, 1982), 29–43; W. W. Newcomb, Jr., and T. N. Campbell, "Tonkawa," *Handbook of North American Indians*, 13 (Washington, D.C.: Smithsonian Institution Press, 1982); Newcomb, "Historic Indians," 21–27; Robert S. Reading, *Arrows Over Texas* (San Antonio, TX: The Naylor Company, 1960), 274–279; Atkinson, *The Texas Indians*, 216–17.

8   Swanton, *The Indian Tribes of North America*, 301; Prikryl, "Fiction and Fact," 2–4; Campbell, "Ethnohistoric Notes," 13–14; Troike, "Tonkawa Prehistory," 26–36; Johnson and Campbell, "Sanan: Traces," 185–212; Johnson, "The Reconstructed Crow Terminology of the Titskanwatits," 150, 377–413.

9   Newcomb and Campbell, "Southern Plains Ethnohistory," 29–43; Newcomb, "Historic Indians," 22–28; Reading, *Arrows Over Texas*, 274–79; Atkinson, *The Texas Indians*, 216–17; Schilz, "People of the Cross-timbers," 27–30.

10   Vehik, "Oñate's Expedition," 13–33; Prikryl, "Fiction and Fact," 4–6; Newcomb, "Historic Indians," 24–25.

11   Ralph A. Smith, trans., "Account of the Journey of Benard de La Harpe: Discovery Made by Him of Several Nations Situated in the West," *Southwestern Historical Quarterly*, 62, No. 3 (January 1959): 374–79, 385; Schilz, "People of the Cross-timbers," 58–59.

12   Ibid.; Bolton, "The Founding of the Missions on the San Gabriel River," 330–32, 338–39; Winfrey, *Indian Tribes of Texas*, 151–53.

13   Béxar Archives, Thomas D. Moorman, trans., Vol. 34: University of Texas at San Antonio, San Antonio, Texas, 105–107, 116–18, 121–25 128–35, hereafter cited as Béxar Archives.

14   Bolton, "The Founding of the Missions on the San Gabriel River," 323–27, 340–41, 354–56, 360–61, 364, 366–73, 377–79; Bolton, *Texas in the Middle Eighteenth Century* 50, 182, 185, 187, 190, 197–98, 231–33; William Edwards Dunn, "The Apache Mission on the San Sabá River, Its Founding and Failure," *Southwestern Historical Quarterly*, 17, No. 4 (April 1914): 383–86, 388; Prikryl, "Fiction and Fact," 17–18; Newcomb and Campbell, "Tonkawas," 4; Newcomb, "Historic Indians," 22, 25–27; Schuetz, *Indians of the San Antonio Missions*, 33–34; Hasskarl, "Culture and History," 221; Smith, "Benard de La Harpe," 376, 385.

15   Ibid.

16   Béxar Archives, 35: 16; 139: 29–35, July 3, 1786, Domingo Cabello to Jacobo de Ugarte y Loyola; Newcomb, "Historic Indians," 22; Dunn, "The Apache Mission on the San Sabá River," 404–11; Robert S. Weddle, *The San Sabá Mission: Spanish Pivot in Texas* (Austin, TX: The University of Texas Press, 1964), 73, 102–103, 114, 190.

[17] Ibid.
[18] Bolton, *Texas in the Middle Eighteenth Century*, 121, 122, 125–26, 153–54; Herbert E. Bolton, ed., *Athanase de Mezieres and the Louisiana–Texas Frontier, 1768–1780*, 2 vols., (Cleveland, OH: Arthur H. Clark Company, 1914), 289–90; Béxar Archives, 57: 88–94, Deposition of Joseph Manuel Diaz; Russell B. Magnaghi, ed. and trans., "Texas as Seen by Governor Winthuysen, 1741–1744," *Southwestern Historical Quarterly*, 88, No. 2 (October 1984): 169; Prikryl, "Fiction and Fact," 17–20; Newcomb, "Historic Indians," 22, 25–27; Schuetz, *Indians of the San Antonio Missions*, 9; Smith, "Benard de La Harpe," 376–77 (footnote 59).
[19] Béxar Archives, 56: 3–5, January 1774, El Bailio Frey Don Antonio Bucareli y Ursua to Señor Barón de Ripperdá; 17–18, March 1774, Bucareli to de Ripperdá; Prikryl, "Fiction and Fact," 18–20; Newcomb, "Historic Indians," 22, 25; Troike, "Tonkawa Prehistory," 26–36.
[20] Béxar Archives, Carmela Leal, trans., Vol. 45: 127–30, March 6, 1768, Melchor Afan de Rivera to Hugo Oconor; Prikryl, "Fiction and Fact," 18–20; Lawrence and Lucia B. Kinnaird, "Choctaws West of the Mississippi, 1766–1800," *Southwestern Historical Quarterly*, 83, No. 4 (April 1980): 358; John C. Ewers, "The Influence of Epidemics on the Indian Populations and Cultures of Texas," *Plains Anthropologist*, 18, No. 60 (1973): 104–109.
[21] Hasskarl, "Culture and History," 221–22; Smith, "Benard de La Harpe," 376–77; Ewers, "Influence of Epidemics," 105.
[22] Béxar Archives, 78: 15–16, February, 9, 1779, Señor Commanding General [Teodoro] de Croix to Domingo Cabello; 86: 33–34, 36–37, August, 20, 1779, Cabello to de Croix; 162–64, August 30, 177, Cabello to de Croix; 99–100, Proclamation by Cabello, September 29, 1779; 92: xv, de Croix decree, January 29, 1780; 79–84, January 18, 1780, Pedro Galindo Nazarro to de Croix; Bolton, *Texas in the Middle Eighteenth Century*, 424–25, 433–35, 442; James Curtis Hasdorff, *Four Indian Tribes in Texas, 1785–1858: A Reevaluation of Historical Sources* (Albuquerque, NM: University of New Mexico Press, 1971), 45–46.
[23] Ibid.
[24] Ibid.
[25] Béxar Archives, 88: 29–32, October 8, 1779, Proclamation by Cabello; 67–71, 76–80, October 19, 1779, Cabello to De Croix; 83–88, Accounting of Expenditures by Joseph Antonio de Bustillo y Zevallos; Elizabeth A. H. S. John, *Storms Brewed in Other Men's Worlds: The Confrontation of Indians, Spanish, and French in the Southwest, 1540–1795* (College Station, TX: Texas A&M University Press, 1975), 635–36, 665–67; Winfrey, *Indian Tribes of Texas*, 129, 153–59.
[26] Ibid.
[27] Béxar Archives, 88: 71–81, October 19, 1779, Cabello to De Croix; 89: 56–57, November 2, 1779, Cabello to de Croix.
[28] Béxar Archives, 94: 2, March 14, 1780, Cabello to de Croix; 99: 8–13, June 17, 1780, Cabello to de Croix; 101: 24–25, July 17, 1780, Cabello to de Croix; 120: 97–104, November 30, 1783, Daily Records of Presidio San Antonio; 121: 24–29, December 18, 1783, Felipe de Neze to Cabello; 123: 66–68, March 29, 1784, Cabello to Phelipe de Nede; John, *Storms*, 635–36, 665–67; Winfrey, *Indian Tribes of Texas*, 129, 153–59; Hasskarl, "Culture and History," 221–22.
[29] Ibid.
[30] Béxar Archives, 121: 24–29, December 18, 1783, Felipe de Neze to Cabello; 121: 36–38, December 26, 1783, (no adressee or signature [probably de Croix to Cabello]); 122: 39–41, January 31, 1784, Daily Reports of Presidio San Antonio; 122: 42–44, February 20, 1784, Summary of the Events Appertaining to the Administration Concerning Warfare which occurred at the Presidios of San Antonio de Béxar and La Bahiá del Esprítu Santo;

66–67, March 29, 1784, Cabello to de Neze; 127: 25–26, July 15, 1784, Cabello to de Neze; 40–41, July 20, 1784, Cabello to de Neze; 129: 110–11, December 31, 1784, José Antonio Rendel to Cabello; 131: 79–80, April 4, 1785, Cabello to Ibarvo, et al.; 133: 112, August 25, 1785, Rendel to Cabello; 136, Draft Letter, [no date], Cabello to Rendel; John, *Storms*, 635–36, 665–67; Winfrey, *Indian Tribes of Texas*, 129, 153–59.

31  John, *Storms*, 635–36, 665–67; Béxar Archives, 138: 90–93, June 12, 1786, Cabello to Ugarte; 121–28, Daily Reports of Presidio San Antonio de Béxar, June 30, 1786; 139: 29–35, July 3, 1786, Cabello to Ugarte; 140: 171–73, August 28, 1786, Cabello to Ugarte; 141: 60, September 10, 1786, Cabello to Ugarte; Winfrey, *Indian Tribes of Texas*, 153–59.

32  Béxar Archives, 146: 109–13, September 20, 1787, Report on Supply and Distribution of Indian presents by Rafael Martínez Pacheco; 147: 112, 122, October 27 & 28, 1787, Pacheco to Ugarte; 148: 20, November 5, 1787, Report on Gifts to Indians Visiting Presidio San Antonio de Béxar by Pacheco; 37, November 10, 1787, Ugarte to Pacheco; 47–48, November 11, 1787, Pacheco to Ugarte; 154: 41–42, June 15, 1788, Report on Gifts to Indians; 155: 19, June 20, 1788, Pacheco to Ugarte; John, *Storms*, 635–36, 665–67; Newlin, *The Tonkawa People*, 17–18; Winfrey, *Indian Tribes of Texas*, 153–59; Hasskarl, "Culture and History," 221–22.

33  Ibid.

34  Béxar Archives, 148: 62, November 12, 1787, Ibarvo to Pacheco; 152: 51, February 6, 1788, Pacheco to Ibarvo; 153: 14, February 23, 1788, Pacheco to Ugarte; 98, May 22, 1788, Pacheco to Ugarte.

35  Béxar Archives, 155: 7–9, June 7, 1788, Pacheco to Ugarte; 19–20, June 20, 1788, Pacheco to Ugarte; John, *Storms*, 635–36, 665–67; Newlin, *The Tonkawa People*, 1–12.

## CHAPTER 2

1  Kelly F. Himmel, *The Conquest of the Karankawas and the Tonkawas, 1821–1859* (College Station, TX: Texas A&M University Press, 1999), 22–24, 28–30; Mardith Keithly Schuetz, *The Indians of the San Antonio Missions, 1718–1821* (Austin, TX: The University of Texas Press, 1980), 7–9, 61; Jean Louis Berlandier, C. H. and Katherine K. Muller, eds., Sheila M. Ohlendorf, Josette M. Bigelow, and Mary M. Standifer, trans., *Journey to Mexico: During the Years 1826–1834*, Vol. II (Austin, TX: Texas State Historical Association and University of Texas Press, 1980), 310–13; Jean Louis Berlandier and J. C. Ewer, eds., *The Indians of Texas in 1830* (Washington, D.C.: Smithsonian Institution Press, 1969), 51.

2  William K. Jones, *Notes on the History and Material Culture of the Tonkawa Indians* (Washington, D.C.: Smithsonian Press, 1969), 77; Daniel J. Prikryl, "Fiction and Fact about the Titskanwatits, or Tonkawa, of East–central Texas" (San Antonio, TX: Institute of Texan Cultures), 13–15; Robert A. Hasskarl, Jr., "The Culture and History of the Tonkawa Indians," *Plains Anthropologist* 7, No. 18 (November 1962): 216–18; Mary Jourdan Atkinson, *The Texas Indians* (San Antonio, TX: The Naylor Company, 1935), 214–16.

3  Berlandier et al., *Journey to Mexico*, Vol. II, 310–13; Berlandier, *The Indians of Texas*, 51; James Curtis Hasdorff, *Four Indian Tribes in Texas, 1785–1858: A Reevaluation of Historical Sources* (Albuquerque, NM: University of New Mexico Press, 1971), 59–60; Thomas F. Schilz, "People of the Cross-timbers: A History of the Tonkawa Indians," (PhD diss., Texas Christian University, 1983), 14–17; Robert S. Weddle, "La Salle's Survivors," *Southwestern Historical Quarterly* 75, No. 4 (April 1972): 417–18; Prikryl, "Fiction and Fact," 13–15; Hasskarl, "Culture and History," 216–18; Himmel, *Conquest*, 57–59; Atkinson, *The Texas Indians*, 214–16.

4   Marian Templeton Place, *Comanches and Other Indians of Texas* (New York: Harcourt Brace,
    1970), 58–62; Schuetz, *Indians of the San Antonio Missions*, 73–74; Himmel, *Conquest*, 27–28;
    Hasskarl, "Culture and History," 220–21.

5   Oral History Interviews, June 28–30, 2002, Don Patterson; Harry Hoijer, "Tonkawa:
    An Indian Language of Texas," (PhD diss., University of Chicago, 1931), 131; Andre F.
    Sjoberg, "The Culture of the Tonkawa: A Texas Indian Tribe," *Texas Journal of Science*, No. 5
    (1953): 289–91; Schilz, "People of the Cross-timbers," 32–35.

6   Hasskarl, "Culture and History," 220–21; Schuetz, *Indians of the San Antonio Missions*,
    80–83; J. Evetts Haley, *Charles Goodnight: Cowman and Plainsman* (Norman, OK: University
    of Oklahoma Press, 1936), 93.

7   Hasskarl, "Culture and History," 220–21; Schilz, "People of the Cross-timbers," 4–7;
    Oral History Interviews, June 28–30, 2002, Don Patterson.

8   Berlandier, *Journey to Mexico*, Vol. II, 310–13; Jones, *Notes on the Tonkawa Indians*, 77; Hasskarl,
    "Culture and History," 217–19; Schuetz, *Indians of the San Antonio Missions*, 65–66; Himmel,
    *Conquest*, 23–24; Schilz, "People of the Cross-timbers," 30–32; Atkinson, *The Texas Indians*,
    211–13; John C. Jacobs, "Robin Hood of the Tonkaways," *Frontier Times*, No. 3 (November
    1925): 36–38.

9   Ibid.

10  Oral History Interviews, June 28–30, 2002, Don Patterson; Randolph B. Marcy, *Thirty
    Years of Army Life on the Border*, 1866 edition, Introduction by Edward S. Wallace (New York:
    Harper and Brothers Publishers, 1866), 175–77; Hasskarl, "Culture and History," 220–
    21; Kenneth F. Neighbors, "Tonkawa Scouts and Guides," *West Texas Historical Association
    Year Book* 49 (1973): 90.

11  Oral History Interviews, June 28–30, 2002, Don Patterson; Marcy, *Thirty Years*, 175–77;
    Hasskarl, "Culture and History," 220–21; Neighbors, "Tonkawa Scouts and Guides," 90;
    Atkinson, *The Texas Indians*, 213–14; Schilz, "People of the Cross-timbers," 40–41.

12  Schilz, "People of the Cross-timbers," 4–5.

13  Ibid.

14  Noah Smithwick, *Evolution of a State, or Recollections of Old Texas Days* (H. P. N. Gammel, 1900;
    rpt., Austin, TX: University of Texas Press, 1983), 181–82; Schuetz, *Indians of the San Antonio
    Missions*, 92–93; Berta Hart Nance, "D. A. Nance and the Tonkawa Indians," *West Texas
    Historical Association Year Book* 28 (1952), 92–94; Sjoberg, "Culture of the Tonkawa," 291–93;
    Hasskarl, "Culture and History," 220–21; Atkinson, *The Texas Indians*, 223.

15  Ibid.

16  Smithwick, *Evolution of a State*, 181–82; W. W. Newcomb, Jr., *The Indians of Texas From Prehistoric
    to Modern Times* (Austin, TX: University of Texas Press, 1961), 148; Berlandier, *Journey to
    Mexico*, Vol. II, 384–85; Sjoberg, "Culture of the Tonkawas," 291–92; Hasskarl, "Culture
    and History," 220–21; Oral History Interviews, June 28–30, 2002, Don Patterson;
    Jacobs, "Robin Hood of the Tonkaways," 36–38.

17  Ibid.

18  Schilz, "People of the Cross-timbers," 7–11, 18–21; Berlandier, *Journey to Mexico*, Vol. II,
    311–13; Hasskarl, "Culture and History," 216–17; Schuetz, *Indians of the San Antonio Missions*,
    62–64; Atkinson, *The Texas Indians*, 214–15.

19  Ibid.

20  Herbert E. Bolton, ed., *Athanase de Mezieres and the Louisiana–Texas Frontier, 1768–1780*, 2 vols.
    (Cleveland, OH: Arthur H. Clark Company, 1914), 2:278–80; Himmel, *Conquest*, 29–30;
    Berlandier, *Journey to Mexico*, Vol. II, 311–13; Hasdorff, *Four Indian Tribes in Texas*, 58–59;
    Hasskarl, "Culture and History," 217–19; Atkinson, *The Texas Indians*, 215–16; Schuertz,

Indians of the San Antonio Missions, 100–101; Paul H. Carlson, The Plains Indians (College Station, TX: Texas A&M University Press, 1998), 31, 58, 68, 70.

21  Ibid.

22  Bolton, Athanase de Mezieres, Vol. 2, 280; Himmel, Conquest, 29–30; Berlandier, Journey to Mexico, Vol. II, 311–13; Hasskarl, "Culture and History," 217–19; Donald E. Worcester, "The Spread of Spanish Horses in the Southwest," New Mexico Historical Review, No. 19 (July 1944): 220; Atkinson, The Texas Indians, 215–16; Schuertz, Indians of the San Antonio Missions, 94–95, 101; Carlson, Plains Indians, 31, 58, 68, 70.

23  Oral History Interviews, June 28–30, 2002, Don Patterson; Himmel, Conquest, 29–30; Deborah Lamont Newlin, The Tonkawa People: A Tribal History from Earliest Times to 1893 (Lubbock, TX: West Texas Museum Association, 1982), 21.

24  Hasdorff, Four Indian Tribes in Texas, 46–47; Berlandier, Journey to Mexico, Vol. II, 311–13; Hasskarl, "Culture and History," 217–19; Schilz, "People of the Cross-timbers," 42–43; Carlson, Plains Indians, 31, 71.

25  Schilz, "People of the Cross-timbers," 18–20, 29–31; Schuetz, Indians of the San Antonio Missions, 69–70; Jones, Notes on the Tonkawa Indians, 77–78; Oral History Interviews, June 28–30, 2002, Don Patterson; Hasskarl, "Culture and History," 219–20; Neighbors, "Tonkawa Scouts and Guides," 110–11.

26  Ibid.

27  Åke Hultkrantz and Esselte Studium, Religions of the American Indians. Originally published as: De Amerikanska Indianernes Religioner (Berkeley, CA: University of California Press, 1967), 138–39; Hasdorff, Four Indian Tribes in Texas, 69–70, 112–17, 167–68, 183; Schuetz, Indians of the San Antonio Missions, 89; Ernest Wallace and E. Adamson Hoebel, The Comanches: Lords of the South Plains (Norman, OK: University of Oklahoma Press, 1952), 70, 260; Hasskarl, "Culture and History," 219.

28  Berlandier, Journey to Mexico, Vol. II, 379; George W. Bonnell, Topographical Description of Texas: To Which is Added an Account of the Indian Tribes (Cruger and Bonnell, 1840, new material: James M. Day, 1964), 137–38; Schuetz, Indians of the San Antonio Missions, 34–35, 89; Béxar Archives, William C. Taylor, trans. Vol. 122, 44, February 20, 1784, Summary of the Events Appertaining to the Administration Concerning Warfare which occurred at the Presidios of San Antonio de Béxar and La Bahiá del Espritu Santo; 155, June 23, 1788, Rafael Martínez Pacheco to Juan de Ugarte y Loyola; 57, July 21, 1788, Pacheco to Ugarte; 156, 32, September 1, 1788, Pacheco to Ugarte; Russell B. Magnaghi, ed. and trans., "Texas as Seen by Governor Winthuysen, 1741–1744," Southwestern Historical Quarterly 88, No. 2 (October 1984): 169; Jones, Notes on the Tonkawa Indians, 77–78; John C. Ewers, "The Influence of Epidemics on the Indian Populations and Cultures of Texas," Plains Anthropologist 18, No. 60 (1973): 110–11; Hasdorff, Four Indian Tribes in Texas, 69–70.

29  Berlandier, Journey to Mexico, Vol. II, 379; Hasdorff, Four Indian Tribes in Texas, 59–60, 65; Smithwick, Evolution of a State, 179–81; Neighbors, "Tonkawa Scouts and Guides," 90–91; Stephen B. Oates, ed., Rip Ford's Texas (Austin, TX: University of Texas Press, 1963), 236; Mary Maverick Green, ed., Memoirs of Mary A. Maverick, Arranged by Mary A. Maverick and her son, George Madison Maverick (San Antonio, TX: Alamo Printing Company, 1921), 18–19; Ross Family Papers, "Texas Collection," Baylor University, Waco, Texas, 27 (hereafter cited as Ross Papers); Thomas W. Dunlay, Gray Wolves for the Blue Soldiers: Indian Scouts and Auxiliaries with the United States Army, 1850–90 (Lincoln, NE: University of Nebraska Press, 1982), 23; Atkinson, The Texas Indians, 211, 217–19; Wallace and Hoebel, The Comanches, 287, 299; Jacobs, "Robin Hood of the Tonkaways," 36–38; Martin L. Crimmins, "The Tonkawe Tribe," Frontier Times, No. 3 (June 1926): 43.

[30] Smithwick, *Evolution of a State*, 179–81; Ross Papers, 27; Hasskarl, "Culture and History," 219–21.

[31] Smithwick, *Evolution of a State*, 179–81; Hasskarl, "Culture and History," 219–22; Atkins, *The Texas Indians*, 222–23.

[32] John Holland Jenkins, *Recollections of Early Texas: The Memoirs of John Holland Jenkins* (Austin, TX: University of Texas Press, 1958), 77–78; Dorman H. Winfrey, *Indian Tribes of Texas* (Waco, TX: Texian Press, 1971), 151–52.

[33] Hasskarl, "Culture and History," 221; Newlin, *The Tonkawa People*, 23–24; Atkinson, *The Texas Indians*, 217–18.

[34] Herman J. Lehmann, J. Marvin Hunter, ed., *Nine Years Among the Indians, 1870–1879: The Story of the Captivity and Life of a Texan Among the Indians* (Albuquerque, NM: University of New Mexico Press, 1999), 153–56; Atkinson, *The Texas Indians*, 219–21; Winfrey, *Indian Tribes of Texas*, 150–55.

[35] Ibid.

## CHAPTER 3

[1] Kelly F. Himmel, *The Conquest of the Karankawas and the Tonkawas, 1821–1859* (College Station, TX: Texas A&M University Press, 1999), 5–7; William K. Jones, *Notes on the History and Material Culture of the Tonkawa Indians* (Washington, D.C.: Smithsonian Press, 1969), 65–67.

[2] Herbert E. Bolton, *Texas in the Middle Eighteenth Century: Studies in Spanish Colonial History and Administration* (Berkley, CA: University of California Press, 1915), 146; Himmel, *Conquest*, 28–29; Jones, *Notes on the Tonkawas*, 67.

[3] Jean Louis Berlandier, John C. Ewers, ed., Patricia Reading Leclercq, trans., *The Indians of Texas in 1830* (Washington, D.C.: Smithsonian Press, 1969), 146–47; Andres F. Sjoberg, "The Culture of the Tonkawa, A Texas Indian Tribe," *Texas Journal of Science* 5 (1953): 283; Robert A. Hasskarl, Jr., "The Culture and History of the Tonkawa Indians," *Plains Anthropologist* 7, No. 18 (November 1962): 21–22; James Curtis Hasdorff, *Four Indian Tribes in Texas, 1785–1858: A Reevaluation of Historical Sources* (Albuquerque, NM: University of New Mexico Press, 1971), 48–50, 56–58; Mardith Keithly Schuetz, *The Indians of the San Antonio Missions, 1718–1821* (Austin, TX: The University of Texas Press, 1980), 85; Marilyn McAdams Sibley, *Travelers in Texas, 1761–1860* (Austin, TX: University of Texas Press, 1967), 79–80; Deborah Lamont Newlin, *The Tonkawa People: A Tribal History from Earliest Times to 1893* (Lubbock, TX: West Texas Museum Association, 1982), 21–22.

[4] Hasdorff, *Four Indian Tribes in Texas*, 46–47; J. H. Kuykendall, "Reminiscences of Early Texans," *Quarterly of the Texas State Historical Association* 6 (January 1903): 252–53; Himmel, *Conquest*, 34–35, 39–41.

[5] Hasdorff, *Four Indian Tribes in Texas*, 49–50; Virginia H. Taylor, "Calendar of the Letters of Antonio Martinez, Last Spanish Governor of Texas, 1817–1822," *Southwestern Historical Quarterly* 61, No. 2 (October 1957): 293; Jones, *Notes on the Tonkawas*, 67.

[6] Jones, *Notes on the Tonkawas*, 67; Himmel, *Conquest*, 34–35, 39–41.

[7] Hasdorff, *Four Indian Tribes in Texas*, 50–51; Gregg Cantrell, *Stephen F. Austin: Emprassario of Texas* (New Haven, CT: Yale University Press, 1999), 136–40; Hasskarl, "Culture and History," 221–22.

[8] Kuykendall, "Reminiscences of Early Texans," 252–53; Himmel, *Conquest*, 40–43, 58; Cantrell, *Stephen F. Austin*, 136–40; Hasskarl, "Culture and History," 221–22.

[9] Himmel, *Conquest*, 44–45; J. H. Kuykendall, "Reminiscences of Early Texans," *Quarterly of the Texas State Historical Association* 7 (July 1903): 29–30; Cantrell, *Stephen F. Austin*, 136–40;

Hasskarl, "Culture and History," 222; Dorman H. Winfrey et al., *Indian Tribes of Texas* (Waco, TX: Texian Press, 1971), 154–58.

10  Kuykendall, "Reminiscences of Early Texans," 7: 29–30; Cantrell, *Stephen F. Austin*, 136–40; Hasdorff, *Four Indian Tribes in Texas*, 51–52; Winfrey, *Indian Tribes of Texas*, 154–57.

11  Kuykendall, "Reminiscences of Early Texans," 7: 323–28; Himmel, *Conquest*, 55–56.

12  Himmel, *Conquest*, 55–56; Hasdorff, *Four Indian Tribes in Texas*, 52–53.

13  Himmel, *Conquest*, 55–57; Hasdorff, *Four Indian Tribes in Texas*, 55–56.

14  Kuykendall, "Reminiscences of Early Texans," 7: 29–30; George W. Bonnell, *Topographical Description of Texas: To Which is Added an Account of the Indian Tribes* (Cruger and Bonnell, 1840, New Material: James M. Day, 1964), 137–38; Cantrell, *Stephen F. Austin*, 136–40; Newlin, *The Tonkawa People*, 24–25; Hasskarl, "Culture and History," 222.

15  Hasdorff, *Four Indian Tribes in Texas*, 53–54; Himmel, *Conquest*, 57–58; Hasskarl, "Culture and History," 222; Newlin, *The Tonkawa People*, 24–25.

16  Jean Louis Berlandier, C. H. Muller and Katherine K. Muller, eds., Sheila M. Ohlendorf, Josette M. Bigelow, and Mary M. Standifer, trans., *Journey to Mexico, During the Years 1826–1834* Vol. II (Austin, TX: Texas State Historical Association and University of Texas Press, 1980), 306, 310–13, 383.

17  Edward A. Lukes, "DeWitt Colony of Texas," (PhD diss., Loyolla University, 1971), 152–54, 156–59; Jones, *Notes on the Tonkawas*, 67.

18  De Witt Colony Archives, Center for American History, University of Texas at Austin, no date, Green De Witt to the Commandant of Arms at La Bahiá; De Witt Archives, General Headquarters, Matamoros: Jan. 4, 1838, Vicente Filisola to Illustrious Ayuntamiento of Reynosa; Lukes, "De Witt Colony of Texas," 152–54, 156–59.

19  Ibid.

20  De Witt Colony Archives, April 23, 1829, De Witt to Ramón Musquiz; Himmel, *Conquest*, 58–61; Newlin, *The Tonkawa People*, 22.

21  Noah Smithwick, *Evolution of a State, or Recollections of Old Texas Days* (H. P. N. Gammel, 1900; rpt., Austin, TX: University of Texas Press, 1983), 179–81; J. W. Wilbarger, *Indian Depredations in Texas*, 2nd ed. (Austin, TX: Hutchings Printing House, 1890), 239–41; Kenneth F. Neighbors, "Tonkawa Scouts and Guides," *West Texas Historical Association Year Book* 49 (1973): 91.

22  Ibid.

23  Hasdorff, *Four Indian Tribes in Texas*, 54–55.

24  Bonnell, *Topographical Description of Texas*, 137–38; John Henry Brown, *Indian Wars and Pioneers of Texas* (Austin, TX: L. E. Daniell, 1880, New Material: Silas Emmett Lucas, Jr., 1978), 25–26; Newlin, *The Tonkawa People*, 25.

25  Kuykendall, "Reminiscences of Early Texans," 6: 252–53; Newlin, *The Tonkawa People*, 24–26.

**CHAPTER 4**

1  Dorman H. Winfrey, and James M. Day, eds., *The Indian Papers of Texas and the Southwest 1825–1916*, 5 vols. (Austin, TX: Texas State Historical Association, 1995), I: 28–29, 30, 45–48, hereafter cited as *Indian Papers*; Deborah Lamont Newlin, *The Tonkawa People: A Tribal History from Earliest Times to 1893* (Lubbock, TX: West Texas Museum Association, 1982), 25–28.

2  Winfrey and Day, *Indian Papers*, I: 46–49; II: 49; William K. Jones, "Notes on the History and Material Culture of the Tonkawa Indians," *Smithsonian Contributions to Anthropology* II, No. 5 (1969): 68; Newlin, *The Tonkawa People*, 27.

3   Ibid.
4   Noah Smithwick, *Evolution of a State, or Recollections of Old Texas Days* (H. P. N. Gammel,
    1900, rpt., Austin, TX: University of Texas Press, 1983), 182–83; Carl H. Hoerig, "The
    Relationship Between German Immigrants and the Native Peoples in Western Texas,"
    *Southwestern Historical Quarterly* 97, No. 3 (January 1994): 423–51; Francis R. Lubbock, "An
    Account of the Tonkawa Indians as the Writer Remembers Them, 1884," November 12,
    1884, Howard Collection, Dallas Historical Society, Dallas, Texas, 2.
5   James Curtis Hasdorff, *Four Indian Tribes in Texas, 1785–1858: A Reevaluation of Historical Sources*
    (Albuquerque, NM: University of New Mexico Press, 1971), 66–67.
6   Ibid., 65–66.
7   Smithwick, *Evolution of a State*, 182–83.
8   Mary Ann Adams Maverick, arranged by Mary A. Maverick and her son, Geo[rge]
    Madison Maverick; Rena Maverick Green, ed., *Memoirs of Mary A. Maverick* (San Antonio,
    TX: Alamo Printing Company, 1921), 18–19; Hasdorff, *Four Indian Tribes in Texas*, 61–62;
    Newlin, *The Tonkawa People*, 27–28.
9   Ibid.
10  Newlin, *The Tonkawa People*, 28–29; Winfrey and Day, *Indian Papers*, II: 4–6, 49, 164.
11  John Henry Brown, *Indian Wars and Pioneers of Texas* (Austin, TX: L. E. Daniell, 1880, new
    material, Silas Emmett Lucas, Jr., 1978), 67–70; Winfrey and Day, *Indian Papers*, II: 4–6,
    49, 164; Kenneth F. Neighbors, "Tonkawa Scouts and Guides," *West Texas Historical
    Association Year Book*, 49 (1973): 91–92; Hasdorff, *Four Indian Tribes in Texas*, 70.
12  Brown, *Indian Wars and Pioneers of Texas*, 74–75; Winfrey and Day, *Indian Papers*, II: 49, 164,
    218; Neighbors, "Tonkawa Scouts and Guides," 91–92.
13  Brown, *Indian Wars and Pioneers of Texas*, 74–75.
14  Ibid., 73–74; J. W. Wilbarger, *Indian Depredations in Texas*, 2nd ed. (Austin, TX: Hutchings
    Printing House, 1890), 288–89, 610; Robert A. Hasskarl, Jr., "The Culture and History
    of the Tonkawa Indians," *Plains Anthropologist* 7, No. 18 (November 1962): 217–22.
15  Ibid.
16  Wilbarger, *Indian Depredations in Texas*, 24–33; Brown, *Indian Wars and Pioneers of Texas*, 106;
    Neighbors, "Tonkawa Scouts and Guides," 92–93.
17  Dorman H. Winfrey, et al., *Indian Tribes of Texas* (Waco, TX: Texian Press, 1971), 151–60.
18  Brown, *Indian Wars and Pioneers of Texas*, 106.
19  Winfrey and Day, *Indian Papers*, II: 150–51, 167–68, 211–12, 254, 261; Brown, *Indian Wars
    and Pioneers of Texas*, 497–98; Newlin, *The Tonkawa People*, 32–33.
20  Winfrey and Day, *Indian Papers*, I: 26–27; Newlin, *The Tonkawa People*, 32–33.
21  Hoerig, "The Relationship Between German Immigrants and the Native Peoples,"
    423–51.
22  Ibid.; Stanley S. McGowen, *Horse Sweat and Powder Smoke: The First Texas Cavalry in the Civil War*
    (College Station, TX: Texas A&M University Press, 1999), 66, 169; Stanley S. McGowen,
    "Battle or Massacre?: The Incident on the Nueces, August 10, 1862," *Southwestern Historical
    Quarterly* 104, No. 1 (July 2000): 66–67.
23  Hoerig, "The Relationship Between German Immigrants and the Native Peoples,"
    423–51.
24  Hasdorff, *Four Indian Tribes in Texas*, 68–69; Oral History Interviews, June 28–30, 2002,
    Don Patterson, et al.
25  Ibid.
26  Winfrey and Day, *Indian Papers*, II: 4, 150–51, 218; Hasskarl, "Culture and History," 222;
    Hasdorff, *Four Indian Tribes in Texas*, 69.

27  Ross Family Papers, "Texas Collection," Baylor University, Waco, 37; Winfrey and Day, *Indian Papers*, II: 65–66.

28  Winfrey and Day, *Indian Papers*, II: 4–6; Daniel J. Gelo, "'Comanche Land and Ever Has Been': A Native Geography of the Nineteenth–Century Comancheria," *Southwestern Historical Quarterly* 103, No. 3 (January 2000): 274.

29  Winfrey and Day, *Indian Papers*, II: 24, 31, 34, 38–41.

30  Ibid., II: 167–68.

31  Ibid., II: 197–98; Hasdorff, *Four Indian Tribes in Texas*, 68–69.

32  Winfrey and Day, *Indian Papers*, II: 202–206.

33  Ibid, II: 198, 205, 206; Hasskarl, "Culture and History," 223.

34  Hasskarl, "Culture and History," 222–23; Newlin, *The Tonkawa People*, 32–36.

35  Ibid.

36  Winfrey and Day, *Indian Papers*, III: 14; Newlin, *The Tonkawa People*, 35–37.

37  Newlin, *The Tonkawa People*, 36–37.

## CHAPTER 5

1  Dorman H. Winfrey and James M. Day, eds., *The Indian Papers of Texas and the Southwest 1825–1916*, 5 vols. (Austin, TX: Texas State Historical Association, 1995), III: 13–14, 53; William K. Jones, "Notes on the History and Material Culture of the Tonkawa Indians," *Smithsonian Contributions to Anthropology* II, No. 5 (1969): 70–71; Robert A. Hasskarl, Jr., "The Culture and History of the Tonkawa Indians," *Plains Anthropologist* 7, No. 18 (November 1962): 224; William A. McClintock, "Journal of a trip through Texas and northern Mexico in 1846–1847," *Southwestern Historical Quarterly* 34, No. 1 (July 1930): 28, 31; Deborah Lamont Newlin, *The Tonkawa People: A Tribal History from Earliest Times to 1893* (Lubbock, TX: West Texas Museum Association, 1982), 41–42.

2  Jones, "Notes on the Tonkawa Indians," 71; Francis R. Lubbock, "An Account of the Tonkawa Indians as the Writer Remembers Them, 1884," November 12, 1884, Howard Collection, Dallas Historical Society, Dallas, Texas, 4–5.

3  Winfrey and Day, *Indian Papers*, III: 97; Jones, "Notes on the Tonkawa Indians," 70; McClintock, "A Trip Through Texas," 31–32; Newlin, *The Tonkawa People*, 43–45.

4  Stephen B. Oates, ed., *John Salmon Ford: Rip Ford's Texas* (Austin, TX: University of Texas Press, 1963), 236; Thomas W. Dunlay, "Friends and Allies: The Tonkawa Indians and the Anglo–Americans, 1823–1884," *Great Plains Quarterly* 1, No. 3 (Summer 1981): 149–50; Kenneth F. Neighbors, "Tonkawa Scouts and Guides," *West Texas Historical Association Year Book* 49 (1973): 91.

5  Newlin, *The Tonkawa People*, 42–43.

6  Dorman H. Winfrey, et al., *Indian Tribes of Texas* (Waco, TX: Texian Press, 1971), 151–68; Robert S. Reading, *Arrows Over Texas* (San Antonio: The Naylor Company, 1960), 40; Newlin, *The Tonkawa People*, 44–45, 51–52.

7  Newlin, *The Tonkawa People*, 44–47; Jones, "Notes on the Tonkawa Indians," 70; Ross Family Papers, "Texas Collection," Baylor University, Waco, Texas, 19, hereafter cited as Ross Papers.

8  Lena Clara Koch, "The Federal Indian Policy in Texas, 1845–1860," *Southwestern Historical Quarterly* 28 (January, April, 1925): 284; Newlin, *The Tonkawa People*, 42–48; Jones, "Notes on the Tonkawa Indians," 70; Ross Papers, 19.

9  Newlin, *The Tonkawa People*, 41–47; James Curtis Hasdorff, *Four Indian Tribes in Texas, 1785–1858: A Reevaluation of Historical Sources* (Albuquerque, NM: University of New Mexico

Press, 1971), 68–70; David Paul Smith, *Frontier Defense in the Civil War: Texas Rangers and Rebels* (College Station, TX: Texas A&M University Press, 1992), 7; Jones, "Notes on the Tonkawa Indians," 70; Hasskarl, "Culture and History," 224.

10  Winfrey and Day, *Indian Papers*, III: 184–85; Hasskarl, "Culture and History," 224; Smith, *Frontier Defense*, 7; Jones, "Notes on the Tonkawa Indians," 70; Berta Hart Nance, "D. A. Nance and the Tonkawa Indians," *West Texas Historical Association Year Book*, 28 (1952): 89; Newlin, *The Tonkawa People*, 48–51, 54–55; Harold B. Simpson, *Cry Comanche: The 2nd U.S. Cavalry in Texas, 1855–1861* (Hillsboro, TX: Hill College Press, 1988), 75–76.

11  Nance, "D. A. Nance and the Tonkawa Indians," 89, 95; Newlin, *The Tonkawa People*, 51; Hasskarl, "Culture and History," 224.

12  Simpson, *Cry Comanche*, 76–77; James K. Greer, ed., *A Texas Ranger and Frontiersman: The Days of Buck Barry in Texas, 1845–1906* (Dallas, TX: Southwest Press, 1932), 103–108; Ty Cashion, *A Texas Frontier: The Clear Fork Country and Fort Griffin, 1849–1887* (Norman, OK: University of Oklahoma Press, 1996), 26.

13  John Henry Brown, *Indian Wars and Pioneers of Texas* (Austin, TX: L. E. Daniell, 1880, new material, Silas Emmett Lucas, Jr., 1978), 121; Greer, *A Texas Ranger and Frontiersman*, 96–98, 100–101, 111–13; George Klos, "'Our People Could Not Distinguish one Tribe from Another,' The 1859 Expulsion of the Reserve Indians from Texas," *Southwestern Historical Quarterly* 97, No. 4 (April 1994): 603–607; Lubbock, "An Account of the Tonkawa Indians," 1–2.

14  Ibid.

15  Rupert N. Richardson, ed., "Documents Relating to West Texas and Its Indian Tribes," *West Texas Historical Association Year Book* (June 1925): 75; Newlin, *The Tonkawa People*, 55–58.

16  Greer, *A Texas Ranger and Frontiersman*, 100, 106–109; John M. Elkins, written by Frank W. McCarty, *Indian Fighting on the Texas Frontier* (Amarillo, TX: Russell & Cockrell, 1929), 78; Newlin, *The Tonkawa People*, 57–59.

17  Ibid.

18  George D. Harmon, "The U.S. Indian Policy in Texas, 1845–1860," *Mississippi Valley Historical Review* 17 (December, 1930): 397; Robert S. Neighbors to Charles E. Mix, January 17, 1858, Robert S. Neighbors to Editor, *Texas Sentinel*, January 21, 1858, Robert S. Neighbors Papers, Center for American History, University of Texas, Austin, hereafter cited as Neighbors Papers.

19  Thomas T. Hawkins to Charles E. Mix, October 30, 1858, Neighbors Papers; Newlin, *The Tonkawa People*, 60–61.

20  J. Evetts Haley, *Charles Goodnight: Cowman and Plainsman* (Norman, OK: University of Oklahoma Press, 1936), 93; Sybil J. O'Rear, *Charles Goodnight, Pioneer Cowman* (Austin, TX: Eakin Press, 1990), 12.

21  Ibid.

22  Ross Papers, 52–56; *Austin State Gazette*, January 30, 1858, Neighbors Papers; "John S. Ford Memoirs," manuscript, Center for American History, University of Texas, Austin, Texas, 653; J. W. Wilbarger, *Indian Depredations in Texas*, 2nd ed. (Austin, TX: Hutchings Printing House, 1890), 320–26; Greer, *A Texas Ranger and Frontiersman*, 107–108; A. R. Johnson, "The Battle of Antelope Hills," *Frontier Times*, No. 1 (February 1924): 12–14, [taken from book called *Partisan Rangers* by Gen. A. R. Johnson]; Thomas W. Dunlay, *Grey Wolves for the Blue Soldiers: Indian Scouts and Auxiliaries with the United States Army, 1860–90* (Lincoln, NE: University of Nebraska Press, 1982), 21; Hasdorff, *Four Indian Tribes in Texas*, 70–71.

23  Wilbarger, *Indian Depredations*, 321–22; Johnson, "The Battle of Antelope Hills," 12–14.

24  Wilbarger, *Indian Depredations*, 321–26.

25 Ibid.; Johnson, "The Battle of Antelope Hills," 12–14; Greer, *A Texas Ranger and Frontiersman*, 158; Reading, *Arrows over Texas*, 31.

26 Ibid.

27 Wilbarger, *Indian Depredations*, 324–26; Ben C. Stuart, "The Battle of Antelope Hills," *Frontier Times*, No. 3 (August 1926): 10–12.

28 Wilbarger, *Indian Depredations*, 320–26; Stuart, "The Battle of Antelope Hills," 10–12.

29 Wilbarger, *Indian Depredations*, 326; Smith, *Frontier Defense in the Civil War*, 13–14; Johnson, "The Battle of Antelope Hills," 12–14.

30 Ross Papers, 37; Brown, *Indian Wars and Pioneers of Texas*, 41–45, 112; Wilbur S. Nye, "The Battle of Wichita Village," *The Chronicles of Oklahoma* XV (June 1937): 226–27; Simpson, *Cry Comanche*, 106–109, 112–13, 118, 120, 128; Schilz, "People of the Cross-timbers," 172; Hasskarl, "Culture and History," 224; Dunlay, *Wolves for the Blue Soldiers*, 22.

31 Ibid.

32 Ibid.

33 Neighbors, "Tonkawa Scouts and Guides," 93; Schilz, "People of the Cross-timbers," 172; Dunlay, *Wolves for the Blue Soldiers*, 22.

34 Greer, *A Texas Ranger and Frontiersman*, 110; Klos, "'Our People Could Not Distinguish one Tribe,'" 609–10.

35 Ibid.

36 Neighbors to Mix, November 13, 1858, Neighbors Papers; Matthew Leeper to Geo[rge] H. Thomas, Major at Ft. Belknap, November 19, 1858, Neighbors Papers.

37 Hardin R. Runnels to Allison Nelson and Citizens of the Frontier, June 6, 1859, Neighbors Papers; John Henry Brown Papers, Center for American History, University of Texas, Austin, Texas, hereafter cited as Brown Papers; Greer, *A Texas Ranger and Frontiersman*, 116–17; Klos, "'Our People Could Not Distinguish one Tribe,'" 611, 617–18; Harmon, "The U.S. Indian Policy in Texas," 401; Koch, *Federal Indian Policy*, 116–18.

38 Greer, *A Texas Ranger and Frontiersman*, 113–16; Elkins, *Indian Fighting*, 27–28; Schilz, "People of the Cross-timbers," 173.

39 Ibid.

40 Census Roll, August 1, 1859, Neighbors Papers; Elias Rector to A. B. Greenwood, August 15, 1859, Neighbors Papers; Klos, "'Our People Could Not Distinguish one Tribe,'" 611, 617; Hasdorff, *Four Indian Tribes in Texas*, 71; Hasskarl, "Culture and History," 224–26; Newlin, *The Tonkawa People*, 64–67, 72–74; Ron Tyler, ed., *The New Handbook of Texas*, 6 vols. (Austin, TX: The Texas State Historical Association, 1996), 4: 971–72; Schilz, "People of the Cross-timbers," 173–74.

41 Greer, *A Texas Ranger and Frontiersman*, 118–19; Newlin, *The Tonkawa People*, 72–73.

## CHAPTER 6

1 Muriel H. Wright, "A History of Fort Cobb," *Chronicles of Oklahoma* 34 (Spring, 1956): 55–57; Robert A. Hasskarl, Jr., "The Culture and History of the Tonkawa Indians," *Plains Anthropologist* 7, No. 18 (November 1962): 225; Deborah Lamont Newlin, *The Tonkawa People: A Tribal History from Earliest Times to 1893* (Lubbock, TX: West Texas Museum Association, 1982), 70–72.

2 Kenneth F. Neighbors, "Indian Exodus out of Texas," *West Texas Historical Association Year Book*, 36 (October 1960): 95; Newlin, *The Tonkawa People*, 71–72, 74.

3 Marvin J. Hunter, "Frank Gholson's Ride," *Frontier Times*, No. 6 (February 1929): 178; Dorman H. Winfrey, et al., *Indian Tribes of Texas* (Waco, TX: Texian Press, 1971), 151–68;

James Curtis Hasdorff, *Four Indian Tribes in Texas, 1785–1858: A Reevaluation of Historical Sources* (Albuquerque, NM: University of New Mexico Press, 1971), 71; Kenneth F. Neighbors, "Tonkawa Scouts and Guides," *West Texas Historical Association Year Book*, 49 (1973): 93; David Paul Smith, *Frontier Defense in the Civil War: Texas Rangers and Rebels* (College Station, TX: Texas A&M University Press, 1992), 22–23.

4   John Henry Brown, *Indian Wars and Pioneers of Texas* (Austin, TX: L. E. Daniell, 1880, new material, Silas Emmett Lucas, Jr., 1978), 41–45; Thomas F. Schilz, "People of the Cross-timbers: A History of the Tonkawa Indians" (PhD diss., Texas Christian University, 1983), 174.

5   Ibid.

6   Arrell M. Gibson, ed., *America's Exiles: Indian Colonization in Oklahoma* (Oklahoma City, OK: Oklahoma Historical Society, 1976), 133; LeRoy Henry Fischer, *The Civil War Era in Indian Territory* (Los Angeles, CA: L. L. Morrison, 1974), 79; Muriel H. Wright, *A Guide to the Indian Tribes of Oklahoma* (Norman, OK: University of Oklahoma Press, 1951), 25; Hasskarl, "Culture and History," 225.

7   Arrell M. Gibson, *The American Indian Prehistory to the Present* (Lexington, MS: D. C. Heath Co., 1979), 367–68; Kinneth McNeil, "Confederate Treaties with the Tribes of Indian Territory," *Chronicles of Oklahoma*, 42 (Winter 1964–65): 419–20; Newlin, *The Tonkawa People*, 76–77.

8   Stanley S. McGowen, *Horse Sweat and Powder Smoke: The 1st Texas Cavalry in the Civil War* (College Station, TX: Texas A&M University Press, 1999), 28–31; Smith, *Frontier Defense in the Civil War*, 33–34, 120.

9   James K. Greer, ed., *A Texas Ranger and Frontiersman: The Days of Buck Barry in Texas, 1845–1906* (Dallas, TX: Southwest Press, 1932), 129; McGowen, *Horse Sweat and Powder Smoke*, 30–33; Annie Heloise Abel, *The American Indian as Participant in the Civil War* (Cleveland, OH: The Arthur H. Clark Company, 1919), 181–82; J. Evetts Haley, *Charles Goodnight: Cowman and Plainsman* (Norman, OK: University of Oklahoma Press, 1949), 93; Smith, *Frontier Defense in the Civil War*, 34.

10  William K. Jones, *Notes on the History and Material Culture of the Tonkawa Indians* (Washington, D.C.: Smithsonian Press, 1969), 71–72; Hasskarl Jr., "Culture and History," 225.

11  Able, *The American Indian as Participant in the Civil War*, 181–83; Hasdorff, *Four Indian Tribes in Texas*, 69–70; Newlin, *The Tonkawa People*, 77–78; Schilz, "People of the Cross-timbers," 175.

12  McNeil, "Confederate Treaties," 419; Newlin, *The Tonkawa People*, 77–79.

13  Jones, *Notes on the Tonkawa Indians*, 71; Schilz, "People of the Cross-timbers," 175–76.

14  Hasdorff, *Four Indian Tribes in Texas*, 70–71; Fischer, *The Civil War Era in Indian Territory*, 80; Jones, *Notes on the Tonkawas*, 71–72; Joseph B. Thoburn, "Horace P. Jones, Scout and Interpreter," *Chronicles of Oklahoma*, 2 (December 1924): 383; Hasskarl, "Culture and History," 225–26; Haley, *Charles Goodnight*, 93.

15  Thomas W. Dunlay, "Friends and Allies: The Tonkawa Indians and the Anglo-Americans, 1823–1884," *Great Plains Quarterly* 1, No. 3 (Summer 1981): 147–52; Wright, "A History of Fort Cobb," 58–61; Jones, *Notes on the Tonkawa Indians*, 71; Hasdorff, *Four Indian Tribes in Texas*, 69–71, 73, 183–84.

16  Jones, *Notes on the Tonkawa Indians*, 71–72; Ross Family Papers, "Texas Collection," Baylor University, Waco, Texas, hereafter cited as Ross Papers; Winfrey, *Indian Tribes of Texas*, 161–68.

17  J. W. Wilbarger, *Indian Depredations in Texas*, 2nd ed. (Austin, TX: Hutchings Printing House, 1890), 326; Jones, *Notes on the Tonkawa Indians*, 71–72.

18   Richard H. Pratt, Robert M. Utley, ed., *Battlefield and Classroom: Four Decades with the American Indians, 1867–1904* (New Haven, CT: Yale University Press, 1964), 55; Haley, *Charles Goodnight*, 95; Newlin, *The Tonkawa People*, 79–80; Jones, *Notes on the Tonkawa Indians*, 72; Greer, *A Texas Ranger and Frontiersman*, 157, 159–62, 166–68, 173–79; Smith, *Frontier Defense in the Civil War*, 94–95, 119–24; Abel, *The American Indian as Participant in the Civil War*, 181–86; Hasskarl, *Culture and History*, 225–26.

19   Greer, *A Texas Ranger and Frontiersman*, 157, 159–62, 166–68, 173–79; Dunlay, "Friends and Allies," 150–52; Smith, *Frontier Defense in the Civil War*, 94–95, 119–24; Thomas Robert Havins, *Camp Colorado, A Decade of Frontier Defense* (Brownwood, TX: Brown Press, 1964), 117; Hasskarl, *Culture and History*, 225–26.

20   Post Records, Fort Griffin, Texas, Box 4, Record Group 393, National Archives and Records Administration, Washington, D.C., hereafter cited as Post Records; Dorman H. Winfrey and James M. Day, eds., *The Indian Papers of Texas and the Southwest 1825–1916*, V vols. (Austin, TX: Texas State Historical Association, 1995), 4:78–79; Smith, *Frontier Defense in the Civil War*, 94–95, 119–24; Greer, *A Texas Ranger and Frontiersman*, 157, 159–62, 164, 166–68; Jones, *Notes on the Tonkawa Indians*, 72; Hasskarl, *Culture and History*, 225–26.

21   Ibid.

22   Greer, *A Texas Ranger and Frontiersman*, 188–95; Smith, *Frontier Defense in the Civil War*, 151–53.

23   Greer, *A Texas Ranger and Frontiersman*, 188–95; Smith, *Frontier Defense in the Civil War*, 153–55; Robert. S. Reading, *Arrows Over Texas* (San Antonio, TX: The Naylor Company, 1960), 84–85.

24   Ibid.

25   Post Records; Neighbors, "Tonkawa Scouts and Guides," 96; Ty Cashion, *A Texas Frontier: The Clear Fork Country and Fort Griffin, 1849–1887* (Norman, OK: University of Oklahoma Press, 1996), 104–105, 199; Jones, *Notes on the Tonkawa Indians*, 72; Hasskarl, *Culture and History*, 225–26; Schilz, "People of the Cross-timbers," 175–76, 183–84.

26   T. H. Stribling and P. Smythe to the President, United States, October 14, 1865, IV:87–88, J. W. Throckmorton to U.S. Indian Commissioner, September 20, 1866, IV:110–12, Winfrey and Day, *Indian Papers*; George Rainey, *The Cherokee Strip* (Guthrie, OK: Co-operative Publishing Co., 1933), 161; Edward Everett Dale, "The Cherokee Strip Live Stock Association," *Chronicles of Oklahoma*, 5 (March 1927): 59; Robert C. Carriker, *Fort Supply: Indian Territory, Frontier Outpost on the Plains* (Norman, OK: University of Oklahoma Press. 1978), 182.

27   Throckmorton to Cooley, November 3, 1866, Winfrey and Day, *Indian Papers* IV: 123; Alan Lee Hamilton, *Sentinel of the Southern Plains: Fort Richardson and the Northwest Texas Frontier, 1866–1878* (Fort Worth, TX: Texas Christian University Press, 1988), 20–21; Newlin, *The Tonkawa People*, 80–82; Jones, "Culture and History," 72; Ron Tylor, ed., *The New Handbook of Texas*, VI vols. (Austin, TX: The Texas State Historical Association, 1996), 6:485–86, 525–26.

28   Wilbarger, *Indian Depredations*, 127–29.

29   Haley, *Charles Goodnight*, 93; Schilz, "People of the Cross-timbers," 183.

30   Haley, *Charles Goodnight*, 93; Schilz, "People of the Cross-timbers," 183–84.

31   John M. Elkins, written by Frank W. McCarty, *Indian Fighting on the Texas Frontier* (Amarillo, TX: Russell & Cockrell, 1929), 46–47.

32   W. J. Maltby, *Captain Jeff, or Frontier Life in Texas with the Texas Rangers* (Colorado City, TX: Whipkey Printing Co., 1906), 48–49; William C. Pool, ed., "Westward I Go Free: The Memoirs of William E. Cureton, Texas Frontiersman," *Southwestern Historical Quarterly* 81, No. 2 (October 1977): 176; Greer, *A Texas Ranger and Frontiersman*, 96; Reading, *Arrows Over Texas*, 66, 72.

[33] Carl Coke Rister, Fort Griffin on the Texas Frontier (Norman, OK: University of Oklahoma Press, 1956), 59–77; Jones, Notes on the Tonkawa Indians, 72; Cashion, A Texas Frontier, 118, 144, 256.


## CHAPTER 7

[1] Post Reports and Tonkawa Scout Muster Rolls, Fort Griffin, Texas, 1869–1878, Record Group 393, Microfilm #354637, Roll 1, National Archives and Records Administration, Washington, D.C., hereafter cited as URMR; Headquarters, Fifth Military District, Austin, Texas, to Commander Fort Griffin, Texas, February 8, 1869, Special Orders [SO], 110, Fort Griffin, Texas, June 26, 1872: Paymaster Report, Tonkawa Scouts, December 1872: Muster Roll, Tonkawa Scouts, Fort Chadbourne, Texas, May 22, 1873: HQ Fort Griffin to AAG Dept. of Texas, August 6, 1873, Post Records, Fort Griffin, Texas, Box 4, Record Group 393, National Archives and Records Administration, Washington, D.C., hereafter cited as Post Records; R. G. Carter, On the Border with Mackenzie, or Winning West Texas from the Comanches (Manatuck, NY: J. M. Carroll and Co., 1935), 68–69; Thomas W. Dunlay, "Friends and Allies: The Tonkawa Indians and the Anglo-Americans, 1823–1884," Great Plains Quarterly 1, No. 3 (Summer 1981): 151–53; William K. Jones, "Notes on the History and Material Culture of the Tonkawa Indians," Smithsonian Contributions to Anthropology II, No. 5 (1969): 72; Robert A. Hasskarl, Jr., "The Culture and History of the Tonkawa Indians," Plains Anthropologist 7, No. 18 (November 1962): 226.
[2] Ibid.
[3] J. Evetts Haley, Charles Goodnight: Cowman and Plainsman (Norman, OK: University of Oklahoma Press, 1949), 95; Kenneth F. Neighbors, "Tonkawa Scouts and Guides," West Texas Historical Association Year Book, 49 (1973): 97; Thomas F. Schilz, "People of the Cross-timbers: A History of the Tonkawa Indians," (PhD diss., Texas Christian University, 1983), 186.
[4] Richard H. Pratt and Robert M. Utley, eds., Battlefield and Classroom: Four Decades with the American Indians, 1867–1904 (New Haven, CT: Yale University Press, 1964), 55–58; J. J. Bragg, "Days of Peril on the Clear Fork," Frontier Times, No. 3 (April 1926): 44–46; Haley, Charles Goodnight, 40; John C. Jacobs, "Robin Hood of the Tonkaways," Frontier Times, No. 3 (November 1925): 36–38; Neighbors, "Tonkawa Scouts and Guides," 96–99; Schilz, "People of the Cross-timbers," 177, 183; Thomas W. Dunlay, Wolves for the Blue Soldiers: Indian Scouts and Auxiliaries with the United States Army, 1860–90 (Lincoln, NE: University of Nebraska Press, 1982), 94; Charles M. Robinson, III, Bad Hand: A Biography of General Ranald S. Mackenzie (Austin, TX: State House Press, 1993), 147–48.
[5] Jones, Notes on the Tonkawa Indians, 72–73.
[6] Ty Cashion, A Texas Frontier: The Clear Fork Country and Fort Griffin, 1849–1887 (Norman, OK: University of Oklahoma Press, 1996), 101–104.
[7] John M. Elkins, written by Frank W. McCarty, Indian Fighting on the Texas Frontier (Amarillo, TX: Russell & Cockrell, 1929), 46; Cashion, A Texas Frontier, 105–106.
[8] John Warren Hunter, "The Fight at Ledbetter's Salt Works," Frontier Times, No. 4 (February 1927): 17–18; Cashion, A Texas Frontier, 106.
[9] Hunter, "The Fight at Ledbetter's Salt Works," 17–18; Martin L. Crimmins, "The Tonkawe Tribe," Frontier Times, No. 3 (June 1926): 43; Cashion, A Texas Frontier, 106.
[10] Leckie, The Buffalo Soldiers, 89–91.
[11] Ibid.
[12] Schilz, "People of the Cross-timbers," 188.

[13]  Alan Lee Hamilton, *Sentinel of the Southern Plains: Fort Richardson and the Northwest Texas Frontier,* *1866–1878* (Fort Worth, TX: Texas Christian University Press, 1988), 54–60; Ron Tyler, ed., *The New Handbook of Texas,* 6 vols. (Austin, TX: The Texas State Historical Association, 1996), 5:899–900.

[14]  Ibid.

[15]  Hamilton, *Sentinel of the Southern Plains,* 60.

[16]  Ibid, 60.

[17]  Ernest Wallace, ed., *Ranald S. Mackenzie's Official Correspondence Relating to Texas, 1871–1873* (Lubbock, TX: West Texas Museum Association, 1967), William T. Sherman to W. H. Wood, May 19, 1871, 24–25, hereafter cited as *Official Correspondence, 1871–1873*; Carter, *On the Border,* 89–90; Tyler, ed., *The New Handbook of Texas,* 5:898–900.

[18]  Carter, *On the Border,* 90, 93, Hamilton, *Sentinel of the Southern Plains,* 89–91.

[19]  Carter, *On the Border,* 90–91; Hamilton, *Sentinel of the Southern Plains,* 89–91.

[20]  Carter, *On the Border,* 91–95, 98–105; Schilz, "People of the Cross-timbers," 190; Tyler, *The New Handbook of Texas,* 5:898–899.

[21]  Hamilton, *Sentinel of the Southern Plains,* 140; Carter, *On the Border,* 91–95, 98–105, 114–23; Robinson, *Bad Hand,* 255; Tyler, ed., *The New Handbook of Texas,* 3:1089–1090.

[22]  Carter, *On the Border,* 105, 114–123; Hamilton, *Sentinel of the Southern Plains,* 83, 88, 96–98; Michael D. Pierce, *The Most Promising Young Officer: A Life of Ranald Slidell Mackenzie* (Norman, OK: University of Oklahoma Press, 1993), 68; Tyler, ed-in-chief, *The New Handbook of Texas,* 3: 1089–1090.

[23]  Ibid.

[24]  Carter, *On the Border,* 123–29.

[25]  Ibid, 128–30; Hamilton, *Sentinel of the Southern Plains,* 103–105.

[26]  Carter, *On the Border,* 127–31.

[27]  Ibid, 131–36.

[28]  Ibid, 135–36; Hamilton, *Sentinel of the Southern Plains,* 105–106.

[29]  Carter, *On the Border,* 135–36.

[30]  Ibid, 136–37; Hamilton, *Sentinel of the Southern Plains,* 105–106.

[31]  Carter, *On the Border,* 138–43, 146–47.

[32]  Ibid, 143–44; Hamilton, *Sentinel of the Southern Plains,* 108–12.

[33]  Carter, *On the Border,* 148; Wallace, *Official Correspondence, 1871–1873,* 10–11; Hamilton, *Sentinel of the Southern Plains,* 110–19; Pierce, *The Most Promising Young Officer,* 96–98.

[34]  Ibid.

[35]  Hamilton, *Sentinel of the Southern Plains,* 111–13; Pierce, *The Most Promising Young Officer,* 97–98.

[36]  Carter, *On the Border,* 146–49; Pierce, *The Most Promising Young Officer,* 99; Schilz, "People of the Cross-timbers," 191–92; Hamilton, *Sentinel of the Southern Plains,* 116–19.

[37]  Carter, *On the Border,* 146–50; Neighbors, "Tonkawa Scouts and Guides," 110.

[38]  Carter, *On the Border,* 145–49; Wallace, *Official Correspondence, 1871–1873,* 10–11; Hamilton, *Sentinel of the Southern Plains,* 116–18; Pierce, *The Most Promising Young Officer,* 98–100.

[39]  Pierce, *The Most Promising Young Officer,* 100–101; Dunlay, *Wolves for the Blue Soldiers,* 94; Robert S. Reading, *Arrows Over Texas* (San Antonio, TX: The Naylor Company, 1960), 41–42.

[40]  Neighbors, "Tonkawa Scouts and Guides," 111.

[41]  Ibid., 111–12.

[42]  Wallace, *Official Correspondence, 1871–1873,* 60–61.

[43]  Hamilton, *Sentinel of the Southern Plains,* 125–26.

[44]  Wallace, *Official Correspondence, 1871–1873,* 76–78.

[45]  Ibid.

46  Wallace, *Official Correspondence, 1871–1873*, 79–80, 133; Neighbors, "Tonkawa Scouts and Guides," 104–105; Schilz, "People of the Cross-timbers," 192–93.
47  Wallace, *Official Correspondence, 1871–1873*, 116–19; Schilz, "People of the Cross-timbers," 193–94; Robinson, *Bad Hand*, 252–53.
48  Wallace, *Official Correspondence, 1871–1873*, 133–34; Hamilton, *Sentinel of the Southern Plains*, 128–29.
49  Ibid.
50  Wallace, *Official Correspondence, 1871–1873*, 141–45; Hamilton, *Sentinel of the Southern Plains*, 129–33; Robinson, *Bad Hand*, 253.
51  Neighbors, "Tonkawa Scouts and Guides," 107; Wallace, *Official Correspondence, 1871–1873*, 141–45; Schilz, "People of the Cross-timbers," 194; Robinson, *Bad Hand*, 253.
52  Henry W. Strong, *My Frontier Days and Indian Fights on the Plains of Texas* (Waco, TX: 1926), 17–120; Neighbors, "Tonkawa Scouts and Guides," 106–107.
53  Wallace, *Official Correspondence, 1871–1873*, 141–45; Schilz, "People of the Cross-timbers," 194; Hamilton, *Sentinel of the Southern Plains*, 134; Hasskarl, "Culture and History," 226.
54  Hamilton, *Sentinel of the Southern Plains*, 134; Hasskarl, "Culture and History," 226; Robinson, *Bad Hand*, 254.

## CHAPTER 8

1   HQ Fort Griffin, Texas, to AAG Department of Texas, January 31, 1873: HQ Fort Griffin to AAG Dept. of Texas, February 27, 1873: AAG Dept. of Texas to Commanding Officer, Fort Griffin, March 22, 1873, Post Records, Fort Griffin, Texas, Box 4, Record Group 393, National Archives and Records Administration, Washington, D.C., hereafter cited as Post Records; Ernest Wallace, ed., *Ranald S. Mackenzie's Official Correspondence Relating to Texas, 1871–1873* (Lubbock, TX: West Texas Museum Association, 1967), Mackenzie to Christopher G. Augur, May 23, 1873, 173, hereafter cited as *Official Correspondence, 1871–1873*; Charles M. Robinson, III, *Bad Hand: A Biography of General Ranald S. Mackenzie* (Austin, TX: State House Press, 1993), 147–48, 255.
2   Wallace, Official Correspondence, 1871–1873, 173; Robinson, *Bad Hand*, 147–48, 255.
3   Special Orders [SO] 140, Fort Griffin, Texas, August 9, 1872: SO 187, Fort Griffin, October 30, 1872: E. M. Heyl to AAG, Department of Texas, June 24, 1873, Post Records; Kenneth F. Neighbors, "Tonkawa Scouts and Guides," *West Texas Historical Association Year Book*, 49 (1973): 101–103; Ty Cashion, *A Texas Frontier: The Clear Fork Country and Fort Griffin, 1849–1887* (Norman, OK: University of Oklahoma Press, 1996), 154.
4   Ibid.
5   Heyl to AAG, Department of Texas, June 24, 1873, Post Records; Neighbors, "Tonkawa Scouts and Guides," 101–103.
6   Statement of Tonkawa Indians concerning the death of William, Tonkawa Scout, [date illegible], Post Records; Neighbors, "Tonkawa Scouts and Guides," 101–103.
7   Heyl to AAG, Dept. of Texas, Post Records; Neighbors, "Tonkawa Scouts and Guides," 101–103.
8   HQ Fort Griffin, Texas, to AAG, Department of Texas, June 1, 1873: Department of Texas to Commanding Officer, Fort Clark, June 15, 1873; HQ Dept. of Texas to CO Fort Griffin, June 30, 1874, Post Records; Neighbors, "Tonkawa Scouts and Guides," 101–103.
9   Department of the Interior to Secretary of War, June 17, 1873: AAG US War Dept. to Commanding Officer, Fort Griffin, June 24, 1873; Dept. of Texas to CO Fort Griffin, July 19, 1873, Post Records; Thomas F. Schilz, "People of the Cross-timbers: A History of

the Tonkawa Indians" (PhD diss., Texas Christian University, 1983), 196–97; Thomas
W. Dunlay, "Friends and Allies: The Tonkawa Indians and the Anglo–Americans, 1823–
1884," *Great Plains Quarterly*, 1, No. 3 (Summer 1981): 154.

10  R. H. Pratt, Commander of Scouts, Fort Griffin, Texas, to AAG Department of Texas,
September 9, 1873: Dept. of Texas, Office of Chief Ordnance Officer to AAG [Dept. of
Texas], September 20, 1873: AAG Dept of Texas to CO Fort Griffin, September 22, 1873,
Post Records; Neighbors, "Tonkawa Scouts and Guides," 111; Thomas W. Dunlay, *Wolves
for the Blue Soldiers: Indian Scouts and Auxiliaries with the United States Army, 1860–90* (Lincoln, NE:
University of Nebraska Press, 1982), 71–72; Schilz, "People of the Cross-timbers," 197.

11  Schilz, "People of the Cross-timbers," 197–98; Neighbors, "Tonkawa Scouts and
Guides," 112.

12  Richard H. Pratt, Robert M. Utley, ed., *Battlefield and Classroom: Four Decades with the American
Indians, 1867–1904* (New Haven, CT: Yale University Press, 1964), 58; William H. Leckie,
*The Buffalo Soldiers: A Narrative of the Negro Cavalry in the West* (Norman, OK: University of
Oklahoma Press, 1967), 79–80; Schilz, "People of the Cross-timbers," 198; Alan Lee
Hamilton, *Sentinel of the Southern Plains: Fort Richardson and the Northwest Texas Frontier, 1866–1878*
(Fort Worth, TX: Texas Christian University Press, 1988), 143, 209–10; Ron Tyler, ed.,
*The New Handbook of Texas*, 6 vols. (Austin, TX: The Texas State Historical Association,
1996), III:1089.

13  John M. Elkins, Written by Frank W. McCarty, *Indian Fighting on the Texas Frontier* (Amarillo,
TX: Russell & Cockrell, 1929), 69; Pratt, *Battlefield and Classroom*, 58.

14  Leckie, *The Buffalo Soldiers*, 79; Schilz, "People of the Cross-timbers," 198–200; Hamilton,
*Sentinel of the Southern Plains*, 143–44.

15  Schilz, "People of the Cross-timbers," 198–200; Pratt, *Battlefield and Classroom*, 65; William
T. Hagan, *Quanah Parker: Comanche Chief* (Norman, OK: University of Oklahoma Press,
1993), 9–12.

16  Schilz, "People of the Cross-timbers," 198–99; Pratt, *Battlefield and Classroom*, 65; Hamilton,
*Sentinel of the Southern Plains*, 151–52; Tyler, ed., *The New Handbook of Texas*, I:34–35.

17  Ernest Wallace, ed., *Ranald S. Mackenzie's: Official Correspondence Relating to Texas, 1873–1879*
(Lubbock, TX: West Texas Museum Association, 1968), 80–82, hereafter cited as *Official
Correspondence, 1873–1879*; Pratt, *Battlefield and Classroom*, 65–66; R. G. Carter, *On the Border
with Mackenzie, or Winning West Texas from the Comanches* (Manatuck, NY: J. M. Carroll and
Co., 1935), 474; Leckie, *The Buffalo Soldiers*, 125–26; Robinson, *Bad Hand*, 163–64; Robert
M. Utley, *Frontier Regulars: The United States Army and the Indian, 1866–1891* (Lincoln, NE:
University of Nebraska Press, 1973), 234.

18  Henry W. Strong, *My Frontier Days and Indian Fights on the Plains of Texas* (Waco, TX: 1926), 50;
Wallace, *Official Correspondence, 1873–1879*, 80–82; Carter, *On the Border*, 474; Robinson, *Bad
Hand*, 163–64.

19  Wallace, *Official Correspondence, 1873–1879*, 112.

20  Dunlay, *Wolves for the Blue Soldiers*, 94.

21  Wallace, *Official Correspondence, 1873–1879*, 113–14.

22  Wallace, *Official Correspondence*, 114; Carter, *On the Border*, 483–84.

23  Auger to Mackenzie, August 28, 1874, Wallace, *Official Correspondence, 1873–1879*, 118–20;
Carter, *On the Border*, 476; Robinson, *Bad Hand*, 168.

24  Charles Hatfield, "Campaign in northwest Texas," *Galveston News*, October 16, 1884;
Carter, *On the Border*, 485; *Official Correspondence, 1873–1879*, 120–22; Utley, *Frontier Regulars*, 80.

25  Ibid.

26  Hatfield, "Campaign in northwest Texas;" Robinson, *Bad Hand*, 169–70.

27  Carter, *On the Border*, 487; Hatfield "Campaign in northwest Texas;" *Official Correspondence*, 1873–1879, 122.

28  Wallace, *Official Correspondence, 1873–1879*, 122.

29  Wallace, *Official Correspondence, 1873–1879*, 122; Robinson, *Bad Hand*, 170–71.

30  Tyler, ed., *The New Handbook of Texas*, 5:28; William G. Tudor, "Ghost Writer of the Palo Duro," *Southwestern Historical Quarterly* 99, No. 4 (April 1996): 533, 536, 539.

31  Wallace, *Official Correspondence, 1873–1879*, 117–18, 146; Tyler, ed., *The New Handbook of Texas*, 5:28; Neighbors, "Tonkawa Scouts and Guides," 107–108; Hamilton, *Sentinel of the Southern Plains*, 157; Tudor, "Ghost Writer," 539–41.

32  Barbara Neal Ledbetter, "Indian Woman is Famous Frontier Scout," *Graham Leader*, [TX] August 9, 1992; Joan Farmer, "Remember When," *Albany News*, June 10, 1999; Leckie, *The Buffalo Soldiers*, 89–91; Wallace, *Official Correspondence, 1873–1879*, 117–18, 146; D. K. Taylor to Lieutenant [?] White, January 29, 1873, Post Records; "The Tonkawa Tribe," June 2002, powwow pamphlet; Oral History Interviews, June 29–30, 2002, Don Patterson.

33  Ibid.

34  Ibid., Repatriation Office, National Museum of Natural History, Washington, D.C., Bill Billeck to Stanley S. McGowen, January 22, 2004, email.

35  Neighbors, "Tonkawa Scouts and Guides," 107–108.

36  Wallace, *Official Correspondence, 1873–1879*, 128, 164–65.

37  Wallace, *Official Correspondence, 1873–1879*, 128, 156–57, 164–65, 173–75.

38  Wallace, *Official Correspondence, 1873–1879*, 164–65, 173–75.

39  Leckie, *The Buffalo Soldiers*, 125–26.

40  Ibid.

41  Ibid.

42  Ibid., 125–29; Hamilton, *Sentinel of the Southern Plains*, 155–56.

43  Ibid.

44  Leckie, *The Buffalo Soldiers*, 142–44.

45  Ibid., 144.

46  Ibid., 143–44; *Frontier Echo* [Jacksboro, Texas], August, 18, 1875; Tyler, ed., *The New Handbook of Texas*, IV:914.

47  Leckie, *The Buffalo Soldiers*, 144–45.

48  Camp on Hill Creek, General Order #5, November 28, 1874; HQ Dept. of Texas to CO Fort Griffin, August 9, 1873, Post Records; Neighbors, "Tonkawa Scouts and Guides," 108–109; Thomas T. Smith, "US Army Combat Operations in the Indian Wars of Texas, 1849–1881," *Southwestern Historical Quarterly* 99, No. 4 (April 1996): 518; Dunlay, "Friends and Allies," 151–52; Michael D. Pierce, *The Most Promising Young Officer: A Life of Ranald Slidell Mackenzie* (Norman, OK: University of Oklahoma Press, 1993), 100–101; Dunlay, *Wolves for the Blue Soldiers*, 94; Robert S. Reading, *Arrows Over Texas* (San Antonio, TX: Naylor, 1960), 41–42.

49  Post Reports and Muster Roll, Tonkawa Scouts, December 1875–February 1876, Fort Griffin, Texas, Record Group 393, Microfilm #354637, Roll 1, National Archives and Records Administration, Washington, D.C., hereafter cited as URMR.

50  HQ Fort Griffin to AAG Dept. of Texas, August 6, 1873, Post Records; Neighbors, "Tonkawa Scouts and Guides," 112; Schilz, "People of the Cross-timbers," 189; Cashion, *A Texas Frontier*, 151–52.

51  Robert A. Hasskarl, Jr., "The Culture and History of the Tonkawa Indians," *Plains Anthropologist* 7, No. 18 (November 1962): 226; Neighbors, "Tonkawa Scouts and Guides," 97; Cashion, *A Texas Frontier*, 146.

[52] J. J. Bragg, "Days of Peril on the Clear Fork," *Frontier Times*, No. 3 (April 1926): 44–46; Edgar Rye, "Old Times in Texas, or Frontier Reminiscences," *Albany News*, March 20, 1891, "Tonkawa file," Robert Nail Archives, The Old Jail Art Center, Albany, TX; Cashion, *A Texas Frontier*, 149–50.

[53] Pratt, *Battlefield and Classroom*, 55; Schilz, "People of the Cross-timbers," 187; Cashion, *A Texas Frontier*, 150–51.

[54] Pratt, *Battlefield and Classroom*, 55–57; Dunlay, *Wolves for the Blue Soldiers*, 119; Schilz, "People of the Cross-timbers," 187.

[55] Pratt, *Battlefield and Classroom*, 55–57.

[56] Ibid.

## CHAPTER 9

[1] Headquarters, Fort Griffin, Texas, to AAG Department of Texas, August 9, 1873, Post Records, Fort Griffin, Texas, Box 4, Record Group 393, National Archives and Records Administration, Washington, D.C., hereafter cited as Fort Griffin Records; Ty Cashion, *A Texas Frontier: The Clear Fork Country and Fort Griffin, 1849–1887* (Norman, OK: University of Oklahoma Press, 1996), 256–58; Robert A. Hasskarl, Jr., "The Culture and History of the Tonkawa Indians," *Plains Anthropologist* 18, Vol. 7 (November 1962): 226–27; James Curtis Hasdorff, *Four Indian Tribes in Texas, 1785–1858: A Reevaluation of Historical Sources* (Albuquerque, NM: University of New Mexico Press, 1971), 70–71.

[2] Ibid.

[3] Cashion, *A Texas Frontier*, 256–57; Carl Coke Rister, *Fort Griffin on the Texas Frontier* (Norman, OK: University of Oklahoma Press, 1956), 23.

[4] Ibid.; Henry W. Strong, *My Frontier Days and Indian Fights on the Plains of Texas* (Waco, TX: 1926), 50; Deborah Lamont Newlin, *The Tonkawa People: A Tribal History from Earliest Times to 1893* (Lubbock, TX: West Texas Museum Association, 1982), 85–86.

[5] Sandra L. Myers, ed., "A Woman's View of the Texas Frontier, 1874: The Diary of Emily K. Andrews," *Southwestern Historical Quarterly* 86, No. 1 (July 1982): 60.

[6] John C. Jacobs, "Robin Hood of the Tonkaways," *Frontier Times*, No. 3 (November 1925): 36–38.

[7] John Brown, *Twenty-five Years a Parson in the Wild West: Being the Experience of Parson Ralph Riley* (Fall River, MA: 1896), 37, 171–72; Berta Hart Nance, "D. A. Nance and the Tonkawa Indians," *West Texas Historical Association Year Book* 28, (1952): 90–92; Cashion, *A Texas Frontier*, 257.

[8] *Frontier Echo*, Jacksboro, TX, June 8, 1877, Vol. II, No. 48, Microfilm J12, Reel 2, Southwest Collection, Texas Tech University, Lubbock, TX; Cashion, *A Texas Frontier*, 181.

[9] Cashion, *A Texas Frontier*, 145–46, 214–18.

[10] *Frontier Echo*, Jacksboro, TX, April 28, 1876, Microfilm J12, Reel 2, Southwest Collection; Richard H. Pratt and Robert M. Utley, eds. *Battlefield and Classroom: Four Decades with the American Indians, 1867–1904*, (New Haven, CT: Yale University Press, 1964), 59–60.

[11] United States Census Bureau, Twentieth Census of the U.S., Shackleford County, Texas, (1880), Washington, D.C.; Cashion, *A Texas Frontier*, 257–58, 274.

[12] Cashion, *A Texas Frontier*, 146; Thomas F. Schilz, "The People of the Cross-timbers: A History of the Tonkawa Indians," (PhD diss., Texas Christian University, 1983), 192–93; Hasdorff, *Four Indian Tribes in Texas*, 71–72.

[13] Jacobs, "Robin Hood of the Tonkaways," 37–38; Pratt, *Battlefield and Classroom*, 55; 1880 U.S. Census, Shackleford County, TX; Thomas W. Dunlay, "Friends and Allies: The

Tonkawa Indians and the Anglo–Americans, 1823–1884," *Great Plains Quarterly* 1, No. 3 (Summer 1981): 155–56; Cashion, *A Texas Frontier*, 146–47; Haley, *Charles Goodnight*, 93; Nance, "D. A. Nance and the Tonkawas," 90; Hasdorff, *Four Indian Tribes in Texas*, 71–72.

14 Neighbors, "Tonkawa Scouts and Guides," 90; Elsa M. Turner, "Tonkawas in Griffin," *Albany News*, June 1989.

15 Kenneth F. Neighbors, "Tonkawa Scouts and Guides," *West Texas Historical Association Year Book*, 49 (1973): 90, 111; Nance, "D. A. Nance and the Tonkawa Indians," 90–93.

16 Records, Fort Griffin, Texas, Box 4, Record Group 393, National Archives and Records Administration, Washington, D.C., hereafter cited as Post Records; Neighbors, "Tonkawa Scouts and Guides," 90, 110–111; *Albany Echo*, July 28, 1883, "Shirley Caldwell, Private Collection," Albany, TX; Turner, "Tonkawas in Griffin;" Cashion, *A Texas Frontier*, 147–48.

17 Berlin B. Chapman, "Establishment of the Iowa Reservation," *Chronicles of Oklahoma*, 21 (December 1943): 372.

18 *Fort Griffin Echo*, February 14, 1880, Vol. II, No. 6, Microfilm J12, Reel 2, Southwest Collection, Texas Tech University, Lubbock, TX; Chapman, "Establishment of the Iowa Reservation," 373; Dunlay, "Friends and Allies," 155; Newlin, *The Tonkawa People*, 85–86.

19 A cemetery near the Oakland Reservation contains the graves of more than one hundred Nez Perce children. The Tonkawas claim that every Nez Perce child born in Indian Territory died. Ibid.

20 Chapman, "Establishment of the Iowa Reservation," 374; Hasskarl, "Culture and History," 226–27; Hasdorff, *Four Indian Tribes in Texas*, 70–71; *Albany Star*, June 1, 1883, "Shirley Caldwell Private Collection," Albany, TX; Cashion, *A Texas Frontier*, 274.

21 Ibid.

22 Chapman, "Establishment of the Iowa Reservation," 374; Grant Foreman, *The Last Trek of the Indians* (New York: Russell and Russell, 1972), 286–87; Newlin, *The Tonkawa People*, 86–87.

23 Chapman, "Establishment of the Iowa Reservation," 374–75; Hasskarl, "Culture and History," 226–27; Hasdorff, *Four Indian Tribes in Texas*, 70–71.

24 Chapman, "Establishment of the Iowa Reservation," 375–77.

25 Nance, "D. A. Nance and the Tonkawas," 94; Cashion, *A Texas Frontier*, 282–83; Chapman, "Establishment of the Iowa Reservation," 375–77; Hasskarl, "Culture and History," 226–27; "Last of Fort Griffin Tonkawas Dies," *Albany News*, April 1, 1943, Tonkawa file, Robert Nail Collection, The Old Jail Art Center, Albany, TX.

26 Chapman, "Establishment of the Iowa Reservation," 375–77.

27 Chapman, "Establishment of the Iowa Reservation," 375–77; Hasskarl, "Culture and History," 226–27; Cashion, *A Texas Frontier*, 282–83.

28 Hasskarl, "Culture and History," 226–27; Muriel H. Wright, *A Guide to the Indian Tribes of Oklahoma* (Norman, OK: University of Oklahoma Press, 1951), 251; Newlin, *The Tonkawa People*, 88–91.

29 Charles J. Kappler, ed. and comp., *Indian Affairs: Laws and Treaties* 1, (Washington, D.C., Government Printing Office, 1904), 494–95; W. F. Semple, *Oklahoma Indian Land Titles* (St. Louis, MO: Thomas Law Book Co., 1952), 871–73, Appendix D; Laurence Frederick Schmeckebier, *The Office of Indian Affairs: Its History, Activities, and Organization* (Baltimore, MD: Johns Hopkins Press, 1927), 22; Newlin, *The Tonkawa People*, 89–90.

30 Ibid.

31 Oral History Interviews, June 28–30, 2002, Don Patterson; Mardith Keithly Schuetz, *The Indians of the San Antonio Missions, 1718–1821* (Austin, TX: The University of Texas Press, 1980), 97–98; George R. Morgan and Omer Stewart, "Peyote Trade in South Texas," *Southwestern Historical Quarterly* 87, No. 3 (January 1984): 285–87; Omer Stewart, "Origin of

the Peyote Religion in the United States," *Plains Anthropologist* 65, No. 19 (1974): 211–23; William T. Hagan, *Quanah Parker: Comanche Chief* (Norman, OK: University of Oklahoma Press, 1993), 52, 53, 55–56; Omer Stewart, *Peyote Religion: A History* (Norman, OK: University of Oklahoma Press, 1987), 88, 99, 118.

[32] Oral History Interviews, June 28–30, 2002, Don Patterson; Schuetz, *Indians of the San Antonio Missions*, 102; Stewart, "Origin of the Peyote Religion," 211–23; Morgan and Stewart, "Peyote in South Texas," 270–73.

[33] Ibid.

[34] Oral History Interviews, June 28–30, 2002, Don Patterson; Stewart, "Origin of the Peyote Religion," 211–23; Morgan and Stewart, "Peyote in South Texas," 270.

[35] Ibid.

[36] Oral History Interviews, June 28–30, 2002, Don Patterson; Hagan, *Quanah Parker*, 53, 55, 116, 118; Stewart, "Origin of the Peyote Religion," 211–23; Donald E. Worcester, *The Apaches: Eagles of the Southwest* (Norman, OK: University of Oklahoma Press, 1979), 236; Stewart, *Peyote Religion: A History*, 118; Daniel J. Gelo, "'Comanche Land and Ever Has Been': A Native Geography of the Nineteenth–Century Comancheria," *Southwestern Historical Quarterly* 103, No. 3 (January 2000): 275.

[37] Morgan and Stewart, "Peyote in South Texas," 270–76, 280–82, 287–95; Stewart, *Peyote Religion: A History*, 118–19.

[38] Oral History Interviews, June 28–30, 2002, Don Patterson; Hagan, *Quanah Parker*, 53, 55; Stewart, "Origin of the Peyote Religion," 211–23; Morgan and Stewart, "Peyote in South Texas," 283–85, 289–95.

[39] Ibid.

[40] Newlin, *The Tonkawa People*, 67–70, 93–95.

[41] Dunlay, "Friends and Allies," 154–55; Neighbors, "Tonkawa Scouts and Guides," 112; Brown, *Twenty-five Years a Parson*, 172.

[42] Newlin, *The Tonkawa People*, 67–70, 93–95.

[43] Ibid., 93–95.

[44] United States Census Bureau, Twenty-second Census of the U.S. (1900), Washington, D.C.; Hasskarl, "Culture and History," 227–28.

[45] Hasskarl, "Culture and History," 227–28; Brown, *Twenty-five Years a Parson*, 37; Oral History Interviews, June 28–30, 2002, Don Patterson.

## CHAPTER 10

[1] Extant records offered no explanation why the tribal population dropped 49% between 1880–1900, but disease might be expected. United States Census Bureau, Twentieth Census of the U.S., Shackleford County, TX, (1880), Washington, D.C.; Twenty-second Census of the U.S., Oklahoma Territory, (1900), Washington, D.C.; W. W. Newcomb, Jr., *The Indians of Texas from Prehistoric to Modern Times* (Austin, TX: University of Texas Press, 1995), 359; Robert Medley, "Remaining Tonkawa Indians Won't Accept Reports of Their Extinction," *Dallas Morning News*, September 21, 1988.

[2] Robert A. Hasskarl Jr., "The Culture and History of the Tonkawa Indians," *Plains Anthropologist* 7, No. 18 (November 1962): 228.

[3] Ibid.

[4] Ibid, Oral History Interviews, June 28–30, 2002, Don Patterson.

5   Harry Hoijer and M. Eleanor Culley, eds., *Chiricahua and Mescalero Apache Texts* (Chicago, IL: University of Chicago Press, University of Virginia, electronic text, 1938), 9.3; Oral History Interviews, June 2002, Don Patterson.
6   Hasskarl, "Culture and History," 228; Oral History Interviews, June 28–30, 2002, Don Patterson.
7   Oral History interviews, June 28–30, 2002; Hasskarl, "Culture and History," 229.
8   Hasskarl, "Culture and History," 229; Oral History Interviews, June 29–30, 2002, Don Patterson; Telephone interviews with Carl Martin, Tonkawa Tribe President, December 12, 2003.
9   Oral History Interviews, June 28–30, 2002.
10  Harry Hoijer, "Tonkawa: An Indian Language of Texas," (PhD diss., University of Chicago, 1931), xxxiii; "Felix Waldo Allen," *The Tonkawa News*, Tonkawa, OK, June 27, 2002, No. 23:6; Oral History Interviews, June 29–30, 2002, Don Patterson.
11  Ibid.
12  "The Tonkawa Tribe," annual powwow pamphlet; Oral History Interviews, June 29–30, 2002; telephone interview, Carl Martin, December 12, 2003.
13  Ibid.
14  "The Tonkawa Tribe," annual powwow pamphlet, June 2002; Oral History Interviews, June 29–30, 2002, Don Patterson.
15  Oral History Interviews, June 28–30, 2002, Don Patterson.
16  Oral History Interviews, June 29–30, 2002, Don Patterson; John C. Ewers, "The Influence of Epidemics on the Indian Populations and Cultures of Texas," *Plains Anthropologist* 18, No. 60 (1973): 104–15.
17  "Felix Waldo Allen (*Wa–ki–teh*)/Straight Shooter," The Tonkawa News, Tonkawa, OK, June 27, 2002, No. 23:6; Barbara Neal Ledbetter, "Indian Woman is Famous Frontier Scout," *Graham Leader*, [TX] August 9, 1992.
18  Oral History Interviews, 29–30 June, 2002, Don Patterson.
19  Ibid.
20  Hasskarl, "Culture and History," 227–28; John Brown, *Twenty-five Years a Parson in the Wild West: Being the Experience of Parson Ralph Riley* (Fall River, MA: 1896), 37; Oral History Interviews, June 29–30, 2002, Don Patterson.
21  Thomas W. Dunlay, "Friends and Allies: The Tonkawa Indians and the Anglo–Americans, 1823–1884," *Great Plains Quarterly* 1, No. 3 (Summer 1981): 147–50, 155–56; Dorman H., Winfrey, et al., *Indian Tribes of Texas* (Waco, TX: Texian Press, 1971), 150.

# BIBLIOGRAPHY

**PRIMARY SOURCES**
*Government Documents*

Belknap, William W. "Tonkawa Indians at Fort Griffin, Texas." Letter from the Secretary of War. 44th Con., 1st Sess., House Exec. Doc. 102. Washington, D.C.: Dept. of War, 1876. Ser. 1689.

Béxar Archives. Thomas D. Moorman, trans. Vols. 34-35 (1760–1762). University of Texas at San Antonio. San Antonio, TX.

_____. Carmela Leal, trans. Vol. 45 (1767-1768), 56 (January 1774–July 1774). University of Texas at San Antonio. San Antonio, TX.

_____. Nena Farrar Bentley, trans. Vol 57 (August 1774–October 1774), 86 (August 1779), 87 (September 1779), 88, (October 1779), 89, (October 20, 1779–November 7, 1779), 92, (January 1780), 94, (March 1780), 99, (June 1780), 100–101 (July–August 1780). University of Texas at San Antonio. San Antonio, TX.

_____. William C. Taylor, trans. Vol. 103 (September 1780), 120 (October–November 1783), 121 (December 1783–January 1784), 122 (January 17, 1784–February 1784), 123 (March 1784), 127, (July 1784), 129, (September–December 1784), 131 (March–April 1785), 133 (July–September 1785), 136 (January–February 1786), 138 (May–June 1786), 139 (July 1786), 140 (August 1876), 141 (September 1786), 146 (August–September 1787), 147 (October 1787), 148 (November 1787), 152 (February 1788), 154 (April–May 1788), 155 (June–July 1788), 156 (August–September 1788). University of Texas at San Antonio. San Antonio, TX.

Cohen, Felix S. *Handbook of Federal Indian Law, with Reference Tables and Index.* Washington, D.C.: Government Printing Office, 1942.

Gammel, H. P. N. *The Laws of Texas, 1822-1897.* 10 Vols. Austin, TX: Gammel, 1898.

*Handbook of American Indians North of Mexico.* "Tonkawas." Department of the Interior, Office of Indian Affairs. Bulletin 30. Washington D.C., 1910.

Kappler, Charles J., ed. & comp. *Indian Affairs, Laws, and Treaties.* 2nd Edition. 5 Vols. Washington, D.C.: Government Printing Office. 1904.

Noble, John W. "Tonkawa Indian Land Cession." In Message from the President of the United States. 52nd Cong., 1st Sess., Senate Exec. Doc. 13. Department of Interior, Washington, D.C., 1892.

Post Reports and Tonkawa Scout Muster Rolls, Fort Griffin, Texas, 1869-1878, Record Group 393, microfilm #354637, roll 1, National Archives and Record Administration, Washington, D.C.

Post Records, Fort Griffin, Texas, Box 4, Record Group 393, National Archives and Record Administration, Washington, D.C.

Regular Army Muster Roles. Tonkawa Indian Scouts. Record Group 94. Box 2372. United States Archives and Record Administration. Washington, D.C.

Semple. W. F. *Oklahoma Indian Land Titles, Annotated.* St. Louis, MS: Thomas Law Book Co., 1952.

United States Census Bureau, Twentieth Census of the U.S. (1880), Washington, D.C.

_____. Twenty-second Census of the U.S. (1900), Washington, D.C.

United States Congress. 30th Cong., 1st Sess. Sen. Misc. Doc. 122 Ser. 511.

United States Indian Office, Letters Received, 1846-18855. 29 Letters. Brazos Agency, 1855–1859. 13 Letters. Wichita, Agency, 1859–1862. 1 Letter. Bureau of Indian Affairs, Washington, D.C.

Wallace, Ernest, ed. *Ranald S. Mackenzie's: Official Correspondence Relating to Texas, 1871–1873.* Lubbock, TX: West Texas Museum Association, 1967.

_____. *Ranald S. Mackenzie's: Official Correspondence Relating to Texas, 1873–1879.* Lubbock, TX: West Texas Museum Association, 1968.

Wallace, Ernest and David M. Vigness. *Documents of Texas History.* 2nd Edition. Austin, TX: The Stock Co., 1963.

Winfrey, Dorman H. and James M. Day, eds. *The Indian Papers of Texas and the Southwest 1825–1916.* 5 Vols. Austin, TX: Texas State Historical Association, 1995.

## PUBLISHED SOURCES

Baylor, George Wythe. *Into the Far, Wild Country: True Tales of the Old Southwest.* El Paso, TX: Texas Western Press, 1996.

Bolton, Herbert Eugene, ed. *Athanase de Mezieres and the Louisiana-Texas Frontier, 1768–1780.* 2 Vols. Cleveland, OH: Arthur H. Clark Company, 1914.

Berlandier, Jean Louis. John C. Ewers, ed. Patricia Reading Leclercq, trans. *The Indians of Texas in 1830.* Washington, D.C.: Smithsonian Press, 1969.

Berlandier, Jean Louis. C. H. Muller and Katherine K. Muller, eds. Sheila M. Ohlendorf, Josette M. Bigelow, and Mary M. Standifer, trans. *Journey to Mexico: During the Years 1826–1834.* Vol II. Austin, TX: Texas State Historical Association and University of Texas Press, 1980.

Bonnell, George W. *Topographical Description of Texas: To Which is Added an Account of the Indian Tribes.* Cruger and Bonnell, 1840. New Material: James M. Day, 1964.

Britton, Wiley. *Memoirs of the Rebellion on the Border, 1863.* Original Edition 1882. Lincoln, NE: University of Nebraska Press, 1993.

Brown, John. *Twenty-five Years a Parson in the Wild West: Being the Experience of Parson Ralph Riley.* Fall River, MA: n.p., 1896.

Brown, John Henry. *Indian Wars and Pioneers of Texas.* Austin, TX: L. E. Daniell, 1880. New Material, Silas Emmett Lucas, Jr., 1978.

Carter, R. G. *On the Border with Mackenzie, or Winning West Texas from the Comanches.* Manatuck, NY: J. M. Carroll and Co., 1935.

Coombes, Zachariah Ellis. Barbara Neal Ledletter, ed. *The Diary of a Frontiersman, 1858-1859.* Newcastle, TX: n.p., 1962.

Dodge, Richard Irving. *Thirty-three Years Among Our Wild Indians*. New York: Archer House, Inc., 1959.

Elkins, John M. Written by Frank W. McCarty. *Indian Fighting on the Texas Frontier*. Amarillo, TX: Russell & Cockrell, 1929.

Greer, James K. ed. *A Texas Ranger and Frontiersman: The Days of Buck Barry in Texas, 1845–1906*. Dallas, TX: Southwest Press, 1932.

Gulick, Charles Adams, Jr., and Winnie Allen, eds. *The Papers of Mirabeau Buonaparte Lamar*. 6 Vols. Austin, TX: Von-Boeckmann-Jones, 1924.

Jenkins, John Holland. *Recollections of Early Texas: The Memoirs of John Holland Jenkins*. Austin, TX: University of Texas Press, 1958.

Lehmann, Herman, J. Marvin Hunter, ed. *Nine Years Among the Indians, 1870–1879: The Story of the Captivity and Life of a Texan Among the Indians*. Albuquerque, NM: University of New Mexico Press, 1999.

Maltby, W. J. *Captain Jeff, or Frontier Life in Texas with the Texas Rangers*. Colorado, TX: Whipkey Printing Co., 1906.

Marcy, Randolph B. *Thirty Years of Army Life on the Border*. 1866 Edition. Introduction by Edward S. Wallace. New York: Harper and Brothers Publishers, 1866.

Matthews, Sallie Reynolds. *Interwoven: A Pioneer Chronicle*. College Station, TX: Texas A&M University Press, 1936; rpt. 1982.

Maverick, Mary Ann Adams. Arranged by Mary A. Maverick and her son, Geo. Madison Maverick. Rena Maverick Green, ed. *Memoirs of Mary A. Maverick*. San Antonio, TX: Alamo Printing Company, 1921.

Oates, Stephen B., ed. *John Salmon Ford: Rip Ford's Texas*. Austin, TX: University of Texas Press, 1963.

Pratt, Richard H. and Robert M. Utley, eds. *Battlefield and Classroom: Four Decades with the American Indians, 1867–1904*. New Haven, CT: Yale University Press, 1964.

Smithwick, Noah. *Evolution of a State, or Recollections of Old Texas Days*. H. P. N. Gammel, 1900; rpt. Austin, TX: University of Texas Press, 1983.

Sowell, Andrew Jackson. *Rangers and Pioneers of Texas: With a Concise Account of the Early Settlements, Hardships, Massacres, Battles and Wars, by which Texas was Rescued from the Rule of the Savage and Consecrated to the Empire of Civilization*. San Antonio, TX: Shepard Brothers and Co., 1884.

Strong, Henry W. *My Frontier Days and Indian Fights on the Plains of Texas*. Waco, TX: n.p., 1926.

Sumpter, Jesse. Ben Pingenot, ed. Harry Warren, comp. *Paso del Aquila: A Chronicle of Frontier Days on the Texas Border as Recorded in the Memoirs of Jesse Sumpter*. Austin, TX: Encino Press, 1969.

Wilbarger, J. W. *Indian Depredations in Texas*. 2nd ed. Austin, TX: Hutchings Printing House, 1890.

Williams, Amelia W. and Barker, Eugene C. eds. *The Writings of Sam Houston, 1813–1863*. 8 Vols. Austin, TX: University of Texas Press, 1938–1943.

## Journals

Estep, Raymond, ed. "Lieutenant Wm. E. Burnet: Notes on Removal of Indians from Texas to Indian Territory." *Chronicles of Oklahoma*. 38 (Autumn, 1960, Winter, 1960, Spring 1960).

La Vere, David and Katia Campbell, eds. and trans. "An Expedition to the Kichai: The Journal of Francois Grappe, September 24, 1783." *Southwestern Historical Quarterly*. 98, No. 1 (July 1994).

Kuykendall, J. H. "Reminiscences of Early Texans." *Quarterly of the Texas State Historical Association*. VI (January 1903).

Magnaghi, Russell B., ed and trans. "Texas as Seen by Governor Winthuysen, 1741–1744." *Southwestern Historical Quarterly*. 88, No. 2 (October 1984).

Myers, Sandra L, ed. "A Woman's View of the Texas Frontier, 1874: The Diary of Emily K. Andrews." *Southwestern Historical Quarterly*. 86, No. 1 (July 1982).

Pool, William C., ed. "Westward I Go Free: The Memoirs of William E. Cureton, Texas Frontiersman." *Southwestern Historical Quarterly*. 81, No. 2 (October 1977).

Richardson, Rupert N., ed. "Documents Relating to West Texas and Its Indian Tribes." *West Texas Historical Association Year Book*. 1 (June 1925).

### Newspapers

Adair, W. S. "Albany found Real Frontier in Early Days: R. A. Slack Tells About Jail Break Lynching and Shootings." Unidentified newspaper article. Robert E. Nail Archives. The Old Jail Art Center, Albany, TX.

*Frontier Echo*, [Jacksboro, TX] July 7, 1875, Microfilm J12, Reel 2, Southwest Collection, Texas Tech University, Lubbock, TX.

*Frontier Echo*, [Jacksboro, TX] August, 18, 1875, Microfilm J12, Reel 2, Southwest Collection, Texas Tech University, Lubbock, TX.

*Frontier Echo*, [Jacksboro, TX] April 28, 1876, Microfilm J12, Reel 2, Southwest Collection, Texas Tech University, Lubbock, TX.

*Frontier Echo*, [Jacksboro, TX] June 23, 1876, Vol I, No. 51, microfilm J12, reel 2, Southwest Collection, Texas Tech University, Lubbock, TX.

*Frontier Echo*, [Jacksboro, TX] June 8, 1877, Vol II, No. 48, microfilm J12, reel 2, Southwest Collection, Texas Tech University, Lubbock, TX.

*Frontier Echo*, [Jacksboro, TX] January 18, 1878, Vol III, No. 27[?], "More Indian Troubles," microfilm J12, reel 2, Southwest Collection, Texas Tech University, Lubbock, TX.

*Fort Griffin Echo*, June 7, 1879, Vol I, No. 23, microfilm J12, reel 2, Southwest Collection, Texas Tech University, Lubbock, TX.

*Fort Griffin Echo*, February 14, 1880, Vol II, No. 6, microfilm J12, reel 2, Southwest Collection, Texas Tech University, Lubbock, TX.

*Albany Echo*. July 28, 1883, January 1884. "Shirley Caldwell, Private Collection," Albany, TX.

*Albany Star*, June 1, 1883, "Shirley Caldwell Private Collection," Albany, TX.

## UNPUBLISHED SOURCES

Bill Billeck (National Museum of Natural History) to Stanley S. McGowen. Email. January 22, 2004.

Brown, John Henry. "Papers." Center for American History. University of Texas, Austin, TX.

Carter, Robert G. "Winning the West: A Vivid Story of a Fierce Battle with the Savage Apaches. The Tragedies of Canyon Blanco—Gallant Stand of a Company of Regular Cavalry." Typed manuscript. Tonkawa File. Panhandle Plains Museum, Canyon, TX.

Collinson, Frank to L. F. Sheffy. Letter. March 12, 1930. "Tonkawa File." Panhandle Plains Museum, Canyon, TX.

Collinson, Frank. "Three Texas Triggermen." Manuscript. "Tonkawa File." Panhandle Plains Museum, Canyon, TX.

De Witt, Green. "Colony Archives." Center for American History. University of Texas, Austin, TX.

Ford, John S. "Memoirs." Manuscript. Center for American History. University of Texas, Austin, TX.

Gilbert, [?]. "Memories of Just a Boy." Typed manuscript. "Tonkawa File." Panhandle Plains Museum, Canyon, TX.

Lubbock, Francis R. "An Account of the Tonkawa Indians as the Writer Remembers them, 1884." Handwritten manuscript. "Howard Collection." Dallas Historical Society, Dallas, TX, November 12, 1884.

Neighbors, Robert S. "Papers." Center for American History, University of Texas, Austin, TX.

Ross Family Papers. "Texas Collection." Baylor University, Waco, TX.

Tonkawa file. Robert Nail Archives. The Old Jail Art Center, Albany, TX.

## SECONDARY SOURCES
### Books

Abel, Annie Heloise. *The American Indian as Participant in the Civil War*. Cleveland, OH: The Arthur H. Clark Company, 1919.

Atkinson, Mary Jourdan. *The Texas Indians*. San Antonio, TX: The Naylor Company, 1935.

_____. *Indians of the Southwest*. San Antonio, TX: The Naylor Company, 1958.

Betdford, Hillary G. *Texas Indian Trouble*. Dallas, TX: Hargreaves Printing Co., Inc., 1905.

Berkhofer, Robert F. *The White Man's Indian: The History of an Idea from Columbus to the Present*. New York: Knopf, 1978.

Bishop, Morris. *The Odyssey of Cabeza de Vaca*. New York: Century Company, 1933.

Bolton, Herbert E. *Texas in the Middle Eighteenth Century: Studies in Spanish Colonial History and Administration*. Berkley, CA: University of California Press, 1915.

Brown, John Henry. *The History of Texas from 1685 to 1892*. 2 Vols. St. Louis, MO: Bectold and Co., 1892.

Cantrell, Gregg. *Stephen F. Austin: Empresario of Texas*. New Haven, CT: Yale University Press, 1999.

Carlson, Paul H. *The Plains Indians*. College Station, TX: Texas A&M University Press, 1998.

Carriker, Robert C. *Fort Supply Indian Territory; Frontier Outpost on the Plains*. Norman, OK: University of Oklahoma Press, 1978.

Cashion, Ty. *A Texas Frontier: The Clear Fork Country and Fort Griffin, 1849–1887*. Norman, OK: University of Oklahoma Press, 1996.

Chalfant, William Y. *Cheyennes at Dark Water Creek: The Last Fight of the Red River War*. Norman, OK: University of Oklahoma Press, 1997.

Christensen, Thomas P. *The Historic Trail of the American Indians*. Cedar Rapids, IO: Laurance Press Company, 1933.

Clarke, Mary Whatley. *Chief Bowles and the Texas Cherokees*. Norman, OK: University of Oklahoma Press, 1971.

Collins, Hubert E. *WarPath and Cattle Trail*. Niwot, CO: University Press of Colorado, 1998.

Connor, Seymour V. *Adventure in Glory: The Saga of Texas, 1836–1849*. Austin, TX: Steck-Vaughn Company, 1965.

Day, James M. *The Texas Almanac, 1857–1873*. Waco, TX: Texian Press, 1967.

Dillon, Richard H. *North American Indian Wars*. Secaucus, NJ: Chartwell Books, Inc., 1993.

Dunlay, Thomas W. *Wolves for the Blue Soldiers: Indian Scouts and Auxiliaries with the United States Army, 1860–90.* Lincoln, NE: University of Nebraska Press, 1982.

Edmunds, R. David, ed. *American Indian Leaders.* Lincoln, NE: University of Nebraska Press, 1980.

Faulk, Odie B. *A Successful Failure: The Saga of Texas, 1519–1810.* Austin, TX: Steck-Vaughn Company, 1965.

Fehrenbach, T. R. *Comanches: The Destruction of a People.* New York: Alfred A. Knopf, 1979.

Fischer, LeRoy Henry. *The Civil War Era in Indian Territory.* Los Angeles, CA: L. L. Morrison, 1974.

Foreman, Grant. *The Last Trek of the Indians.* New York: Russell and Russell, 1972.

Francaviglia, Richard V. *The Cast Iron Forest: A Natural and Cultural History of the North American Cross Timbers.* Austin, TX: University of Texas Press, 2000.

Gibson, Arrell M. *The American Indian Prehistory to the Present.* Lexington, MS: D. C. Heath Co., 1979.

_____. *America's Exiles: Indian Colonization in Oklahoma.* Oklahoma City, OK: Oklahoma Historical Society, 1976.

Gregory, Jack and Rennard Strickland. *Sam Houston with the Cherokees, 1829–1833.* Austin, TX: University of Texas Press.

Hagan, William T. *Quanah Parker: Comanche Chief.* Norman, OK: University of Oklahoma Press, 1993.

Haley, J. Evetts. *Charles Goodnight: Cowman and Plainsman.* Norman, OK: University of Oklahoma Press, 1949.

Haley, James L. *Apaches A History and Culture Portrait.* Garden City, NY: Doubleday and Co., Inc., 1981.

Hallenbeck, Cleve. *Alvar Nunez Cabeza De Vaca: The Journey and Route of the First European to Cross the Continent of North America 1534-1536.* Glendale, CA: The Arthur H. Clark Company, 1940.

Hamilton, Alan Lee. *Sentinel of the Southern Plains: Fort Richardson and the Northwest Texas Frontier, 1866–1878.* Fort Worth, TX: Texas Christian University Press, 1988.

Hasdorff, James Curtis. *Four Indian Tribes in Texas, 1785–1858: A Reevaluation of Historical Sources.* Albuquerque, NM: University of New Mexico Press, 1971.

Havins, Thomas Robert. *Camp Colorado, A Decade of Frontier Defense.* Brownwood, TX: Brown Press, 1964.

Hill, Edward E. *The Office of Indian Affairs, 1824–1880: Historical Sketches.* New York: Clearwater Publishing Co., 1974.

Himmel, Kelly F. *The Conquest of the Karankawas and the Tonkawas, 1821–1859.* College Station, TX: Texas A&M University Press, 1999.

Hodge, Frederick Webb. *Handbook of American Indians North of Mexico.* Washington, D.C.: Government Printing Office, 1912.

Hodge, Frederick W., ed. "The Narrative of Alvar Nuñez, Cabeza de Vaca." Frederick W. Hodge and Theodore H. Lewis. *Spanish Explorers in the Southern United States 1528–1543.* New York: Charles Scribner's Sons, 1907.

Hoebel, E. Adamson and Ernest Wallace. *The Comanches: Lords of the South Plains.* Norman, OK: University of Oklahoma Press, 1952.

Hoijer, Harry. M. and Eleanor Culley, eds. *Chiricahua and Mescalero Apache Texts.* Chicago, IL: University of Chicago Press, University of Virginia, [electronic text] 1938.

Holt, Ray D. *Heap Many Texas Chiefs.* San Antonio, TX: Naylor, 1966.

Hoopes, Alban W. *Indian Affairs and their Administration, 1849–1860.* Philadelphia, PA: University of Pennsylvania Press, 1932.

Hultkrantz, Åke and Studium, Esselte. *Religions of the American Indians*. Originally published as: *De Amerikanska Indianernes Religioner*. Berkley, CA: University of California Press, 1967.

Hyer, Julian. *The Land of Beginning Again*. Atlanta, GA: Tupper and Love, Inc., 1952.

Institute of Texan Cultures. *The Indian Texans*. San Antonio, TX: n.p., 1970.

Iverson, Peter. *We Are Still Here: American Indians in the Twentieth Century*. Wheeling, IL: Harlan Davidson, Inc., 1998.

John, Elizabeth A. H. S. *Storms Brewed in other Men's World's: The Confrontation of Indians, Spanish, and French in the Southwest, 1540–1795*. College Station, TX: Texas A&M University Press, 1975.

Josephy, Alvin M., Jr. *The Indian Heritage of America*. New York: Bantam Books, 1969.

Kenner, Charles L. *Buffalo Soldiers and Officers of the Ninth Cavalry 1867–1898*. Norman, OK: University of Oklahoma Press, 1999.

Leckie, William H. *The Buffalo Soldiers: A Narrative of the Negro Cavalry in the West*. Norman, OK: University of Oklahoma Press, 1967.

Mayhall, Mildred P. *Indian Wars of Texas*. Waco, TX: Texian Press, 1965.

McConnell, Joseph Carroll. *The West Texas Frontier; or, a Descriptive History of Early Times in Western Texas; Containing an Accurate Account of Much Hitherto Unpublished History*. Jacksboro, TX: Gazette Print, 1933.

McGowen, Stanley S. *Horse Sweat and Powder Smoke: The 1st Texas Cavalry in the Civil War*. College Station, TX: Texas A&M University Press, 1999.

Morfi, Juan Agustin. Carlos Castaneda, trans. *History of Texas, 1673–1779*. Albuquerque, NM: Quivira Society, 1935.

Morril, Sibley S. *The Texas Cannibals; or, Why Father Serra Came to California*. Oakland, CA: Cadleon Publishing Co., 1964.

Nance, Joseph Milton. *After San Jacinto The Texas-Mexican Frontier, 1836–1841*. Austin, TX: University of Texas Press, 1963.

_____. *Attack and Counter-Attack: The Texas-Mexican Frontier, 1842*. Austin, TX: University of Texas Press, 1964.

Neighbours, Kenneth F. *Robert Simpson Neighbors and the Texas Frontier, 1836–1859*. Waco, TX: Texian Press, 1975.

Newcomb, W. W., Jr. *The Indians of Texas From Prehistoric to Modern Times*. Austin, TX: University of Texas Press, 1961.

Newcomb, W. W., Jr. and T. N. Campbell. Don G. Wyckoff and Jack L. Hofman, eds. "Southern Plains Ethnohistory: A Re-Examination of the Escanjaques, Ahijados, and Cuitoas." *Pathways to Plains Prehistory: Anthropological Perspectives of Plains Natives and Their Pasts*. Memoir 3, Duncan, OK: Oklahoma Anthropological Society, 1982.

_____. "Tonkawa." *Handbook of North American Indians*. Vol. 13. Plains. Washington, D.C.: Smithsonian Institution Press, 1982.

Newlin, Deborah Lamont. *The Tonkawa People: A Tribal History from Earliest Times to 1893*. Lubbock, TX: West Texas Museum Association, 1982.

O'Rear, Sybil J. *Charles Goodnight, Pioneer Cowman*. Austin, TX: Eakin Press, 1990.

Place, Marian Templeton. *Comanches and Other Indians of Texas*. New York: Harcourt, Brace, 1970.

Pierce, Michael D. *The Most Promising Young Officer: A Life of Ranald Slidell Mackenzie*. Norman, OK: University of Oklahoma Press, 1993.

Rainey, George. *The Cherokee Strip*. Guthrie, OK: Co-operative Publishing Co., 1933.

Reading, Robert S. *Arrows Over Texas*. San Antonio, TX: Naylor, 1960.

Richardson, Rupert Norval. *The Comanche Barrier to South Plains Settlement*. Abilene, TX: Hardin-Simmons University, 1991.

Rister, Carl Coke. *Fort Griffin on the Texas Frontier*. Norman, OK: University of Oklahoma Press, 1956.

_____. *The Southwestern Frontier, 1865–1881, a History of the Coming of the Settlers*. New York: Russell and Russell, 1969.

Robinson, Charles M., III. *Bad Hand: A Biography of General Ranald S. Mackenzie*. Austin, TX: State House Press, 1993.

Schmeckebier, Laurence Frederick. *The Office of Indian Affairs: Its History, Activities, and Organization*. Baltimore, MD: Johns Hopkins Press, 1927.

Sibley, Marilyn McAdams. *Travelers in Texas, 1761–1860*. Austin, TX: University of Texas Press, 1967.

Simpson, Harold B. *Cry Comanche: The 2nd U.S. Cavalry in Texas, 1855-1861*. Hillsboro, TX: Hill Junior College Press, 1988.

Slotkin, James. "The Peyote Religion: A Study in Indian White Relations." *The Encyclopedia of World Religions*. New York: Farrar, Straus, and Giroux, 1975.

Smith, David Paul. *Frontier Defense in the Civil War: Texas Rangers and Rebels*. College Station, TX: Texas A&M University Press, 1992.

Stein, Pearl, ed. *Brazos Minutemen: on the Texas Frontier Along the Clear Fork and Fort Belknap-on-the-Brazos*. Dallas, TX: AAA Press, 1992.

Stewart, Omer. *Peyote Religion: A History*. Norman, OK: University of Oklahoma Press, 1987.

Swanton, John R. *The Indian Tribes of North America*. Washington, D.C.: Smithsonian Institution Press, 1952; rpt. 1969.

Thompson, Jerry Don. *Colonel John Robert Baylor: Texas Indian Fighter and Confederate Soldier*. Hill Junior College Monographs in Texas and Confederate History, No. 5. Hillsboro, TX: Hill Junior College Press, 1971.

Tyler, Ron, ed. *The New Handbook of Texas*. 6 Vols. Austin, TX: The Texas State Historical Association, 1996.

Utley, Robert M. *Frontiersmen in Blue: The United States Army and the Indian, 1848–1865*. Lincoln, NE: University of Nebraska Press, 1967.

_____. *Frontier Regulars: The United States Army and the Indian, 1866-1891*. Lincoln, NE: University of Nebraska Press, 1973.

Vigness, David M. *The Revolutionary Decades*. Vol. 2 of The Saga of Texas Series, 1810–1836. Austin, TX: Steck-Vaughn Co., 1965.

Wallace, Ernest. *Ranald S. Mackenzie on the Texas Frontier*. Lubbock, TX: West Texas Museum Association, 1964.

_____. *Texas in Turmoil*. The Saga of Texas Series, 1849–1875. Austin, TX: Steck-Vaughn Company, 1965.

Washburn, Wilcomb E., ed. *The American Indian and the United States: A Documentary History*. 4 Vols. New York: Random House, 1973.

Weddle, Robert S. *The San Sabá Mission: Spanish Pivot in Texas*. Austin, TX: University of Texas Press, 1964.

_____. *San Juan Bautista Gateway to Spanish Texas*. Austin, TX: University of Texas Press, 1968.

_____. *Wilderness Manhunt: The Spanish Search for La Salle*. Austin, TX: University of Texas Press, 1973.

Winfrey, Dorman H., et al. *Indian Tribes of Texas*. Waco, TX: Texian Press, 1971.

Wooten, Dudley Goodall. *Comprehensive History of Texas, 1685–1897*. 2 Vols. Dallas, TX: W. G. Scarff, 1898.

Wooster, Ralph A. *Texas and Texans in the Civil War*. Austin, TX: Eakin Press, 1995.

Wooster, Robert. *The Military & United States Indian Policy 1865–1903.* Lincoln, NE: University of Nebraska Press, 1988.

_____. *Soldiers, Sutlers, and Settlers: Garrison Life on the Texas Frontier.* College Station, TX: Texas A&M University Press, 1987.

Worcester, Donald E. *The Apaches: Eagles of the Southwest.* Norman, OK: University of Oklahoma Press, 1979.

Wright, Muriel H. *A Guide to the Indian Tribes of Oklahoma.* Norman, OK: University of Oklahoma Press, 1951.

*Young County History and Biography.* Dallas, TX: Dealey and Lowe, 1937.


## UNPUBLISHED SOURCES

Gerdes, Bruce. "The Thompson Cañon Fight." Typed manuscript. "Tonkawa File." Panhandle Plains Museum, Canyon, TX.

Hoijer, Harry. "Tonkawa: An Indian Language of Texas." PhD diss., University of Chicago, 1931.

Mayhall, Mildred Pickle. "The Indians of Texas: The Atakapa, Karankawa, the Tonkawa." Master's thesis, University of Texas at Austin, 1939.

Lukes, Edward A. "DeWitt Colony of Texas." PhD diss., Loyolla University, 1971.

Neighbors, Alice A. "The Life and Works of Robert S. Neighbors." Master's thesis, University of Texas at Austin, 1936.

Prikryl, Daniel J. "Fiction and Fact about the Titskanwatits, or Tonkawa, of East-central Texas." Institute of Texan Cultures, San Antonio, TX.

Schilz, Thomas F. "People of the Cross-timbers: A History of the Tonkawa Indians." PhD diss., Texas Christian University, 1983.

Schuetz, Mardith Keithly. "The Indians of the San Antonio Missions, 1718–1821." PhD diss., University of Texas at Austin, 1979.

Troike, Rudolph Charles. "Tonkawa Prehistory: A Study in Method and Theory." Master's thesis, University of Texas at Austin, 1957.


## Journals/Magazines

Bolton, Herbert E. "The Founding of the Missions on the San Gabriel River, 1745–1749." *Southwestern Historical Quarterly.* Vol. 17, No. 4 (April 1914).

_____. "The Beginnings of Mission Nuestra Sonora del Refugio." *Southwestern Historical Quarterly.* Vol. 19, No. 4 (April 1916).

Cashion, Ty. "(Gun)Smoke Gets in Your Eyes: A Revisionist Look at 'Violent' Fort Griffin." *Southwestern Historical Quarterly.* Vol. 99, No. 1 (July 1995).

Chapman, Berlin B. "Establishment of the Iowa Reservation." *Chronicles of Oklahoma.* Vol. 21 (December 1943).

Crimmins, Martin L. "The Tonkawe Tribe." *Frontier Times.* Vol. 3 (June 1926).

Collinson, Frank. "The Tonkawas: An Old-Timers Recollections." *Ranch Romances.* Vol. LXXXI, No. 2 (July 1938).

Crouch, Carrie J. "When Redskins Left Texas: Migration of Indians to Oklahoma." *National Republic.* Vol. 19 (September 1931).

Dale, Edward Everett. "The Cherokee Strip Live Stock Association." *Chronicles of Oklahoma*. Vol. 5 (March 1927).

Dunlay, Thomas W. "Friends and Allies: The Tonkawa Indians and the Anglo-Americans, 1823–1884." *Great Plains Quarterly*. Vol. 1, No. 3 (Summer 1981).

Dunn, William Edwards. "Mission Activities Among the Eastern Apaches Previous to the Founding of the San Sabá Mission." *Quarterly of the Texas State Historical Association*. Vol. 15, No. 3 (January 1912).

_____. "The Apache Mission on the San Sabá River, Its Founding and Failure." *Southwestern Historical Quarterly*. Vol. 17, No 4 (April 1914).

Ewers, John C. "The Influence of Epidemics on the Indian Populations and Cultures of Texas." *Plains Anthropologist*. Vol. 18, No. 60 (1973).

Gelo, Daniel J. "'Comanche Land and Ever Has Been': A Native Geography of the Nineteenth-Century Comancheria." *Southwestern Historical Quarterly*. Vol. 103, No. 3 (January 2000).

Hasskarl, Jr., Robert A. "The Culture and history of the Tonkawa Indians." *Plains Anthropologist*. Vol. 7, No. 18 (November 1962).

Harmon, George D. "The U.S. Indian Policy in Texas, 1845–1860." *Mississippi Valley Historical Review*. Vol. 17 (December 1930).

Hatcher, Mattie Austin, trans. "Descriptions of the Tejas or Asinai Indians, 1691–1722." *Southwestern Historical Quarterly*. Vol. 30, No. 4 (April 1927).

Hoerig, Carl H. "The Relationship Between German Immigrants and the Native Peoples in Western Texas." *Southwestern Historical Quarterly*. Vol. 97, No. 3 (January 1994).

Hunter, J. Marvin. "Frank Gholson's Ride." *Frontier Times*. Vol. 6 (February 1929).

Johnson, A. R. "The Battle of Antelope Hills." *Frontier Times*. Vol. 1 (February 1924).

Johnson, L., Jr. "The Reconstructed Crow Terminology of the Titskanwatits, or Tonkawas, with Inferred Social Correlates." *Plains Anthropologist*. Vol. 150, No. 39 (1994).

Johnson, L., Jr. and T. N. Campbell. "Sanan: Traces of a Previously Unknown Aboriginal Language in Colonial Coahuila and Texas." *Plains Anthropologist*. Vol. 140, No. 37 (1992).

Jones, William K. "Notes on the History and Material Culture of the Tonkawa Indians." Smithsonian Contributions to Anthropology. Vol. II, No 5 (1969).

Kinnaird, Lawrence and Lucia B. Kinnarid. "Choctaws West of the Mississippi, 1766–1800." *Southwestern Historical Quarterly*. Vol. 83, No 4 (April 1980).

Klos, George. "'Our People Could Not Distinguish one Tribe from Another': The 1859 Expulsion of the Reserve Indians from Texas." *Southwestern Historical Quarterly*. Vol. 97, No. 4 (April 1994).

Koch, Lena Clara. "The Federal Indian Policy in Texas, 1845–1860." *Southwestern Historical Quarterly*. Vol. 28 (January April 1925).

Lewis, Anna. "La Harpe's First Expedition in Oklahoma." *Chronicles of Oklahoma*. 2 (Winter 1924).

McClintock, William A. "Journal of a trip through Texas and northern Mexico in 1846–1847." *Southwestern Historical Quarterly*. Vol. 34, No. 1 (July 1930).

McGowen, Stanley S. "Battle or Massacre?: The Incident on the Nueces, August 10, 1862." *Southwestern Historical Quarterly*. Vol. 104, No. 1 (July 2000).

McNeil, Kinneth. "Confederate Treaties with the Tribes of Indian Territory." *Chronicles of Oklahoma*. 42 (Winter 1964).

Mooney, James. "The Tonkawas; Our Last Cannibal Tribe." *Harper's*. 103 (September 1901).

Morgan, George R. and Omer Stewart. "Peyote Trade in South Texas." *Southwestern Historical Quarterly*. Vol. 87, No. 3 (January 1984).

Nance, Berta Hart. "D. A. Nance and the Tonkawa Indians." *West Texas Historical Association Year Book*. 28 (1952).

Neighbours, Kenneth F. "Indian Exodus Out of Texas." *West Texas Historical Association Year Book*. 36 (1960).

_____. "Tonkawa Scouts and Guides." *West Texas Historical Association Year Book*. 49 (1973).

Nielsen, George R. "Matthew Caldwell." *Southwestern Historical Quarterly*. Vol. 64, No 4 (April 1961).

Newcomb, W. W., Jr. "Historic Indians of Central Texas." *Bulletin of the Texas Archeological Society*. No. 64 (1993).

Nye, Wilbur S. "The Battle of Wichita Village." *The Chronicles of Oklahoma*. XV (June 1937).

Paige, John C. "Wichita Indian Agent, 1857–1869." *Journal of the West*. 12 (July 1973).

Ratcliffe, Sam D. "'*Escenas de Martirio*': Notes on The Destruction of Mission San Sabá." *Southwestern Historical Quarterly*. Vol. 94, No. 4 (April 1991).

Richardson, Rupert N. "The Comanche Reservation in Texas." *West Texas Historical Association Year Book*. Vol 3.

Sjoberg, Andre F. "The Culture of the Tonkawa, A Texas Indian Tribe." *Texas Journal of Science*. 5 (1953).

Smith, Ralph A., trans. "Account of the Journey of Benard de La Harpe: Discovery Made by Him of Several Nations Situated in the West." *Southwestern Historical Quarterly*. Vol. 62, No. 3 (January 1959).

Smith, Thomas T. "Fort Inge and Texas Frontier Military Operations, 1849–1869." *Southwestern Historical Quarterly*. Vol. 96, no. 1 (July 1992).

_____. "US Army Combat Operations in the Indian Wars of Texas, 1849–1881." *Southwestern Historical Quarterly*. Vol. 99, No. 4 (April 1996).

Stewart, Omer. "Origin of the Peyote Religion in the United States." *Plains Anthropologist*. Vol. 19, No. 65 (1974).

Stuart, Ben C. "The Battle of Antelope Hills." *Frontier Times*. 3 (August 1926).

Taylor, Virginia H. "Calendar of the Letters of Antonio Martinez, Last Spanish Governor of Texas, 1817–1822." *Southwestern Historical Quarterly*. Vol. 61, No. 2 (October 1957).

Thoburn, Joseph B. "Horace P. Jones, Scout and Interpreter." *Chronicles of Oklahoma*. 2 (December 1924).

Tjarks, Alicia V. "Comparative Demographic Analysis of Texas, 1777–1793." *Southwestern Historical Quarterly*. Vol. 77, No. 3 (January 1974).

Tudor, William G. "Ghost Writers of the Palo Duro." *Southwestern Historical Quarterly*. 99 (April 1996).

Vehik, S. C. "Oñate's Expedition to the Southern Plains: Routes, Destinations, and Implications for Late Prehistoric Cultural Adaptations." *Plains Anthropologist*. Vol. 111, No. 31 (1986).

Wade, Mariah. "Go-between: The Roles of Native American Women and Álvar Núñez Cabeza de Vaca in Southern Texas in the 16th Century." *Journal of American Folklore*. Vol. 112, Issue 445 (Summer 1999).

Wright, Muriel H. "A History of Fort Cobb." *Chronicles of Oklahoma*. 34 (Spring 1956).

Weddle, Robert S. "La Salle's Survivors." *Southwestern Historical Quarterly*. Vol 75, No. 4 (April 1972).

Worcester, Donald E. "The Spread of Spanish Horses in the Southwest." *New Mexico Historical Review*. No. 19 (July 1944).

*Newspapers*

Farmer, Joan. "Remember When." *Albany News.* June 10, 1999.

Ledbetter, Barbara Neal. "Indian Woman is Famous Frontier Scout." *Graham Leader.* August 9, 1992.

Medley, Robert. "Remaining Tonkawa Indians Won't Accept Reports of Their Extinction." *Dallas Morning News.* September 21, 1988.

Turner, Elsa M. "Tonkawas in Griffin," *Albany News.* June 1989.

Waldo Allen (*Wa-ki-teh*)/Straight Shooter. *The Tonkawa News.* Tonkawa, OK. No. 23:6. June 27, 2002.

# INDEX